Sparks

SLAVERY AND METHODISM

SLAVERY
AND METHODISM

A Chapter
in American Morality
1780-1845

BY

DONALD G. MATHEWS

PRINCETON UNIVERSITY PRESS
PRINCETON, NEW JERSEY
1965

To my father and mother

THE Methodists' confrontation with American Negro slavery was part of a larger drama whose first act ended in the Civil War. The moral alienation which presaged the war, although latent during the early years of the Republic, had by 1820 become involved in national politics. It was increased by the abolitionist crusade in Jacksonian America and partially institutionalized by the Methodist schism of 1844–1845. The story of the Methodist Episcopal Church and slavery, therefore, offers an excellent opportunity for investigating American sentiments and attitudes on this issue from 1780 to 1845.

There are several justifications for a study of the slavery controversy as it evolved within the Methodist Episcopal Church. First of all, that sect became the largest Protestant church in the United States and was spread fairly evenly over the entire country. No nonpolitical organization touched the lives of more people; none reflected the social attitudes of millions of Americans more accurately. Although physically absent from the deliberations of the churchmen, the laity were omnipresent in their influence, for the clergy early learned to make only those decisions which they could enforce. As indicators of public opinion, ministers were almost as reliable as politicians. Along with ubiquity and numbers, the Methodists were uniquely active in the antislavery and colonization movements and in missions to the slaves. Second only to the Quakers in their early protests against slavery, the Methodists' subsequent interest in African colonization suggests that the early antislavery impulse was diverted into that movement. Furthermore, because the Methodists had an antislavery heritage and a reputation for strict morality, the record of their grapple with slavery proved rich in irony, contrast, and human conflict. And finally, their organization provided a structure of conferences where ministers met to decide matters for rather large geographical areas. Since this connexional system lent itself more easily to agitation than did the loose-knit congregationally governed churches, Methodist conference records reveal much about the nature of abolitionism and its harried opposition.

Although this study uses the Methodist Episcopal Church as a framework, it was conceived primarily not as an essay on church history but as an examination of the various reactions to slavery in early America. Eager though they were to be a special people, Methodists actually came to be little different from the other major denominations in their attitudes on slavery and morality. And although the moral issues sometimes hid the material interests involved with slavery, the former were quite real to many Americans and served to affect their relations with their fellows in other parts of the country. Thus, the Methodists' behavior and concepts of morality provide some insight into the common, everyday discourse which dealt with American Negro slavery.

The purpose of this essay is rather modest: it is not designed to overturn previous theories or correct grave misconceptions engrained into American historiography. Hopefully, its readers will learn a little more about the early antislavery movement and the kinds of people who supported the colonization cause; perhaps they will see the abolitionists and their opponents in a new light; possibly they will find out more about the dissemination and influence of antislavery ideas in Jacksonian America. The thesis includes several points. Although Methodist leaders failed to identify the Wesleyan conscience with antislavery ideas, they attempted to help Negroes through such philanthropic agencies as the American Colonization Society and the Mission to the Slaves. When abolitionists converted by William Lloyd Garrison aroused antislavery sentiment through their revivalism, they polarized reactions to slavery to such an extent that they split the church. All sides in the controversy defended themselves with moral arguments legitimatized either by experience or principle, creating a hopeless situation that could end only in conflict.

This is not the first study of slavery and Methodism. Charles Elliott, in his partisan, bulky, and unreadable *History of the Great Secession from The Methodist Episcopal Church in the year 1845* (Cincinnati, 1855), emphasized the perfidy of the South and the irresponsibility of the abolitionists. Lucius C. Matlack, an abolitionist, wrote two books on the Methodists and slavery: *The History of American Slavery and Methodism from 1780 to 1849* (New York, 1849) and *The Anti-Slavery Struggle and Triumph in the Methodist Episcopal Church* (New York, 1881). Both give the abolitionists their due but fail to see the connection between the early antislavery movement, the Colonization Society, and the missions to the slaves. John Norwood in *The Schism in the Methodist Episcopal Church: 1844* (Alfred, New York, 1923) focuses on the schism and almost completely disregards the developments prior to 1835. Although Charles Swaney in *Episcopal Methodism and Slavery* (Boston, 1926) tries to give a more complete picture than the others, he is often too hasty in his judgments, inaccurate in the use of evidence, and deficient in perspective.

For their interest, aid, and patience in this new attempt to explain the Methodists and slavery, the author is greatly indebted to the librarians of the following institutions: the Boston Public Library, Boston University, Cornell University, DePauw University, Drew University, Duke University, Emory University, Emory and Henry College, Garrett Theological Seminary, Georgia State Historical Society, Illinois Wesleyan University, Johns Hopkins University, the Library of Congress, the Lovely Lane Museum and Library in Baltimore, Maryland, the Maryland Historical Society, Millsaps College, the Mississippi Conference Historical Society, the New York Public Library, Ohio Wesleyan University, the Philadelphia Conference Historical Society at Old St. George's Church in Philadelphia, Princeton University, Randolph-Macon College, Syracuse University, the University of North Carolina, Wesleyan University, Wofford College, the World Methodist Building, Lake Junaluska, North Carolina, and Yale University.

The author is also grateful to Princeton University Press for allowing him to reprint portions of "Orange Scott: the Methodist Evangelist as Revolutionary" in Martin B. Duberman *et al., The Antislavery Vanguard: New Essays on the Abolitionists* (Princeton, 1965). He is indebted as well to the editors of the *Journal of American History* for their permission to reprint "The Methodist Mission to the Slaves, 1829–1844," LI (March 1965), which appears here as the major portion of Chapter III.

Many people have helped produce this book. Professor Leslie Van Horne Brock of the College of Idaho long ago awakened the author's interest in historical scholarship which finally developed into this study. Professors Robert A. Lively of Princeton and William Catton of Middlebury College read portions of the manuscript; Professors Harold T. Parker, H. Shelton Smith, Robert F. Durden, and Robert H. Woody of Duke University raised penetrating questions and opened new paths of research. Professor Woody, advisor and friend, has been especially helpful as the manuscript became a seminar paper, a Ph.D. thesis, and finally a book. His interest, astute judgment and scholarly integrity will always be appreciated. I also wish to express appreciation to the Princeton University Research Committee for its financial aid.

Unlike many wives, Jane DeHart Mathews did not type the manuscript. Instead, she read it, criticized it, trimmed it, and improved its style even though she had to take much valuable time from her own writing to do so. Only she could know the depths of my gratitude.

In spite of the communal nature of scholarship, the writer bears full responsibility for any errors or oddities of style which appear in this book.

Princeton, New Jersey   DONALD G. MATHEWS

CONTENTS

PART I

THE CHURCH AND SLAVERY

CHAPTER I

COMPROMISE AND CONSCIENCE:
The Church and Slavery
1780–1816

S LAVERY is unjust, un-Christian, and un-natural," proclaimed the early Methodist prophets.

Mendicant preachers of emancipation for bodies as well as souls, the first generation of circuit riders tried to translate their offended consciences into moral rules that would arouse Wesleyans against slavery until it was destroyed. For over a generation a small, energetic, saintly, English blacksmith's son, Francis Asbury, led the Methodist ministry in repeated assaults upon Negro servitude, but he and his fellows failed to loosen the Negro's bonds. They failed partially because as evangelists they hoped to preach to both whites and blacks, an aspiration endangered by their antislavery enthusiasm. They also failed for other reasons, and these reasons are in part the story not only of Methodism but of America, its institutions and its social morality.

By 1780, when American Methodist preachers first formally denounced Negro servitude, it was well established by law and custom in a majority of the rebellious English colonies. Slavery had met no resistance as it evolved from part of the economic system into a pattern of social adjustment. The first ripples of moral protest did not question the justice of owning men as property, but merely suggested that masters purge the system of what they considered its more flagrant abuses—harsh treatment of slaves and neglect of their religious care.[1] This placation of conscience was not, how-

---

[1] Mary Stoughton Locke, *Anti-Slavery in America from the Introduction of African Slaves to the Prohibition of the Slave Trade,*

3

ever, enforced by law or general public sentiment, and the Negro slave had few champions.

Most of those few champions were members of the Society of Friends. Although the first Friend, George Fox, had become convinced of the evil of slavery in 1671, not until the Quakers had weathered years of persecution and internecine controversy did they direct their energies against slaveholding. Nevertheless, by 1714 prophetic pamphleteering Friends began to use the Quaker doctrine of the Divine presence in every man against the institution of slavery. An extended literary campaign, the devoted service of apostle John Woolman, and the persistence of yearly meetings cleansed the society of Friends of all but the last taint of slavery by 1830.[2] The judgments made at each meeting exerted a broad-based and powerful influence against slavery—derived not from a moral appeal handed down by a special class of preachers, but from long, reasoned, steady discussions among religious peers. Furthermore, the Quaker valued his peculiarity as a Friend, and once the sense of the meeting had decided against slavery, he had recourse only to "the world" which he had renounced, to other sects which could not fulfill his religious needs, or to schism which required too large a number of dissidents and slaveholders. Thus, the Quakers moved against slavery and earned for their small sect an admired position in American social history.

The Methodists were less fortunate, primarily because their early and vigorous opposition to slavery was effaced

---

1619–1808, Boston, 1901, pp. 9–15. Ulrich Bonnell Phillips, *American Negro Slavery,* New York, 1940, pp. 75–83. See John C. Hurd, *Law of Freedom and Bondage,* Boston, 1862, vol. I for a discussion of the statutes concerning the regulation of slavery before 1776. For a description of the difficulties faced by ministers who wished to convert the Negroes, see Joseph B. Earnest, *The Religious Development of the Negro in Virginia,* Charlottesville, 1914, pp. 27–29.

[2] Thomas Drake, *Quakers and Slavery in America,* New Haven, 1950, pp. 5, 23, 34–37, 47. For a discussion of Woolman's activities and influence see especially pp. 51–84.

by compromise. Nevertheless, during the last twenty years of the eighteenth century, American Methodists acquired a well-deserved reputation for antagonism to Negro servitude. That antagonism was fostered by English precedents, American revolutionary ideas, the Methodist "conscience," evangelical concern for the Negro, and the antislavery enthusiasm of men like Francis Asbury and Thomas Coke, both bishops of the Methodist Episcopal Church after 1784.

Methodism was formed in England by the creative devotion of the Anglican priest, John Wesley, and the urgent preaching of his itinerants, who proposed to "reform the nation, more particularly the Church; to spread scriptural holiness over the land." Scriptural holiness was the transformation of ones personal life from "disobedience and hate" into "obedience and love." This transformation issued in avoiding evil, doing good, and attending the ordinances of the Church of England. To help his fellows determine what avoiding evil and doing good meant, Wesley outlined a guide to Christian ethics in the General Rules. Methodists were to exemplify their salvation by refraining from drunkenness, slave trading, fighting, buying smuggled goods, charging excessive interest, or enjoying any self-indulgence. Furthermore, Wesleyans were expected to obey the Biblical injunctions to feed the hungry, clothe the naked, and visit the sick. Thus, the Methodists, who brought these General Rules with them to America, had a personal philanthropic activism built into their understanding of the Christian life.[3]

Wesley believed that Negro slavery was one of the greatest evils that a Christian should fight. In 1743 when he wrote the General Rules, he had prohibited "the buying or selling the bodies and souls of men, women, and children, with

[3] Wade Crawford Barclay, *To Reform the Nation*, New York, 1950, vol. 2 of *Early American Methodism, 1789–1844,* Part One of his History of Methodist Missions, pp. 1, 63. See also *Doctrines and Discipline of the Methodist Episcopal Church in the United States of America,* Baltimore, 1789, pp. 48–50; usually called the *Discipline.*

an intention to enslave them." In 1774, after reading an antislavery pamphlet by Anthony Benezet, an American Quaker, Wesley wrote his *Thoughts Upon Slavery,* reviling the enslavement of the noble savage by barbarous and inferior white men. He utterly repudiated those who argued the necessity of continuing so evil an institution as slavery. "Villainy" was never necessary, he ejaculated. "It is impossible that it should ever be necessary for any reasonable creature to violate all the laws of Justice, Mercy, and Truth. No circumstances can make it necessary for a man to burst asunder all the ties of humanity."[4] Methodists made it a habit to read the work of Wesley, their spiritual father; although Wesley never proposed a plan for getting rid of slavery, he did provide early Methodists with an incipient antislavery sentiment as well as the moral urgency to enforce it.

Antipathy to slavery was nourished also by the American Revolution and its apologists. Freedom was what Americans were fighting for, and to some enlightened men that same freedom would have to include Negroes if the words of the Declaration of Independence were not sheer hypocrisy. James Otis had already denounced slavery; Henry Laurens of South Carolina privately abhorred so unjust an institution, and Thomas Paine publicly wrote aaginst it. The pamphleteer's eloquence, however, could not match that of the Negroes themselves, whose very presence in the Revolutionary armies forced thoughtful Americans to reflect upon the injustice of servitude. At the same time, morality, politics, and economics were merging into laws that restricted the slave trade; and in 1780 Pennsylvania began the legal process that would abolish slavery in that state. By 1804 the end of slavery was guaranteed above Mason and Dixon's line, and the Northwest had been closed to it by the vision and common sense of Thomas Jefferson and Con-

[4] John Wesley, *Thoughts Upon Slavery,* London, 1774, p. 35. Drake, *Quakers and Slavery,* p. 91.

gress. At the same time, philanthropists were organizing abolition societies dedicated to carrying out the ideals which revolutionaries applied to all humanity.[5] But emancipationist ideas, no matter how well publicized, were expressed by only a small minority throughout the new nation.

Francis Asbury was included in that minority. More than any other man, he was responsible for the establishment of the Methodist movement in America. In 1771, at the age of twenty-six, he had volunteered to go to the American colonies to strengthen the Methodist Societies there. From the beginning of his American ministry, Asbury was pleased when the "poor Negroes" were "affected" by his preaching because their reaction signified to him that God was "no respecter of persons." His willingness to accept the Negro on the basis of religious equality developed into a conscientious antagonism against slavery through conversations with antislavery men. He decided by 1778 that the Methodists would have to emulate Quaker exertions "for the liberation of the slaves" or suffer God's displeasure. Furthermore, in the intimate company of Methodist preachers, Asbury could not fail to be impressed by the ideas and actions of Freeborn Garrettson who, upon his conversion in 1775, emancipated his slaves and began to preach "the doctrine of freedom" as often and as eloquently as he could. It is not surprising, therefore, that Asbury encouraged the Methodists to mold Wesleyan background, moral enthusiasm, revolutionary

[5] Benjamin Quarles, *The Negro in the American Revolution,* Chapel Hill, 1961, pp. 33–50. William Frederick Poole, *Anti-Slavery Opinions before the year 1800,* Cincinnati, 1873, pp. 43–58. Locke, *Anti-Slavery in America,* pp. 46–57, 73, 77. William Sumner Jenkins, *Pro-Slavery Thought in the Old South,* Chapel Hill, 1935, pp. 23, 27. Thomas Jefferson, *Notes on the State of Virginia,* William Peden, ed., Chapel Hill, 1955, pp. 138, 162–163. Dwight L. Dumond, *Antislavery: The Crusade for Freedom in America,* Ann Arbor, 1961, pp. 26–34. Vermont, Massachusetts, Connecticut, Rhode Island, and Pennsylvania had begun programs for emancipation before 1787. New York passed a gradual emancipation law in 1799 and New Jersey followed suit in 1804. Slavery still existed in the North but it had arrived at the "moment of truth."

ideals, and Quaker example into a mild but aspiring disapproval of slavery.[6]

❧ At Baltimore in the spring of 1780 Asbury, as president of a conference of Methodist preachers, introduced and supervised the passage of a statement on slavery—the preachers were not only to provide for the religious instruction of slaves but also attempt to exert pressure which might bring about eventual emancipation. Hoping their example would encourage others, the conference required itinerant preachers to free what slaves they held, and advised all other Methodists to do the same. The pronouncement was based on the assumption that slavery was contrary to divine, human, and natural justice, a violation of the Golden Rule, and inconsistent with "pure religion."[7] The new rule was not very harsh since it did not dispossess many Methodists of their slaves, but it was a first step toward more determined action.

Like most first steps, it was a tottering one. The decision to fight slavery had only the power of enlightened morality behind it. The Methodists were weak and few in number. A small minority within the unpopular Church of England, they were distrusted by American patriots because of Wesley's Toryism as well as their own pacifism; as if public suspicion were not bad enough, they were also divided among themselves as to whether or not to remain within the Anglican Church. Methodist preachers were laymen, and most of those in Virginia were encouraged by the American Revolution and a scarcity of priests to separate from

[6] Elmer T. Clark ed., *The Journal and Letters of Francis Asbury,* Nashville, 1958, I, 9–10, November 17, 1771; p. 25, April 3, 1772: Asbury talked with Daniel Roberdeau, a friend of George Whitefield's and a leading Philadelphia emancipationist; p. 43, September 11, 1772; p. 56, December, 7, 1772; p. 57, December 8, 1772; p. 273, May 10, 1778. Hereafter cited as, Asbury, *Journal.* Also Freeborn Garrettson, *The Experience and Travels of Mr. Freeborn Garrettson,* Philadelphia, 1791, pp. 36–37, 40ff., 76–77.

[7] *Minutes of the Annual Conferences of the Methodist Episcopal Church,* New York, 1845, I, 12.

the Church of England, form a presbyterian polity, and administer the sacraments. Because Asbury objected to such proceedings, he was gambling with Methodist unity when he and his preachers passed the first rule against slavery. Almost two-thirds of the American Wesleyans—all in slaveholding territory—were beyond his jurisdiction in 1780. Nevertheless, he persuaded the Southerners to return to the Church of England, and in 1783 a Virginia conference followed the lead of the Baltimore meeting of 1780. Asbury was elated. "We all agree in the spirit of African liberty," he wrote, "and strong testimonies were borne in its favor. . . ."[8]

Although acquiescence to the rules was not overwhelming among the majority of Methodists, it was great enough to encourage further disciplinary action. In the spring of 1784 circuit riders voted to expel members who sold slaves or bought them for nonhumanitarian reasons—a policy much like that of the Quakers, who believed that by cutting off the slave trade they were draining the lifeblood of slavery. The itinerants also decided to warn and then suspend local preachers who would not *"emancipate slaves in the states where the laws admit it."*[9] Thus into the Paradise of moral requirements, the Methodists had to admit the serpent of civil law. Such an admission was necessary for a law-abiding people who valued social order, but the possibilities of self-justification were limitless. For the moment, however, Methodists could hide their morality behind legality only in North Carolina; the other states allowed emancipation with few legal disabilities.[10]

[8] Asbury, *Journal,* I, 441, May 7, 1783. John J. Tigert, *A Constitutional History of American Episcopal Methodism,* Nashville, 1916, pp. 61–68, 97–125.
[9] *Minutes of Annual Conferences,* I, 46–47. Drake, *Quakers and Slavery,* p. 67.
[10] By 1777 North Carolina had passed a law forbidding manumission save for "meritorious service." The law did not necessarily forbid emancipation, but it did make manumission difficult enough to discourage the faint-hearted. See Hurd, *Law of Bondage,* I, 295.

9

The cautious antislavery activity promoted by Asbury and his ministers was violently transfigured at the organization of the Methodist Episcopal Church. Because the independence of the United States had severed ecclesiastical as well as political bonds with Great Britain, John Wesley decided to ordain the American Methodist preachers, an action which led to the separation of the societies from the Church of England. To help organize American Methodism, Wesley chose plump little Thomas Coke, Anglican priest, Doctor of Civil Law, and furious opponent of slavery. Together with Francis Asbury, Coke was to superintend the societies which became the Methodist Episcopal Church at a special conference in Baltimore during the Christmas season of 1784.

In creating the new church, the Christmas Conference conformed to the organization and rules of the English societies except where the American situation called for changes. The most significant departure was a new and detailed antislavery rule that reflected the legal training of Dr. Coke. With control of the sacraments for the first time, the conference of preachers made one change in the terms of communion. Any Methodist who did not free his slaves as directed by the *Discipline* of the new church was to be denied the elements of the Lord's Supper and expelled. The structure of the rule came from a Virginia law of 1782 which prescribed procedure and age limits for voluntary manumission; the conference simply added a few refinements and made the law an imperative for all Methodists.[11] Although Virginians were to have two years' grace within which to comply, and although emancipation was to conform to the civil law, the prophetic message was clearly a departure

[11] "An Act to authorize the Manumission of Slaves [1782]," in *A Collection of all such Public Acts of the General Assembly and Ordinances of the Conventions of Virginia Passed since the year 1768 as are now in force,* Richmond, 1785, pp. 159–160. Robert Emory, *History of the Discipline of the Methodist Episcopal Church,* New York, 1844, pp. 23ff. The Methodist Rules Concerning Slavery are printed in the Appendix to the present study.

10

from previous suggestions and "disapprobations." Hereafter Methodist laymen as well as preachers ought not and would not hold slaves.

This departure from the more cautious course under Asbury was obviously the work of the fiery Dr. Coke and the result of the Methodists' newly acquired autonomy. Coke was so emphatically opposed to Negro servitude that he could not at first discuss it diplomatically, and as Wesley's special representative to America he had a signal opportunity to affect the action of the new church on slavery.[12] Furthermore, with an extant antislavery sentiment, the opportunity to control communion, a desire to begin their church with a clean moral slate, and the natural impetuosity of evangelical preachers in the act of optimistic creativity, the conference quite naturally overextended its moral demands. The all-inclusiveness and uncompromising character of the new rule portended much greater difficulties than the previous rules; ecclesiastical discipline now had to achieve at one blow what persuasion and preaching had been suggesting for only a few years.

The preachers had not long to await the results of their bold action. Although some masters in Maryland emancipated their slaves, a great number in Virginia, where almost half of all Methodists lived, raised a resounding furor which frightened the ministry into reconsidering what they had done.[13] Virginia and North Carolina preachers exchanged threats and denunications on the subject of slavery in their conference the early spring of 1785. At the center of the controversy, Dr. Coke defended the new rule with characteristic vigor. His chief antagonist, calm, intelligent Jesse Lee,

[12] For Dr. Coke's attitude on slavery, see Samuel Drew, *The Life of the Rev. Thomas Coke, LL.D.*, New York, 1818, pp. 134ff.
[13] Jesse Lee, *A Short History of the Methodists*, Baltimore, 1810, p. 88. Barclay, *Reform the Nation*, p. 91. Drew, *Life of Coke*, p. 133. Warren Thomas Smith, "Thomas Coke and Early American Methodism," unpublished Ph.D. thesis, Boston University, 1953, p. 203.

the antislavery son of a slaveholder, maintained that the new rule had been ill-timed and ill-advised since it had excited "strong prejudices" against the preachers. Masters thus prejudiced, he argued, kept the ministers from the slaves and closed their own minds to prudent antislavery measures. Devereaux Jarratt, an Anglican rector and the patron of Virginia Methodism, agreed with Lee. He told one Methodist minister that the rule had "already done more harm than the united effort of all the Preachers . . . [would] ever do good."[14] Although Lee and Jarratt failed to convince the more rabid antislavery preachers, they had the logic of circumstances on their side. In June another conference at Baltimore suspended the rule on behalf of the entire church. Aware that the action in December had been precipitous, the preachers nevertheless defended the principles upon which they had acted: "We do hold in the deepest abhorrence, the practice of slavery; and shall not cease to seek its destruction by all wise and prudent means."[15]

The implication of the Baltimore announcement was that the Christmas Conference had acted imprudently, and—given the nature and mission of the Methodist Episcopal Church—indeed it had. The Quakers were removing slavery from their society only through a long and steady process which was not seriously complicated by a greatly expanding membership. What was difficult for the Friends was almost impossible for the Methodists because of their revivalism. American Methodists increased their numbers more than twofold between 1780 and 1785, leaving little time to create a special sense of community upon which

---

[14] Devereaux Jarratt to Edward Dromgoole, May 31, 1785, Edward Dromgoole Papers, Southern Historical Collection, the University of North Carolina. Also Asbury, *Journal,* I, 488, May 30, 1785. Minton Thrift, *Memoir of the Rev. Jesse Lee with Extracts from His Journals,* New York, 1823, p. 79. Drew, *Life of Coke,* p. 135. W. L. Grissom, *History of Methodism in North Carolina,* Nashville, 1905, p. 229.

[15] *Minutes of Annual Conferences,* I, 24.

to base rather stringent social and moral demands. Coke himself had to admit that the church was "in too infantile a state to push things to extremity."[16]

Furthermore, the mission of the Church was to "preach the Gospel to every creature," Negro as well as white. If indignant masters kept them from the slaves, the preachers reasoned, Negroes would never know of God's love for them. And the master, alienated by harsh rules, would shut himself away, not only from his own salvation, but also from influences that would work ultimately to free the slaves. Therefore the Methodists conscientiously withdrew their unenforceable rule in the best interests of slaves, masters, and Church alike. Although still certain that slavery was wrong, the preachers had learned that enlightened efforts must be carried out in a real world of selfish men, incomplete institutions, and complicating circumstances. The problem for the early Wesleyans, as for most men, was to know how much to yield to complicating circumstances without betraying their God.

For the present, however, no Methodist preacher could believe that he had betrayed God. On the contrary, the great success of Methodist preaching was interpreted as the result of Divine pleasure. Excited evangelical oratory, emotional ecstasy, and the constant organization of new societies swept converts into the new Zion at such a speed that it grew from 15,000 members in 1784 to 58,000 in 1790. Confronted with such spectacular results, many preachers might have turned away from enthusiasm for emancipation and contented themselves with religious instruction of the slaves. Antislavery fires, however, still warmed some ministers' Christianity, and although their rules were curtailed, their voices were not. Continuing to preach an emancipationist ethic, itinerants insisted that the piety of a prayerful, honest man who was emotionally aware of the love of God should be expressed through opposition to slavery.

[16] Quoted in Smith, "Thomas Coke and Methodism," p. 203.

13

The attack on slavery took many forms. Ministers joined Quakers in petitioning the North Carolina legislature to allow emancipation, and they circulated memorials in Virginia praying for the freedom of the slaves. Asbury was distressed at "the resentment expressed by Virginia legislators against general abolition-ists," but proud of Methodist endeavors for "liberty—emancipation."[17] He himself wrote John Wesley's old rule against slavery into the General Rules of the Methodist Episcopal Church. And his preachers throughout the South condemned slavery, in some instances likening slaveholders to "horsethieves & Hogstealers" and other nefarious riffraff.[18] Under such preaching, Methodists enlisted along side the Baptists and Presbyterians to fight slavery in Kentucky, and they joined abolition societies in the Old Dominion in alliance with the Quakers.[19]

The Methodists also relied upon the written word. From Maryland to Georgia the preachers sold or gave away pamphlets against slavery—James O'Kelly's *Essay on Negro-Slavery,* John Wesley's *Thoughts Upon Slavery,* or *Othello on Slavery,* or *Slavery Inconsistent with Justice and Good*

[17] Asbury, *Journal,* I, 498, November 15, 1785; p. 582, November 1, 1788. Drew, *Life of Coke,* pp. 135–136. Wesley March Gewehr, *The Great Awakening in Virginia, 1740–1790,* Durham, 1930, pp. 243, 248.

[18] Devereaux Jarratt to Edward Dromgoole, March 22, 1788, Dromgoole papers. Also James Meacham's "Journal" for August 1, 1789, in William K. Boyd, ed., "A Journal of James Meacham," *Historical Papers* (Trinity College Historical Society), Series IX (1912), 82. Meacham was a rather outspoken circuit rider who carried on a personal and violent battle against slaveholders. Also Emory, *History of the Discipline,* pp. 79–80 for discussion of the editing chores of the early bishops. See also the *Discipline* for 1789, p. 49.

[19] Asa Earl Martin, *The Anti-Slavery Movement in Kentucky Prior to 1850,* Louisville, 1918, pp. 17–18. Stephen B. Weeks, *Southern Quakers and Slavery* (Johns Hopkins University Studies in Historical and Political Science, extra vol. 15), Baltimore, 1896, p. 213. James Meacham's "Journal," August 27, 1792 in William K. Boyd, ed., "A Journal of James Meacham," *Historical Papers* (Trinity College Historical Society), Series X (1914), 102.

Policy by the Presbyterian clergyman, David Rice.[20] Bishops Asbury and Coke wrote a scriptural argument against the slave trade in the 1798 edition of the Methodist *Discipline*, and the able young Ezekiel Cooper, who later saved the Methodist Publishing House from bankruptcy, condemned slavery in the *Virginia Gazette,* the *Maryland Gazette,* and the *Maryland Journal.* Except for the bishops' short discussion, these appeals were based upon the broad general principles of justice, the "benevolent purposes of the Christian religion," and the ideal of freedom for which Americans had fought their Revolution.

The most thorough antislavery pamphlet was that written by Rice, whose arguments were first presented in a speech at Danville, Kentucky, and later published by the Methodists in 1792; this Presbyterian apostle had affirmed the injustice of depriving a rational human being of his will and dignity, the lack of wisdom in continuing so antirepublican and immoral an institution as slavery, and the economic waste involved in it.[21] Rice's young Methodist counterpart in Maryland, Ezekiel Cooper, had but one major point to emphasize: the thorough inconsistency of slavery in a supposedly free nation. "I blush," he wrote, "at the conduct of many who are free men in principle, have declared for, and supported the cause of liberty and still persist in holding their fellow creatures in bondage." Such refusal to give Negroes the freedom which belonged to them as a human right was contrary to reason, charity, and the enlightened standards of the eighteenth century. Consequently Cooper believed that lawmakers should provide for emancipation as soon as pos-

[20] *Friend of Man,* August 30, 1837, p. 43. Francis Asbury to George Roberts, January 5, 1803 in Asbury, *Journal,* III, 258. Journals of the Philadelphia Conference, I, May 3, 1802, Philadelphia Conference Historical Society Papers, Old St. George's Church, Philadelphia.

[21] David Rice, *Slavery Inconsistent with Justice and Good Policy* . . . , Philadelphia, 1792, *passim,* but especially pp. 4, 7, 12, 18, 34–36.

sible. Freedom was as much a right of an American Negro as an American white man. "The same that wounds and pains us wounds and pains them. All our feelings are in them. . . . O compassion awake in the breasts of men!" he cried.[22]

Cooper's coreligionist, the influential James O'Kelly, also pleaded for compassion no matter what the cost. Affected by Wesley's *Thoughts Upon Slavery,* O'Kelly emphasized the moral necessity of liberating the Negroes even if this worked hardship upon whites. Christian morality was not always easy to follow, he implied; and because the Methodists had a reputation for strict morality, O'Kelly taunted them where they were most vulnerable. "We are pained at small matters," he charged, "We strain at gnats, while camels choak [sic] us not."[23]

Such arguments were met with self-righteous counterarguments. One preacher reported the not too surprising response of one Methodist who claimed that "God Almighty gave [his slaves] to him, and he intended to keep them."[24] Such a Providential view of the origins of slavery could be embellished with a defense based upon the Old Testament, which recorded the Israelites' enslavement of their enemies with impunity, or the New Testament, which urged obedience but not emancipation. Others less sure of the morality of slavery complained that the laws and decisions of former generations had entailed the system upon them.

[22] A Student [Ezekiel Cooper] to Goddard and Angell [*Maryland Journal*] April 18, 1792; A Freeman to a True Friend of the Union for the *Maryland Gazette,* n.d.; A Freeman to Mr. Love-Truth, Ezekiel Cooper Papers, Garrett Theological Seminary. Also *Maryland Gazette,* November 11, 1790, p. 3; December 2, 1790, pp. 2–3; December 30, 1790, p. 2; January 20, 1791, p. 2. *Virginia Gazette,* November 28, 1791, p. 2.

[23] James O'Kelly, *Essay on Negro Slavery,* Philadelphia, 1789, p. 31.

[24] William Colbert, "A Journal of the Travels of William Colbert, Methodist Preacher through parts of Maryland, Pennsylvania, New York, Delaware, and Virginia in 1790 to 1828," Typescript copy in World Methodist Building, Lake Junaluska, N.C., August 6, 1791.

Furthermore, they argued that emancipation would work unnecessary hardship upon slaveholders by depriving them of their property, and revolutionize society by creating a numerous race of mulattoes.

These rationalizations were countered in turn. It was confidently argued that the Old Testament never allowed perpetual slavery, that the New Testament preached freedom to the oppressed; and, as Cooper said in a point typical of the Enlightenment, that the historical age of institutions did not justify their existence. If antiquity had its slaves, it also had its kings, and the eighteenth century had condemned both. If laws inherited from previous generations upheld slavery, change them! Difficulty and hardship for the master were no excuse to maintain slavery since the Negroes deserved justice; if men feared that such justice woud produce racial amalgamation in the future, why did they so unjustly force miscegenation in the present?[25] The arguments shifted back and forth in heated private discussion, in letters, and in conferences; many opponents of slavery must have wondered if all the energy expended was actually worth the fight.

To some Methodists the preaching, the pamphlets, and the arguments had indeed been persuasive. Ever since the first public pronouncement against slavery there had been a trickle of manumissions in Maryland. As the antislavery preaching continued, a handful of Virginia Methodists emancipated their Negroes, and by 1789 the hopeful Asbury was led to anticipate a decline of slavery in the two states. His enthusiasm probably resulted from the fact that people whom he knew intimately were freeing their slaves. One of those slaveholders was Philip Gatch, a Methodist preacher, who signed a deed of manumission "from a clear

[25] Rice, *Slavery Inconsistent,* pp. 23, 26, 28. *Maryland Gazette,* November 11, 1790, p. 3; January 13, 1791, p. 2: January 20, 1791, p. 2. A Student to Goddard and Angell, April 18, 1792, Cooper Papers.

conviction of the injustice of depriving fellow creatures of their natural Right."[26]

Only the exceptional man, often one who had heard a call to preach, could live by principle and justice when economic and social position were at stake. Yet in Maryland, where Wesleyan preaching had first begun in the South, over 1,800 slaves were freed in predominantly Methodist territory between 1783 and 1799. In Amelia County, Virginia, another Wesleyan stronghold, Methodists registered a popular protest against slavery with the state legislature.[27] Such evidence does suggest that the Methodists could have maintained a consistent opposition to slavery at the cost of creating a small sect rather than an all-embracing evangelical church. Such a sect, if continuously revivalistic, might have become the religious expression of economic and social antagonism to slaveholders, at least in the upper South. More likely, however, such a sect would have shrunk into obscurity or emigrated from the South, as did many antislavery Quakers, Methodists, Baptists, and "seceding" Presbyterians. The Methodist clergy would have to make the choice between purity and popularity.

Although the choice was not yet obvious to the itinerants, their next attempt to transform antislavery ideals into rules revealed their predicament: they wanted to oppose slavery while avoiding social ostracism. Since any attempt at regulation was bound to provoke antagonism, the reasons for the ministry's decision to pass new rules are not altogether clear. Perhaps by 1796 they had reached the point where their

[26] William Warren Sweet, *Virginia Methodism: A History,* Richmond, 1955, p. 194.

[27] Kenneth L. Carroll has done a thorough study of the effects of Methodist and other antislavery preaching in Maryland in "Religious Influences on Manumission of Slaves in Caroline, Dorchester, and Talbot Counties," *Maryland Historical Magazine,* LVI (June, 1961), 176–197, especially pp. 191ff. Gewehr, *Great Awakening,* pp. 235ff. reports other manumissions in Virginia. See also *Journal of the House of Delegates of Virginia,* Session 1785–1786 [Richmond, n.d.], p. 25, Tuesday, November 8, 1785.

antislavery preaching demanded action, or perhaps they had acquired more confidence as the failure of 1785 receded into the past. Perhaps, also, the secession of the prominent antislavery preacher, James O'Kelly, forced regular Methodists to emphasize their opposition to slavery. In any event, their decision came after O'Kelly had left the church in 1792 and after Virginia and South Carolina preachers in 1795 had resolved neither to hold slaves nor to ordain slaveholders.[28]

But no matter how enthusiastically opposed to slavery they might be, the preachers would be hard put to make a meaningful rule within the bounds of the 1785 decision to avoid unduly antagonizing the slaveholders. Bishop Asbury was fully aware of his problem as he presided over the quadrennial General Conference of 1796—the second meeting of the whole church. Although convinced that slavery should be regulated and finally abolished, he was determined that the action of the conference should not curtail the preaching of the Gospel. He was more than ever persuaded that Christianity would "soften" the masters' attitudes towards the slaves, and "sweeten the bitter cup" of servitude. "There are thousands here of slaves," he wrote, "who if we would come out to them would embrace religion. It is of vast moment for us to send the news far and wide. It hath its influence."[29]

[28] Asbury, *Journal*, II, 33, November 25, 1794. Barclay, *Reform the Nation*, p. 79. Document of Agreement on Slavery, January 2, 1795, South Carolina Conference Historical Society Papers, Wofford College. See also Asbury, *Journals*, III, 420n. Robert Paine, *Life and Times of William M'Kendree*, Nashville, 1870, I, 54, 60, 62.

[29] Francis Asbury to George Roberts, February 11, 1797 in Asbury, *Journal*, III, 160. The General Conference was in effect the national Methodist governing body, made up entirely of clergy. The annual conferences were also clerical and directed the business of regions which were outlined by the quadrennial General Conference. The quarterly meeting conferences conducted the primary business of a minister's charge which would include one or more churches, and at this level the laity exerted their influence.

It is not surprising, therefore, that the rule on slavery passed in 1796 was formalized frustration as much as it was opposition to a social wrong and a guide to the "extirpation of the crying evil of African slavery." The frustration was revealed in the General Conference's "recommendation that the Church require its lay officials to emancipate their slaves as soon as possible, if laws and "the circumstances of the case" would allow it. Yearly conferences could make other appropriate rules for their localities on the slaveholding of church officials. If strictly enforced, however, these regulations could have asserted the church's authority over slavery: they forbade the selling of slaves on pain of expulsion, and prescribed procedures by which local quarterly conferences would determine the length of a Negro's servitude when bought by a Methodist. If a church member refused to register a deed of manumission for any slave he had purchased, or for that slave's children, he was to be expelled also. Furthermore, no slaveholder would be admitted into membership until he understood that the Church opposed slavery; and to make that opposition more effective, the Conference appealed to all Methodists for advice on how to eradicate "this enormous evil from that part of the church of God to which they are united."[30]

As the rule of 1796 merged with the continuing antislavery preaching, the clergy were inspired to widen their appeal by exerting pressure aginst the laws around which they had had to bend their regulations. At the General Conference of 1800 they rejected antislavery rules similar to those which had disrupted the peace of the Church in 1785, but agreed to prevent themselves and their colleagues from holding slaves in states where laws allowed emancipation. Then they directed the annual conferences to draw up and circulate petitions for the gradual emancipation of all slaves in states which still lacked laws for that purpose—a campaign which

---

[30] *Discipline,* 1798, pp. 169–171. See Appendix to this study.

20

should be "continual from year to year till the desired end be fully accomplished." The directive was published in a special address and circulated over the signatures of Bishops Asbury, Coke, and Richard Whatcoat, and the influential ministers, William McKendree, Jesse Lee, and Ezekiel Cooper.[31] If circumstances prohibited the exclusion of slaveholders from the Church, the Methodists would move against the circumstances.

But once again, new tactics against slavery failed. The annual conferences simply did not do what was required of them. The papers of the Baltimore and Virginia conferences, with churches in four slaveholding states, mention no attempts to draw up any petitions on slavery; and the South Carolina conference was cowed into silence by the reaction of Carolinians who believed the Address of the General Conference to be an incendiary and dangerous broadside. The white inhabitants of Charleston, who could forget neither the slave insurrection in Santo Domingo nor the recent Gabriel plot in Virginia, read with great alarm the Methodists' statement that they regarded slavery "as repugnant to the unalienable rights of mankind, and to the spirit of the Christian religion." Such opinions were especially dangerous among a group of men who continually preached to the Negroes. Furthermore, the Methodists had had the temerity to print the address for free distribution. Refusing to allow this, the good citizens of Charleston promptly burned the leaflets on arrival. They then turned upon George Dougherty, a Methodist preacher, and dragged him through the streets to the town pump where they tried unsuccessfully to drown him. A mob of respectable gentle-

[31] *Journals of the General Conference of the Methodist Episcopal Church,* New York, *1855,* I, 40–41, 44. Charles Elliott, *History of the Great Secession from the Methodist Episcopal Church in the Year 1845,* column 39. Also, The Address of the General Conference of the Methodist Episcopal Church to all their Brethren and Friends in the United States, Baltimore Conference Papers, Lovely Lane Museum and Library, Baltimore.

men also surrounded the home of John Harper, Dougherty's colleague, and threatened him with violence.[32]

So intense was public hostility that magistrates told the ministers that they could not "expect peace in this State, unless [the Methodists] objured [their] principles respecting slavery." Harper wrote Ezekiel Cooper that if Bishop Asbury came to Charleston it would be "at the Peril of his life."[33] But Asbury did come and found that the Address had caused a reaction not only in Charleston, but also in the back country. Suspicious masters were forbidding ministers to preach to the slaves, who formed a majority of Methodists in some areas. Moreover, the legislature made a direct attack by forbidding Negroes to meet behind closed doors or at night, which was how and when Methodists of both races met.[34] The violent reaction of Carolinians and the inaction of ministers in the upper South revealed that antislavery activity in the South as early as 1800 was neither prudent nor easy. The revolutionary ideals of freedom, the enlightened belief in equality, and the Christian affirmation of suffering love were neither widespread nor powerful enough to command men to love or free a race which many believed unequal to their own.

The reasons for the great repudiation of Methodist antislavery ideals and action are not difficult to determine. In the first place, recalcitrant Methodist laymen simply did not want to free slaves which they either already owned or someday hoped to buy. The Church was growing rapidly not

[32] John Harper to [Ezekiel Cooper], [November], 1800, Cooper Papers. The Gabriel Plot was a slave conspiracy in Virginia in 1800 which was linked by rumor with Methodist antislavery preaching. See Herbert Aptheker, *American Negro Slave Revolts,* New York, 1943, pp. 101–103.

[33] *Ibid.*

[34] H. M. Henry, *The Police Control of the Slave in South Carolina,* Emory, Va., 1914, pp. 134–135. James Jenkins, *Experience, Labours, and Sufferings of Rev. James Jenkins of the South Carolina Conference,* Charleston, 1842, p. 96. Asbury, *Journals,* II, 271, December 17, 1800; p. 272, December 21, 1800; p. 281, January 30, 1801.

only among the dispossessed Negroes but also among the possessing whites, who craved a share of the prosperity which has always been the "American dream." Part of that dream for many Southerners became the owning of slaves as cotton ascended to its throne after 1793. If the occasional conscience-stricken master were convinced that the evils of slavery were great, he would be more tempted to mitigate the evils than to emancipate his Negroes. Methodism was a people's movement, and the people either wanted slavery or feared emancipation. Asbury had concluded by 1798 that slavery would exist in Virginia "for ages; there [was] not a sufficient sense of religion nor of liberty to destroy it; Methodists, Baptists, Presbyterians, in the highest flights of rapturous piety, still maintain and defend it."[35]

In this climate of opinion the preachers' individual convictions had begun to lose their cutting edge. Antislavery men began to find themselves able to live with slavery. The impecunious Asbury himself could not follow the example of the Quaker saint, John Woolman, who refused to accept the free hospitality of slaveholders. The Bishop slept in many a master's house but at the expense of a guilty conscience: "O," he cried in anguish, "to be dependent on slaveholders is in part to be a slave, and I was free born."[36] Nevertheless, he cautioned antislavery Methodists to "*give the credit due to multitudes who do not enslave the minds of their servants, but allow them full liberty to attend the preaching of the gospel.*"[37]

This kind of accession to the institution of slavery was gradually written into the rules of the Church, since the clergy tried to appease slaveholders by not demanding impracticable, unreasonable, or illegal manumissions. The rule

[35]Asbury, *Journal*, II, 151, January 9, 1798.

[36] *Ibid.* Also Drake, *Quakers and Slavery,* p. 59.

[37] *Discipline,* 1798, p. 138. There was no mitigation in Methodist hostility to the slave trade. They reprinted an English attack upon it in 1798. See "A Summary View of the Slave Trade," *Methodist Magazine,* II (April, 1798), 164–167.

of 1796, by allowing local quarterly and sectional annual conferences to transform its provisions into action, made a universal and strict ethic on slavery impossible. Anyone with a normal facility for rationalization could develop a circumstantial argument for retaining his slaves, and when enough slaveholders were admitted to membership they could soon prejudice the action of the quarterly conferences. Enforcement of the rule on slavery would vary with the congregations and their preachers. If pressures were strong enough to make a preacher publicly deny the danger of his antislavery sentiments, he might eventually place his spiritual and physical concern for the slaves above emancipation. In addition economic pressures might encourage relaxation of discipline, for Asbury found some ministers who feared that by expelling those who "trade in slaves, the preachers [would] not be supported."[38]

Thus, gradually, the Methodist ministry was becoming identified with the South and its institutions. Local preachers, part-time ministers who were usually farmers, were quite susceptible to local customs and not surprisingly began to buy slaves. Itinerants were less susceptible to local mores during the early years of American Methodism since they were appointed first to one section of the country and then another; but soon their area of circulation shrank. Although an itinerant would not identify himself so much with a community as a local preacher, he could still identify his interests with the people whom he knew in a group of communities. Asbury feared that this tendency plus the increasing number of Southern marriages among the clergy would eviscerate the purity and vitality of the ministry. His misgivings were justified. The circuit riders, although called to preach the Gospel, might well believe that they ought not to do so

[38] Asbury, *Journal,* II, 8, March 10, 1794. One of the Methodist preachers in Charleston did make a public declaration explaining his pacific beliefs and intentions, reported in a newspaper clipping for October 30, 1800 in the Cooper Papers.

amid their usual abject poverty. If they happened to marry women who eventually received an inheritance of slaves, or if they themselves inherited slaves, they might be more tempted to regard the Negroes as a trust than as subjects for emancipation. In the General Conference of 1796 some preachers even defended the holding of slaves.[39] Thus did the iron economic and social facts of a slaveholding society confront and confound Methodist antislavery activity.

The ideological justification for this retreat was, and continued to be, that the Church must preach to the slave even if it could not emancipate him. The argument may have been a rationalization to some, but not to the preachers who had brought 42,500 Negroes into the Church by 1816—and that fact signified to the Methodists that the Gospel was being faithfully preached. Furthermore, a twenty-five fold increase in membership in one generation brought the Church's numerical strength by 1816 to 172,000 whites. White and black together could "testify" that faith in Christ, trust in His love, and joyful hope in a future life freed them from present cares and bondage. Preaching the Gospel, as far as the Methodists were concerned, led primarily to a willful affirmation of faith in Christ and a determination to be righteous in personal encounters and actions. Although this faith was nourished in the society of true believers, it did not necessarily lead to an assault upon social institutions—as the Methodist clergy found. With such a view of Christian piety Asbury could write, "What is the personal liberty of the African which he may abuse, to the salvation of his soul, how may it be compared."[40] The retreat from the position of 1785, therefore, was not only the result

[39] Colbert, "Journal . . . ," October 31, 1796. Asbury, *Journal*, I, 440, April 5, 1783; II, 156, March 25, 1798. Sweet, *Virginia Methodism*, pp. 144, 154. A description of how marriage might affect the ministers' attitudes towards slavery is in George G. Smith, *The Life and Letters of James Osgood Andrew, Bishop of the Methodist Episcopal Church, South*, Nashville, 1882, pp. 153–155.
[40] Asbury, *Journal*, II, 591, February 1, 1809.

of endemic self-interest, but also of conscientious moral struggle.

Thus when Charleston and South Carolina reacted so explosively to the Address of 1800, Bishop Asbury regretfully concluded that he had been fighting a hopeless fight. Although he allowed the South Carolina Conference to give away antislavery pamphlets, he decided to mitigate the rule on slavery at the next meeting of the General Conference in 1804 and met little opposition. In frustrated resignation, he wrote, "I am called upon to suffer *for Christ's sake*, not for slavery."[41] Tired and angry with himself, he stubbornly refused to act in the Conference upon Freeborn Garrettson's motion to have the three bishops formulate a new Section on Slavery. Taking the cue, the Conference produced an ordinance which further softened the rules on trading in slaves, rescinded the call to petition state legislatures, and insisted that itinerants could not own slaves where emancipation was legal and practicable. It also suggested that ministers "admonish and exhort all slaves to render due respect and obedience to the commands and interests of their respective masters." The Conference's most telling decision, however, was to suspend the whole Section on Slavery south of Virginia. Accordingly, the Methodists printed two *Disciplines* in 1804—one for Virginia and her northern neighbors, and one for the southernmost states.[42]

At the next meeting in 1808 the Conference decided to continue the practice of printing two *Disciplines,* and added still further to the division between North and South by giving the annual conferences the power to determine how to deal with those who bought or sold slaves. Clearly the leaders of the Church believed that they must not appear to be too much opposed to a social and economic institution

[41] *Ibid.,* p. 430, April 10, 1804. Francis Asbury to George Roberts, January 5, 1803 in Asbury, *Journal,* III, 258.

[42] *Journals of the General Conference,* I, 44, 60. *Discipline,* 1804, p. 216.

so thoroughly identified with sectional peculiarities as was Negro servitude. All that Asbury could suggest for opponents of slavery was emigration to Ohio.[43] There was now a pathetic and hollow quality to the preface of the Section on Slavery in the *Discipline:* "We are as much as ever convinced of the great evil of slavery."

At least one rugged antislavery veteran challenged this constant yielding to evil. Samuel Mitchell of the Baltimore Conference addressed his colleagues upon the subject in 1813. It is impossible, he complained, to convince people that "the Methodist conference believe slavery so great a crime as they profess or they would adopt some decisive measures against it, seeing they let no other sin go unpunished. . . ." He admitted that laws often made emancipation difficult, but demanded, "When did laws wash away the guilt of an act prohibited by the word of God?" Mitchell exhorted the Baltimore Conference to act decisively because people believed antislavery preachers to be only "a few disordered minds, who have more zeal than knowledge, while the majority of the more sober and informed think it no crime to hold a fellow man in state of perpetual bondage." The conference answered with a rule to prohibit the ministry from owning slaves and the laity from buying and selling them.[44] Although the rule was not decisive, the ministry of northern Virginia and Maryland, by continuing a part of the antislavery tradition of the Methodist Episcopal Church, showed more determination than did the General Conference of 1816.

That assembly worked not only under the weight of its previous decisions on slavery, but also that of the growing legal entrenchment of Negro servitude. North Carolina in 1796 reaffirmed an old law which prohibited emancipation.

[43] Peter Pelham to Edward Dromgoole, November 19, 1807, Dromgoole Papers.

[44] Samuel Mitchell, Address to the Baltimore Conference, January 30, 1813; Journals of the Baltimore Conference, I, 272, Baltimore Conference Papers.

Other states allowed manumission only within certain limits: South Carolina, Georgia, and Tennessee by 1805 all demanded security for freed slaves lest they become burdens upon the community. Georgians could free slaves only by act of legislature, and Mississippians only on grounds of meritorious service. A Virginia law of 1806 demanded that emancipated slaves leave the state within twelve months or forfeit their freedom, a harsh rule mitigated only slightly in 1816.[45] The laws which made it difficult or at least troublesome to free slaves could easily be used by halfhearted Methodists as excuses for remaining slaveholders; and that is what the national assembly of Methodist ministers finally admitted had happened.

The meeting of 1816 brought the termination of the first phase of Methodist antislavery activity. The end came with little fanfare, for the conference faced many other issues. The basic problem confronting Methodists involved growth and organization. They had developed from a small sect within the Anglican Church into the largest Christian denomination in the United States, and they looked forward to converting the thousands moving westward. Francis Asbury, who had led the Methodists across so many frontiers before, who had preached wherever there was a soul to listen, was dead. It was this small, frail prophet of lonely places and never-ending trails who had introduced opposition to slavery into the councils of the Church, then caution, then compromise; and with his death came the final gasp of ecclesiastical determination to oppose slavery throughout the nation. The Committee on Slavery, whose report the Conference adopted, concluded that "under the present, existing circumstances in relation to slavery, little can be done to abolish, the practice so contrary to the principles of moral justice." Furthermore, "the evil" appeared beyond remedy since Methodists were "too easily contented with laws unfriendly

[45] Hurd, *Law of Bondage*, II, 7, 19–21, 82–86, 89–92, 95–97, 101–103, 142–146.

28

to freedom" and because the General Conference could not change the civil code.[46] There was no talk of hoping that the Gospel would gradually eradicate slavery—only a sense of failure and regret for having to compromise great principles. The compromise, however, was not between sections, North and South, but rather between the Church and the "World." The first Methodist controversy with slavery ended as a candle flickers out when the wax is melted and there is nothing left to burn.

[46] *Journals of the General Conference,* I, 169ff.

CHAPTER II

COMPROMISE CONFIRMED:
The Sectional Adjustment to Slavery
1808–1830

THE despair expressed by the General Conference in 1816 symbolized the end of an era during which the Methodist clergy opposed Negro servitude wherever it existed. The anxious expurgation of the regulation on slavery from the Southern *Disciplines* in 1804 had already indicated the division of the Methodist Episcopal Church into geographical as well as moral sections; the period from 1808 to 1830 continued extant trends. Against a fluid background of economic development, social movement, and political antagonism, Methodists were seduced by prevailing sectional attitudes. While ministers in the deep South joined the laity in owning slaves with impunity, their fellows in the North lamented the trials of Southern brethren laden with the weight of entailed wrong. In the border states it continued to be possible for church officials to regulate the relationship between Methodists and slavery for at least a short while longer. But wherever the ministry compromised with slavery, the compromise became a virtue confirmed by experience if not ideals.

The world in which the Methodist Episcopal Church struggled to be catholic in membership and strict in morality was a rough, explosive world—influenced less by revolutionary ideals of freedom and equality than by economic facts of expansion and accessible wealth. Eli Whitney's cotton gin, new English processing of cotton fibers, and the South's great supply of new lands were primary factors in the increase of cotton culture before the War of 1812 and the explosion in production afterwards. With prosperity, the value of Negro slaves increased as they were sold out of the upper South into South Carolina, Georgia, Alabama, and Mississippi, where involvement with slavery grew with every rise in the price of cotton.[1] Since Methodists were part of this new prosperity, their church became a part of the new South with its deepening addiction to slavery and fear of emancipationist preaching.

After 1808, most antislavery activity in the United States became limited to the area north of South Carolina, and to a mere handful of the thousands who swept on to their dreams of wealth. The foreign slave trade was outlawed and slavery was on the way to extinction in every state north of Mason and Dixon's line and the Ohio River. In this milieu, the antislavery fame of the Methodists continued to be second only to that of the Quakers, who sought to complement their literary attack upon servitude with a boycott of slave-tainted goods. Still persistent was the Wesleyan reputation for hating slavery that had made the Negro insurgents in Gabriel's conspiracy of 1800 exclude the Methodists from their plan of killing all whites. In many areas as far south as Mississippi, people naturally assumed that Methodists, and especially their preachers, did not like slavery.[2]

The Wesleyans were, of course, not the only evangelicals who stood against the institution. A few emancipating Baptists, especially the Friends of Humanity in Kentucky, were

[1] Lewis Cecil Gray, *History of Agriculture in the Southern United States to 1860*, Washington, D.C., 1938, II, 651–666, 679–686, 691–692.

[2] Herbert Aptheker, *A Documentary History of the Negro People in the United States*, New York, 1951, pp. 43, 46. Locke, *Anti-Slavery in America*, p. 190. Helen Tunnicliff Catterall, *Judicial Cases Concerning American Slavery and the Negro*, Washington, D.C., 193, IV, 161. W. F. Strickland, *The Life of Jacob Gruber*, New York, 1860, p. 156, 160ff., 248. William Winans to Ralph Randolph Gurley, February 27, 1827. American Colonization Society Papers, Library of Congress.

excluding slaveholders from membership, and by 1818 David Rice had convinced the Presbyterians that they ought to condemn Negro servitude. Antislavery men were a self-conscious minority who shared their ideas across denominational lines. The established Methodist rule against the "buying and selling of slaves" was understandably similar to that proposed by Presbyterian clergymen in 1815.[3] These other denominations, however, were opposing slavery with no better results than the Methodists. And those spiritual children of John Wesley and Francis Asbury were finding their ethics affected by geography and economics.

This is demonstrated through a survey of Methodist action in various parts of the country between 1808 and 1830. The General Conference, despairing of the possibility of a nationwide ethic on slavery, gave the annual conferences in 1808 the power to "form their own regulations relative to buying and selling slaves." In following this directive, the northernmost of the Southern conferences, such as those of Baltimore and Philadelphia, had a great advantage. They included portions of Pennsylvania, Maryland, and Virginia—territory where slavery was illegal and where it was entrenched. This gave ministers who preached in slave territory the perspective of close association with society in free states; they would eventually ride circuits on both sides of Mason and Dixon's line. And in that settled and often sedate area, the ministry and determined lay officials continued

[3] A. T. McGill, *American Slavery as viewed and acted on by the Presbyterian Church in the United States of America,* Philadelphia, 1865, p. 14. Locke, *Anti-Slavery in America,* pp. 130–131. Alice Dana Adams, *The Neglected Period of Anti-Slavery in America (1808–1831),* Boston, 1908, pp. 117–118, 126–139. William Warren Sweet, *The Baptists* (volume 1 of his *Religion on the American Frontier, 1783–1840*), New York, 1931, pp. 80–85, 89. Walter Posey, "The Slavery Question in the Presbyterian Church in the Old Southwest," *Journal of Southern History,* xv (August, 1949), 312. Also Posey's *The Presbyterian Church in the Old Southwest, 1778–1838,* Richmond, 1952, pp. 74–81. Drake, *Quakers and Slavery,* pp. 114–121, 127–132.

for years to maintain a public disapproval of slavery while doing obeisance to civil law.

The Baltimore Conference was the first to act. In 1808 it adopted the rule passed in 1796 by the General Conference and since repealed. The local quarterly conferences of laymen were to decide how long slaves bought by Methodists would have to serve their masters in order to buy their freedom—perhaps a decade for an adult and a generation for a child. Subsequently, masters were to file deeds of manumission with the county court, and in many cases they did so. Records of only five circuits in Maryland and Virginia reveal no fewer than forty cases involving Methodists who bought slaves between 1799 and 1820; and on the eastern shore of Maryland during the same period, more than 1,200 deeds were reported in predominantly Methodist counties.[4] Besides these cases, there were instances of suspension and expulsion of Methodists from their societies for selling and whipping Negroes.[5] Clearly, some strong-willed people believed that the rules on slavery were meant to be obeyed.

The central figures in applying these regulations were the clergy. The Methodist Episcopal Church beyond the local level was a hierarchy of ministerial conferences which set the tone for their laity. Consequently, conferences might

[4] See quarterly conference records for Fells Point Station, and Harford, Baltimore, and Frederick circuits in Maryland and the Berkeley circuit in Virginia. Note especially the Baltimore Circuit Quarterly Conference Records, October 11, 1800, March 14, 1801, and October 5, 1811; Fells Point Station Quarterly Conference Records, July 17, 1807. All the records are in the Lovely Lane Museum in Baltimore save those of the Frederick Circuit which are in Wesley Seminary Library in Washington, D.C. The statistics on the deeds of manumission are from Carroll, "Religious Influences on Manumission of Slaves in Caroline, Dorchester and Talbot Counties," *Maryland Historical Magazine,* LVI (June, 1961), 194–196. For the rule of 1796, see Appendix to this study.

[5] Baltimore Circuit Quarterly Conference Records, February 12, 1803; November 12–13, 1803. Fells Point Station Quarterly Conference Record, August 9, 1805. Baltimore Conference Papers.

differ from each other not only because of location, but also because of the varying dedication to antislavery ideals of the ministry. The Baltimore Conference, for example, was much more sanguine in regulating the "buying and selling of slaves" than that in Philadelphia—the City of Brotherly Love. Not until 1814 did the Philadelphia Conference act upon the General Conference directive of 1808. Even then, the Philadelphia group was not so indefatigibly dedicated to enforcing its rules as the Baltimore Conference, which included more slaveholding territory.[6] The latter, by comparison, was a model of activity and rigor, and far more wary of devious laymen. When the quarterly conference grew lax in enforcing the slave rules, the clergy became primary prosecutors of the recreant. Since Virginia law made a freedman subject to reenslavement within a year, the strict control practiced in Maryland was impossible in the Old Dominion. But the conference could enforce the expulsion of a Methodist who sold a slave in any state.

As usual, there were sly recalcitrants who used ambiguous phrases to cover their venality. One of these phrases allowed Wesleyans to sell slaves for the sake of "humanity" or "mercy." The clergy had meant that Negroes might be sold to keep families together, but in 1817 they were forced to explain that the "terms humanity and mercy were designed to have exclusive application to the slave."[7] Although there could conceivably be cases wherein masters were forced to sell their slaves to relieve indebtedness, the conference believed that it had conceded enough. Slavery was evil, and white men as well as Negroes might have to suffer for their involvement in it.

Were the laity to be convinced of the wrong of slavery, the ministry had to provide a good example. The preachers

[6] Philadelphia Conference Journals, I, April 31 [sic.], 1813 and April 13, 1814, Philadelphia Conference Historical Society Papers.
[7] *Discipline,* 1808, pp. 210–211. Baltimore Conference Journals, I, 227–230 (1812), 272 (1813); II, 17½ (1817).

of the Baltimore Conference, therefore, followed the *Discipline* in purging themselves of any identification with slavery. To many this was a crisis greater than that of the war with Great Britain. In 1813 they began a surveillance of ministerial connections with slavery that persisted throughout the abolitionist crusade of a later generation.[8] The procedure was simple. In 1813, for instance, the conference required one Richard Tydings to prove that he could not legally free the slaves which his wife would soon inherit. Knowing the feeling of his brethren, Tydings dutifully produced the proof and piously declared that he intended "either not to possess them . . . or to free them" in the future if he could. Only then did he receive his ordination. In 1820 the conference again inquired into Tydings' relation with slavery and found that he was employing his wife's slaves, but only for "their own benefit."[9]

This kind of consistent sensitivity to the wiles and encroachments of slavery derived largely from the influence of Stephen G. Roszel, veteran circuit rider and persistent foe of a slaveholding ministry. He demanded strictness when his fellows tended to be lax. He persuaded the conference to be certain that candidates for the ministry had exhausted all legal means to free themselves from slavery, and year after year he kept close watch lest lack of precision allow some moral sluggard to be ordained.[10] In this quiet and determined manner, the Baltimore Conference attempted to continue its antislavery heritage at least in part.

Although the ministers could easily discredit slavery within the confines of their own limited authority, their public attacks upon it might bring down the wrath of the masters against them. This, at least, is what Jacob Gruber discovered. In August 1818, at a Maryland camp meeting of 3,000

[8] Baltimore Conference Journals, I, 248 (1813).
[9] *Ibid.*, pp. 227, 244f. (1813); II, 75f., 87 (1820). Also Baltimore Conference Papers for 1813.
[10] *Ibid.*, II, 11–14, 20, 26, 35, 70, 90, 97, 101, 106, 110, 129ff., 157 (1817–1822).

35

whites and 400 Negroes, the presiding elder from Carlisle, Pennsylvania, chose as his text, "Righteousness exalteth a nation; but sin is a reproach to any people (Proverbs, xiv, 34)." The sins which Gruber had in mind were infidelity, intemperance, and slavery. He said that slavery was not only contrary to the Declaration of Independence but also dangerous to the peace of society; if continued, it could possibly lead to the murder of all slaveholders. For this warning, Gruber was indicted by a grand jury for "maliciously intending and endeavoring to disturb the tranquility, good order, and government of the State of Maryland, and to endanger the persons and property" of many of its citizens.[11]

Stephen G. Roszel persuaded Gruber to accept the services of the influential young attorney, Roger B. Taney. The future Chief Justice emphasized that Gruber's indictment was based upon what he intended to do, and he obviously had meant to convict his hearers of sin—not to raise an insurrection. Taney pointed out that Methodists were famous for their disapproval of slavery, and masters had brought their slaves to meeting in full knowledge of this fact. The lawyer then demanded to know if a preacher who "maliciously" intended to incite slaves to acts of violence would do so in the presence of 3,000 whites? The jury agreed with Taney that Gruber was not guilty, but the Baltimore Conference was worried about the whole affair.[12] It advised its preachers to "be more cautious" and to "forbear as much as possible the use of epithets and allusions calculated unnecessarily to irritate without reforming the people." This advice was meant to achieve caution, not silence, but two years later another Methodist minister got involved in a

[11] Strickland, *Life of Jacob Gruber,* pp. 130ff., 137–139, 142, 146ff., 156, 160ff., 248. Stephen G. Roszel to Jacob Gruber, October 11, 1818, Baltimore Conference Papers. Stephen G. Roszel to William McKendree, September 16, 1818, William McKendree Papers, Emory University.
[12] Baltimore Conference Papers for 1820.

lawsuit for his all too relevant remarks upon the problem of slavery.[13] Clearly there were others who would have agreed with Gruber when he mused, "I have heard of Republican slaveholders, but I understand no more what it means than sober drunkards."[14]

In a world where public denunciation of slavery was such a tenuous occupation, the Baltimore Conference attempted to give Methodism the aspect of a free Church in a slave society. It did not vigorously denounce slavery by resolution or publication and it allowed slaveholders to become Methodists. But through the efforts of a majority led by Stephen G. Roszel the ministry was zealous to confine the influence of slavery to those outside the company of preachers. Although the conference achieved a very limited goal, it had used what little power it possessed to formalize the Methodist antislavery ideal. Such a position was not always clear and consistent, and the great temptation to be satisfied with it was always present. But it was an attempt to continue a concrete example of the Church's stated belief that it was "as much as ever convinced of the evil of slavery" in an unsure, fluid world. The laws that allowed emancipation in Maryland, and the fact that the conference included free Pennsylvania territory, helped to keep the impulse alive. In the itinerant system of transferring ministers from circuit to circuit across state lines, a slaveholding preacher would be excluded from a free state contrary to the theory of itineracy. Therefore, the Baltimore Conference, with a combination of fortuitous laws, geography, conscientious men, and the true Methodist heritage, developed its own peculiar antislavery tradition.

To the south, across the Rappahannock River, the Virginia Conference was less active in discrediting and limiting

---

[13] Baltimore Conference Journal, ɪɪ, 146 (1823).
[14] Strickland, *Life of Jacob Gruber,* p. 253. Also Stephen G. Roszel to Jacob Gruber, February 20, 1821, Baltimore Conference Papers.

the influence of slavery. Including within its bounds the highest concentration of slaves in Virginia and northeastern North Carolina, the conference naturally had more difficulty than the Baltimore Conference. Furthermore, Virginia law made emancipation tenuous for the slave, and North Carolina law made it impossible for the master except in rare cases. Nevertheless, until 1820 the Virginia ministry joined their northern brethren in inquiring into ministerial relations with slavery. Now and again the conference could extract a promise of emancipation from a ministerial candidate, or suspend a deacon for "trying to buy Negroes," or refuse ordination to a slaveholder.[15] But the record was sporadic, revealing none of the constancy and relentless pursuit exhibited by the Baltimore Conference. The southern area had neither proper laws, nor an intrepid Stephen Roszel, nor a geographical situation to help keep the ministry free from slavery. Without the possibility of transferring ministers between free and slave territory, pragmatic fact did not reinforce ethical ideals.

Until 1820, however, when the General Conference rescinded its delegation of such power, the Virginia Conference did have rules that provided for the expulsion of Methodists who bought and sold slaves. The rule had been passed in 1813 under pressure from the Baltimore Conference, and had to be redefined later as laymen tried to squirm out from under its provisions. Each preacher was supposed to read a copy of the rule to his congregations; but the effect of this directive on a region which had once before caused the Church to rescind rules on slavery can only be guessed.[16] Certainly the old and respectable Amelia Circuit never asked questions about slaves as had circuits of the Baltimore Conference, and a prominent lay preacher like Edward Drom-

[15] Virginia Conference Journals, I, 1812; II, 1813 (Case of Lewis Kimball), 1814, 1820. Randolph-Macon College Library.
[16] *Ibid.,* II, 1813, 1817. Baltimore Conference Journals, I, 212ff. (1812).

goole could acquire slaves with impunity.[17] The Virginia brethern were simply unable to pursue even a limited anti-slavery course for various reasons of law, geography, and personal proclivities, but they were not yet forced into a position of publicly disavowing their heritage like their colleagues in the South Carolina Conference.

Until 1831 that section of the Methodist Episcopal Church included most of the lands drained by the rivers which flowed into the Atlantic Ocean from the Neuse River in North Carolina to the Florida border. Along the coast, and past the malarial tidewater into the rolling back country, the Methodists preached their Gospel of hope and love to thousands of Negro slaves. In 1808, 90 per cent of Charleston Methodists were Negroes; by 1820 one-third of the laymen in the conference were slaves, and one-fourth of the Negro members of the entire church were in the South Carolina Conference. To protect this constituency the Methodists since 1800 had been particularly wary of the tinderbox sensitivities of the outnumbered tidewater whites in South Carolina.

Furthermore, the clergy were definitely becoming connected with slavery. At one time, ministers asked prospective colleagues if they were opposed to slavery, but one recalled that a "system of Jesuitical jugglery and management . . . enable[d] a man to be dreadfully opposed to the sum of all villainies and yet to comfortably pocket the proceeds of the labor of his wife's slaves." The conference seems never to have challenged the influential William Capers for his slaveholding, although the Methodist antislavery heritage did once induce him to allow his Negroes to manage his farm for themselves with disastrous results. The end of an era came formally when one of the foremost antislavery men

[17] Amelia Circuit Quarterly Conference Records, 1800–1832, Randolph-Macon College Library. Edward Dromgoole to George C. Dromgoole, January 16, 1817. Also a tax receipt for 1823, Dromgoole Papers.

of the conference, the rugged old German, Lewis Myers, surrendered completely and became a slaveowner.[18] Acquiescence was the rule throughout the old Southwest as well, even though the moral valor of earlier days still lingered in some minds to preserve a slight trace of antislavery reputation in Mississippi.[19]

The reason for succumbing to the values of a slave society lay not only in the great cottom boom which convinced many whites that slavery was necessary, and in the laws which discouraged manumission, but also in the public opposition to any criticism of slavery—an opposition born of fear. South Carolinians were afraid of insurrection when they burned Methodist pamphlets in 1800, and in 1822 they once again were gripped by fear. The so-called Denmark Vesey conspiracy of that year placed Methodist preaching to Negroes under general suspicion. Vesey, a free Negro carpenter of Charleston, was thought to have organized a slave insurrection of well over 6,000 conspirators. A member of the African Methodist Church in Charleston since 1817, Vesey became influential in class meetings and acted in such a way as to make the authorities think that he was the leader of an insurrection. South Carolinians hanged 37 "conspirators," banished Negro Bishop Moses Brown of the African Methodist Church, passed laws repressive of Negroes, and published pamphlets to vindicate the master class.[20]

[18] William M. Wightman, *Life of William Capers, D.D.*, Nashville, 1859, pp. 185–186. George G. Smith, *The Life and Letters of James Osgood Andrew, Bishop of the Methodist Episcopal Church, South*, Nashville, 1882, pp. 154–155.

[19] William Winans to Ralph Randolph Gurley, February 27, 1827, American Colonization Society Papers. Also John G. Jones, *Complete History of Methodism as connected with the Mississippi Conference of the Methodist Episcopal Church, South*, Nashville, 1908, I, 250ff.

[20] Two of the standard reports of the Denmark Vesey Conspiracy are Aptheker, *American Negro Slave Revolts*, pp. 268–273 and Anne King Gregorie, "Denmark Vesey," in the *Dictionary of American Biography*, New York, 1936, XIX, 258. Professor Richard

Since Vesey had apparently been led into action not only by Northern attacks upon slavery but also by religious enthusiasm, preachers to the slaves were suspect along with Northerners. Edwin C. Holland, Charleston editor and author, inveighed against the hypocrisy of the North for selling slaves to the South and then abusing that section for buying them. He also condemned Christian missionaries who "with the Sacred Volume of God in one hand" scattered "with the other, the firebrands of discord and destruction; and *secretly* dispensed among our Negro Population, the seeds of discontent and sedition." Holland repudiated such dangerous sympathy for those whom he called "the *common enemy of civilized society,* and the barbarians who would, IF THEY COULD, become the DESTROYERS of *our race.*"[21] But another Charlestonian suggested that proper sympathy for the slaves could be directed through the Protestant Episcopal Church. No Episcopalian was among the rebels, he pointed out, for the Prayer Book did not allow emotions to run riot. In the Episcopal Church, he emphasized, "there is nothing to inflame the passion of the ignorant enthusiast; nothing left to the crude, undigested ideas of illiterate black class-leaders."[22]

The Baptists and Methodists were thus placed on the defensive because of their work with the slaves, and because the conspiracy could not have gone so far without the "crude, undigested ideas of illiterate black class-leaders."

C. Wade, however, has raised serious questions which indicate that the conspiracy was probably a few rumors and the extreme wariness of the Charleston citizenry. See Wade's article, "The Vesey Plot: A Reconsideration," *Journal of Southern History,* xxx (May, 1964), 143–161.

[21] Edwin C. Holland, *A Refutation of the Calumnies Circulated Against the Southern and Western States, Respecting the Institution and existence of Slavery Among Them,* Charleston, 1822, pp. 7ff., 11, 60–61, 86.

[22] *Practical Considerations founded on the Scriptures relative to the Slave Population of South-Carolina,* Charleston, 1823, pp. 3, 6, 10ff., 14, 33–34.

41

Clergymen struggled to reassure Carolinians of the friendliness of their denominations to Southern institutions. Richard Furman, for the Baptists, denied that slavery and Christianity were incompatible, for the "right of holding slaves [was] clearly established in the Holy Scriptures, both by precept and example." If Baptists believed such exegesis, Furman implied, they could certainly be trusted to preach to the slaves. The Church did not act to destroy ignorance, poverty, or slavery, he said, but to emphasize peace, obedience, and kindness—a pleasing Gospel, it must be admitted, that would never have got anyone crucified.[23]

The Methodist preachers followed closely behind, lamenting the doctrine that "religion may do murder." There was no evil in slavery worse than depriving the Negroes of the "means of grace" they declared. Then, going on to eulogize the state of the Southern slaves, they assured their fellow Southerners that they believed the Negroes of the Carolinas and Georgia (where they preached) to be better off than many European peasants and white Americans. "We long after a free unsuspected access to them," they added, as if to explain why they had begun to defend an institution which their church still pronounced evil.[24] The approbation of slavery in these public statements did not arise from free, thoughtful, and enlightened scriptural exposition, but from the reaction of the custodians of human institutions caught in pragmatic necessity as they understood it.

The Methodist clergy had made a moral decision. They might have been more circumspect, or they might have developed a slave code that would eventually release Methodists from involvement in slavery and have some effect

---

[23] Richard Furman, *Rev. Dr. Richard Furman's Exposition of the views of the Baptists Relative to the Coloured Population of the United States in a Communication to the Governor of South-Carolina,* Charleston, 1823, pp. 7, 13–19.

[24] "Extracts from the Third Annual Report of the South-Carolina Conference Missionary Society," *Methodist Magazine,* VII (May, 1824), 196–198.

in their communities, but they could not. The compromise of the first generation of Methodist clerics to preach to all men and be quiet on slavery, once regretted, was now affirmed by a second generation with a pious belief in their responsibility to society and to the slaves. Prayer, preaching, and peace were their business; their fathers had "mistakenly" attacked slavery and the sons had learned a new wisdom. Like chameleons they adapted, but like moral men they understood that adaptation in moral terms. Those terms were real as their morality was real; but they had apparently lost a sense of guilt in living with a hated thing—a monster, as Asbury had called it. And when their sense of guilt had gone, they succumbed completely to a world they were ordained to convert.

This changing evaluation of slavery was part of the transformation of the relation of Methodism to society. Once outcast by the "better sort," the Methodist Church helped to create its own "better element" in the new society that was developing in early nineteenth century America. In the wilderness, churches ordered the moral and social lives of a rugged but uprooted people, serving as moral courts by enforcing discipline through the threat of ostracism from a "beloved community." At Sunday meeting, prayer meeting, and camp meeting, neighbors from distant places socialized and learned of such new benevolent institutions as the Bible Society and the American Colonization Society. As the communities aspired to greater things, churches provided colleges for a land devoid of education. They brought peace to family life by deploring "grog" and emphasizing prayer. Since they were the bond of peace for society, their role in such near tragedies as the Denmark Vesey conspiracy was quite clear. Furthermore, it is not surprising that the Methodist Episcopal Church shifted position as more and more of its Southern members acquired respectability and slaves. For, as one circuit rider recalled, the "better" people held slaves and "The narrowest men, when they came South, saw the situation, and enjoyed the warm, elegant, and devoutly Christian hospitality of the slaveholding membership, usually broadened."[25] Although a Methodist minister might join in "reprobating a sycophantic dancing of attendance upon the ungodly rich," the godly "rich" were probably more dangerous to the Church if not less desirable.[26]

How many Methodists mixed their piety and respectability with slaveholding is impossible to determine. The general consensus is that more Methodists and Baptists held slaves than members of any other denominations, but there were more Methodists and Baptists to begin with, so their share was naturally greater.[27] If they wanted to prosper easily in the South they could hardly avoid slavery, and many did want to prosper as easily as possible. This desire helped former opponents of slavery, such as the ambitious and pious Edward Dromgoole, to acquire slaves. Dromgoole was an immigrant Irish convert from Roman Catholicism who had served as a traveling preacher from 1774 to 1786, when he settled in Brunswick County, Virginia, and began to resolve the paradox of piety and economic well-being. Although warned that his new situation would detract from his calling, he manfully persisted in his accumulation of the "cares of this world." He was bothered little about slavery as he disposed of Negroes for the estates of deceased planters and by 1823 had acquired twenty slaves of his own.

[25] Richard Nye Price, *Holston Methodism from its Origin to the Present Time,* Nashville, 1903–1914, III, 335–336.

[26] William Winans to Thomas Nixon, May 26, 1820, William Winans Collection, property of the Mississippi Conference Historical Society in the Millsaps College Library. See also Roy M. Robbins, "Crusade in the Wilderness, 1750–1830," *Indiana Magazine of History,* XLVI (June, 1950), 121–132. Beverly W. Bond, Jr., *The Civilization of the Old Northwest,* New York, 1934, pp. 465–506. William Warren Sweet, *Religion in the Development of American Culture, 1755–1840,* New York, 1952, pp. 137–146, 160–189.

[27] See, for example, John Hope Franklin, *From Slavery to Freedom,* New York, 1947, p. 200. Walter Posey, *The Baptist Church in the Lower Mississippi Valley, 1776–1845,* Lexington, 1957, p. 89.

The Church never disciplined him for buying those slaves, but his antislavery friends and relatives in Ohio urged him to leave Virginia because "a Land of Liberty must be preferable to a Land of Slavery." Dromgoole did come to like the Land of Liberty across the Ohio enough to buy several hundred acres of it, but he continued to live in the Land of Slavery, where he prospered.[28] In a society that recognized the owning of slaves as an indication of success, Dromgoole was undoubtedly a far more popular example of Methodist piety than his colleague, John Jeremiah Jacob, who had emancipated his slaves to "support the Gospel."[29] Dromgoole was not a troublemaker who upset the calm of society or "meddled" in other people's business, but a respectable man in a respectable church.

This respectability and piety could produce a rather interesting and believable apologetic for accepting slavery, especially if expressed by a man like William Winans. A Methodist minister in Mississippi since 1811, Winans had left his antislavery ideas in his Pennsylvania Quaker home when he came south. A rough frontiersman of forbidding temper and rigorous self-discipline, he championed four causes in his lifetime: the American Colonization Society, the demand for a slaveholding Methodist episcopacy, justice for the Cherokee Indians, and the Whig Party. By his strong will and definite views he became the leader of Mississippi Methodism which he represented in every General Conference from 1824 to 1844. By 1820 Winans had married a slaveholder and settled down as a part-time farmer. His

[28] Wade Crawford Barclay, *Missionary Motivation and Expansion* (vol. 1 of his *Early American Methodism*), New York, 1949, p. 57n. Richard Ivy to Edward Dromgoole, March 31, 1786; Richard Lindsay to Dromgoole, March 22, 1788; Peter Pelham to Dromgoole, July 27, 1807 and September 8, 1809; Frederick Benson to Dromgoole, July 19, 1807. Also Tax Receipts for 1821 and 1823. Dromgoole Papers.

[29] Majorie Moran Holmes, "The Life and Diary of the Reverend John Jeremiah Jacob (1757–1839)," Unpublished M.A. thesis, Duke University, 1941, p. 328.

brother, who lived in Ohio, asked if he were a master of slaves. "I shall not hesitate to answer," replied the preacher, "that I am!"

But he thought he should justify himself. He would not favor enslaving Negroes were they already free, he explained, nor would he retain them if he could emancipate them. "So you see," he insisted, "I abhor the thing as much as you do." Congressmen had "shrunk from the task" of emancipation, he pointed out, because it would "ruin" the slaves and "endanger the very existence of the Nation." In such a situation he thought that a Christian should own slaves because he himself had not enslaved them, and because he would treat them far better than a non-Christian. Furthermore, Winans claimed that unbelievers would accept the "exhortations" of slaveholding Christians far sooner than those of the nonslaveholding brethren. The end of the discussion came when Winans pointed out that although slaves were mentioned in the Bible, slavery was never condemned; "the Apostles never [said] 'Set your servants free' " he concluded, but rather enjoined good treatment of them.[30] Certainly the piety which had led some men to denounce slaveholding had been transformed rather easily into acceptance, and then into affirmation.

Although Methodist adaptation to slavery was steadily and silently accepted along the Atlantic coast and the Gulf of Mexico, it came with more difficulty across the Appalachians in Kentucky and Tennessee. In fact, the intensity of the antislavery controversy in the Tennessee Conference forced the Church in 1820 to take back from the annual conferences the power to make their own rules on buying and selling slaves. The Tennessee Conference was as fortunate as the Baltimore in its proximity to free territory and

---

[30] William Winans to Obadiah Winans and his mother, April 14, 1820 and July 1, 1820. See also Winans to Samuel R. Shackleford, April 11, 1827. Winans Collection.

in its less dense concentration of slaves. In addition, the West Tennessee Basin attracted most of the large slaveholders of the area, giving Baptist, Presbyterian, and Methodist antislavery preachers a base in the east where they excoriated slaveholders with unrelenting enthusiasm.[31]

In 1808 the ministers who preached to 19,000 Methodists from northern Ohio to Mississippi repudiated Bishop Asbury's counsel of moderation and forced him and his colleague, William McKendree, to sign a directive expelling any Methodist who sold a slave. Later, anyone who bought a slave was also liable to a church trial. Although many church members were disciplined, from 1812 to 1819 the preachers continually redefined and reworked the rules in order to counter the usual evasiveness of the laity. Through war, peace, prosperity, depression, and expansion, the majority of the Tennessee Conference adhered to their principles. Even after Ohio and Kentucky were separated from them, the Tennessee ministry clung tenaciously to their opposition to slavery. One presiding elder told his brethren that the quarterly conferences refused to apply the rules because of their "officious intermeddling with legal and private rights," but Bishop McKendree told him that he had to keep the rules until they were changed.[32]

A majority of the Tennessee Conference refused to change them. Led by Peter Cartwright and James Axley, they firmly refused to ordain unrepentant slaveholders and resolutely

[31] J. Winston Coleman, *Slavery Times in Kentucky,* Chapel Hill, 1940, p. 4. Phillips, *American Negro Slavery,* p. 170. Martin, *Anti-Slavery in Kentucky,* p. 38. William Birney, *James G. Birney and His Times,* New York, 1890, pp. 74ff.

[32] Western Annual Conference Decision on Slavery, October 7, 1808, Francis Asbury Papers, Emory University. Price, *Holston Methodism,* I, 115, 254–256. William Warren Sweet, *The Rise of Methodism in the West, 1800–1811: The Journal of the Western Conference,* Nashville, 1920, p. 194. John B. McFerrin, *History of Methodism in Tennessee,* Nashville, 1875, II, 226, 400. Paine, *Life of McKendree,* I, 216, 287f.

continued to require that slaves bought by Methodists be freed at a future date.[33] In each meeting of the Tennessee Conference between 1812 and 1819 the battle over anti-slavery rules persisted. Finally, local lay preachers vowed to have no part in enforcing such rules; and when a minority of the itinerants supported their lay brethren, the youthful and excited opponents of slavery condemned them as *"Apostates."* By 1817 the controversy had become exceptionally intense and the conference secretary, Thomas Douglass, was livid with rage. He roundly scolded the bishops, McKendree, Robert Roberts, and Enoch George, for allowing the majority of the conference continually to "set up new standards of communion and Church membership." If the bishops would not "direct the course of the proceedings" to a better end, they ought to be charged with "maladministration," he wrote. "If our Episcopacy suffers our young, *inexperienced* and *furious Sons* of Nimski . . . to drive over the *feelings* and *characters* of men of *age, Wisdom,* and *longstanding* in our Church . . . , farewell to Methodism as it now is."[34]

In reaction to the controversy in Tennessee, the bishops suggested that the party favoring a relaxation of the rules should memorialize the General Conference to establish one uniform law on slavery for the whole Church—one which would require almost nothing. Following this advice, the minority of the Tennessee Conference in 1819 asked the national assembly of churchmen to repudiate the "principle that no man, even in those States where the law does not admit emancipation, be admitted" into the ministry as a slaveholder. Such a principle, they claimed, was contrary

[33] McFerrin, *Methodism in Tennessee,* II, 401, 462ff.; III, 160f., 494. A. H. Redford, *The History of Methodism in Kentucky,* Nashville, 1870, II, 503. Peter Cartwright, *Autobiography of Peter Cartwright,* Cincinnati, 1856, p. 196.

[34] Thomas L. Douglass to Bishops William McKendree, Robert Roberts, and Enoch George, December 25, 1817, McKendree Papers.

to the "order and discipline of the Church."[35] Actually the *Discipline* did state that traveling ministers should emancipate their slaves "if it be practicable" and "conformabl[e] to the laws of the state." But the majority in the Tennessee Conference had decided that they could judge practicability, and knew that the *Discipline* did not in any way force the Methodists to ordain slaveholders. The rule on slavery outlined what a minister could not be, not what he had to be. Antislavery activity in Tennessee, however, proved so contrary to peace, prosperity, and progress that the virtue of a compromise with slavery had to be affirmed by the highest body of the Methodist Episcopal Church in 1820.

It is not surprising that rumor linked the discussion on slavery at the General Conference with the "Missouri question." Only two months before the assembly met, the Congress of the United States had arrived at a compromise between politicians favoring admission of new states into the Union without restriction as to slaves and those opposing creation of any new slave states from the Louisiana Territory. Missouri's request to enter the Union had been the signal for a debate which, for a complex of economic, political, and humanitarian motives, centered upon slavery and its symbiotic association with the Southern section of the country. In the resulting public discussions, the North grew wary of a South seeking to expand through the device of new slave states, and the South grew suspicious of a North becoming hostile on political as well as moral grounds.[36] Inherent in both positions, along with self-righteousness and the use of principle for selfish reasons, was a conscious sectionalism which by the simple act of repeated articulation

---

[35] McFerrin, *Methodism in Tennessee,* III, 160–161. Henry Bidleman Bascom, *Methodism and Slavery,* Frankfort, Kentucky, 1845, p. 7.

[36] Glover Moore, *The Missouri Controversy, 1819–1821,* Lexington, 1953, pp. 42ff., 49, 65, 82, 172ff., 342. Also Allan W. Lane to Ezekiel Cooper, September 11, 1820, Cooper Papers.

could become a basis for the development of separate national identities.

The Missouri question lent political relevancy but not substance to the Methodists' continual, passionate discussion of what Wesley had labeled "the sum of all villainies." Nevertheless, Bishop McKendree told the General Conference that the Church, in its drive to "extirpate" slavery, should not contravene law, custom, and "the interests of society." After a preliminary committee report, the delegates fell into a heated debate over slavery and its establishment by law and custom. Many preachers emphasized that the diversity of laws and attitudes made it impossible for the Church to enforce a uniform, specific, and meaningful regulation of slavery. Others advocated as many restrictions as possible because the Church could not tolerate moral evil. Their opponents claimed that scripture justified Negro servitude, adding that the Church could do nothing about it anyway.[37] The split in this debate was not sectional, since most of the participants were from the Southern or border conferences.

Many Northerners, however, joined in passing a rule which was too weak to be effective except where local customs were already antagonistic to slavery. The action was the natural progeny of men who had declared for years that nothing could be done about slavery. The majority, following past experience and their bishops' suggestion, deprived the annual conferences of the power to regulate the buying and selling of slaves. Since the controversy in Tennessee had been over the use of such power, there would now be peace there even though the Section on Slavery continued to begin with the grandiose question that promised more than it could provide. "What shall be done for the

---

[37] *Journals of the General Conference,* I, 179–180, 205, 228, 229, Samuel Dunwody, *A Sermon upon the Subject of Slavery,* Columbia, S.C., 1837, p. 26. [Ezekiel Cooper] to [Allen W. Lane, Jr.], September 13, 1820, Cooper Papers.

extirpation of the evil of slavery?" the General Conference asked. The reply was that no official or minister could be a slaveholder "where the law of the State in which he lives will admit of emancipation, and permit the liberated slave to enjoy freedom."[38] This was no effective institutional reminder that the Church condemned slavery. The laws of most Southern states rendered the rule meaningless. The General Conference had not only betrayed the antislavery preachers in Tennessee, but had also implied that Methodist ethics on slavery would derive less from Christian morality than from sectional economics, politics, and social adjustment.

With the meeting of 1820, slavery ceased to be a major item of business in the General Conference. Of more moment were controversies over the hierarchical structure of the Church: whether to elect presiding elders, how to define the powers of the episcopacy, whether to allow lay representation in the conferences. Advocates of more "republican" church government even seceded from the Methodist Episcopal Church to form the Methodist Protestant Church. With this and other crises to face, the slavery issue became less important—though never forgotten.[39]

The official attitude was that discussion of slavery had caused too much trouble, and that the decision to say little more was invaluable to the proper work of the Church. Since that work was preaching, the General Conference of 1824, amid some sectional feeling, rejected the attempt to reassign power over slavery to the annual conferences, and turned to religious instruction of Negroes. Although Negroes continued to join the Methodist Episcopal Church, in recent years they had objected to their treatment in the North. In an attempt to remedy grievances in the North and apathy

[38] *Ibid.*, pp. 179–180, 228–229. *Discipline*, 1820, pp. 194–195.
[39] *Ibid.*, pp. 211–213, 218, 230–232, 236–237, Tigert, *Constitutional History of Methodism*, pp. 338–363, 369–385. See also Edward J. Drinkhouse, *History of Methodist Reform*, 2 volumes, Baltimore, 1899.

in the South, the conference urged religious instruction of the slaves, and announced that Negro preachers would have all of the usual organizational privileges of the church where "the usages of the country in different sections justify" them.[40] This action was as bold as prudent judges of public sentiment could make it, and perhaps it could have been made into an effective guide if vigorously pursued. But a majority of the General Conference, including Northerners, would not favor a vigorous and continual fight against slavery, even within the bounds of the compromise already affirmed.

In 1828 they rejected a resolution proposed by Stephen G. Roszel and Peter Cartwright permitting the Church to discipline masters who mistreated their slaves. The resolution provided for objurgation, suspension, and even expulsion as penalties for treating slaves with "inhumanity, either in not supplying them with comfortable and sufficient food or raiment, or in separating husbands and wives or parents and children by buying or selling them in an inhuman traffic of our fellow creatures."[41] That Methodists occasionally mistreated their slaves is suggested by the fact that the proposal was offered by two Southerners who had intimately observed slavery for many years. The majority gave no reason for refusing to enforce Christian morality on behalf of a people who had few enough advocates. They evidently believed that Southern sensitivities would be aroused by attempts even to ameliorate the institution of slavery. As before, the application of Christian ethics to concrete situations would seem "officious intermeddling." And so the ministers officially abdicated their responsibility. In the Roszel-Cartwright resolution they could have demanded what public sentiment could not have denied, weakening slavery by providing an

[40] *Journals of the General Conference,* I, 294, See also, *Discipline,* 1824, pp. 189–190.
[41] *Ibid.,* p. 337.

institutional reminder of the Negro's claims to humanity. But the adoption of the resolution might have required white men to suffer, and the preachers apparently believed that Christianity needed only one cross.

Throughout the 1820's, a few stubborn and dedicated Methodists remained true to their antislavery heritage. They joined the weak and scattered abolition societies in the upper South and read the *Genius of Universal Emancipation,* edited by the ubiquitous and energetic Benjamin Lundy. Some Methodist ministers became agents for the short-lived *Abolition Intelligencer and Missionary Magazine* which the Presbyterian clergyman, John Finley Crowe, published in 1822–1823 in Shelbyville, Kentucky.[42] The Baltimore, Kentucky, and Holston conferences occasionally investigated and acted to curtail a slaveholding ministry, but strictness was not always achieved.[43] Conferences could still oppose slavery in sentiment, which was never too costly. The Kentucky Conference in 1822 expressed approval of the Kentucky Abolition Society's aims of gradual abolition; and the Tennessee Conference in 1824 concurred "in the sentiments" of the Moral Religious Manumission Society of West Tennessee that "slavery is an evil to be deplored, and

[42] *Abolition Intelligencer and Missionary Magazine,* June, 1822, pp. 31–32. The abolition societies and the *Intelligencer* urged general emancipation and education for the slaves. The societies were not part of an organization, but were held together by little more than a community of sentiment. By 1827 there were 130 abolition societies in the United States of which 106 were in the South, and none below the southern border of North Carolina. See Adams, *Neglected Period of Anti-Slavery,* pp. 165–172. Also see the *Genius of Universal Emancipation and Baltimore Courier,* October 1, 1825, p. 42, November 4, 1826, p. 53. *Christian Advocate and Journal,* February 29, 1828, p. 101.

[43] Baltimore Conference Journals, II, 157, 235, 265 (1824–1828). W. E. Arnold, *A History of Methodism in Kentucky,* Louisville, 1936, II, 66. "Minutes of the Holston Annual Conference, 1824–1844," typescript copy in Duke University Library, October 20, 1825, November, 1827; November, 1828; December, 1829.

. . . should be counteracted by every judicious and religious exertion."[44] A few laymen tried to stir their ministers to greater exertions, but they usually failed. The Cambridge Circuit on the eastern shore of Maryland memorialized the General Conference to prevent slaveholders from joining the Church. And one meek but determined Methodist pleaded with the Holston Conference in the Appalachian highlands to aid the Manumission Society of Tennessee in its fight against slavery, "a sin of the greatest magnitude imaginable." He wrote, "Deprive us of the ministers of the Gospel when we engage in trying to reform the nation, and we are, like Sampson [sic], shorne of our Strength."[45]

Manumission societies, importunate moralists, and general antislavery activity were indeed shorn of their strength. Prosperity and politics were deepening the wedge between open antagonism and silent acceptance, even among those who regretted slavery's existence. An example of this sectionalism can be seen in the thoughts of Freeborn Garrettson and Alexander Talley. Garrettson, one of the earliest and most consistent of Methodist antislavery preachers, published *A Dialogue Between Do-Justice and Professing Christian*, probably in 1820. His basic assumption was couched in language that he had learned as an evangelist in revolutionary America: slavery was contrary to natural law and the Christian religion. No man had a right to absolute power over another because only God could have absolute rights. Since slavery broke this moral axiom, Christians must be emancipationists.[46] Talley, a revered local preacher and

[44] *Abolition Intelligencer and Missionary Magazine,* October, 1822, pp. 81–82. McFerrin, *Methodism in Tennessee,* III, 270.

[45] Alexander Logan to the Holston Conference, October 15, 1830, George Aiken (Ekin) Papers, Emory and Henry College, *Genius of Universal Emancipation and Baltimore Courier,* April 8, 1826, p. 252.

[46] Freeborn Garrettson, *A Dialogue Between Do-Justice and Professing Christian,* Wilmington [1820?], pp. 7, 12, 13, 19–22, 29–30, 35–39, 48, 53.

veteran minister of the South Carolina Conference, privately dreamed of a scheme for abolishing slavery. "Are we doomed," he demanded of William Winans, "to pass on until the secret thunder bursts in destructive fury from the gathering storm?" He thought not, provided the South eschew a reactionary course. He suggested that a society be formed to purchase slaves in the cheapest market. It would then put them to work at their chosen occupations and use the resulting profits for the purchase of others while preparing their children for freedom in colonies beyond the United States. Private citizens could offer the money and Congress could give the land for the project.[47]

Both Garrettson and Talley in their own ways regretted slavery. Garrettson was impressed by the necessity of emancipation, Talley by the difficulty. Garrettson suggested emancipation with or without removal of the freedom, whereas Talley assumed that they would have to be removed. For all his profound compassion and sorrow at the existence of slavery, Talley tacitly accepted it as the proper social relationship between white and black men when they lived in the same country. The difference between the two men, however, was not merely that of personality or ideas. Garrettson had spent most of his life outside the South, whereas Talley had settled in the South. The basic difference was sectional. And the sections were coming to demand an allegiance of their own, not only within the body politic but also within the Body of Christ.

It was far easier to be against slavery in the North than in the South. Among the thousands who invaded the Old Northwest Territory after 1800 were Southern Quakers, Methodists, Baptists, and Presbyterians who were fleeing a land of slavery as well as seeking new opportunities. Among those ministers who emigrated from evil were the inimitable Peter Cartwright of Tennessee, Jesse Haile of Arkansas,

[47] Alexander Talley to William Winans, December 8, 1824, Winans Collection.

Joshua Boucher and Daniel De Vinne of Mississippi, John Clark of South Carolina, John Ray and John Sinclair of Kentucky, and a host of Virginians: James Ward, William Craven, Thomas Rice, Samuel Mitchell, Philip Gatch, and John Sale. All are merely names now, but then they were colorful, erratic, determined, and often irascible prophets who had staked their lives on principles that would not bend before human law. And so they went where the law would let them be at peace, for even prophets tire of trying to hold back a flood. In Indiana, Methodists joined Quakers in helping to fight the introduction of slavery. In Illinois they "meddled in politics" again by opposing a constitutional convention backed by proslavery men, and their victory in 1824 apparently made Governor Ninian Edwards try to gain votes years later by awakening Methodist "apprehensions about slavery."[48]

Morality, however, was not the primary denominator of sectional characteristics relating to slavery. The appeal to the people of Illinois concerning the introduction of slavery, written by the transplanted Englishman, Morris Birkbeck, reveals other factors. Birkbeck warned that land values,

[48] Governor Ninian Edwards to Cyrus and B. F. Edwards, July 15, 1830 in E. B. Washburne, ed., *The Edwards Papers*, Chicago, 1884, pp. 530–531. Henry Clay Fox, *Memoires of Wayne County and the City of Richmond, Indiana*, Madison, Wisconsin, 1912, I, 77. Merton L. Dillon, "The Antislavery Movement in Illinois, 1809–1844," unpublished Ph.D thesis, University of Michigan, 1951, pp. 100, 109, 129. William Warren Sweet, *The Methodists*, volume 4 of his *Religion on the American Frontier*, Chicago, 1946, p. 352n. James Leaton, *History of Methodism in Illinois from 1793 to 1832*, Cincinnati, 1883, pp. 31–32, 68, 141, 147. F. C. Holliday, *Life and Times of Rev. Allen Wiley, A.M.*, Cincinnati, 1853, p. 53. Horace Jewell, *History of Methodism in Arkansas*, Little Rock, 1892, pp. 55–56, 129. Jones, *History of Mississippi Methodism*, II, 115. Philip Gatch to Edward Dromgoole, February 11, 1802, June 1, 1805. John Sale to Dromgoole, February 20, 1807. Dromgoole Papers. Also John D. Barnhart, "Sources of Southern Migration into the Old Northwest," *Mississippi Valley Historical Review*, XXII (June, 1935), 53, 60. F. C. Holliday, *Indiana Methodism*, Cincinnati, 1873, pp. 34–36, 102–103.

democratic society, and small farmers would suffer in a slave state. Furthermore, there would always be danger of a slave insurrection.[49] Birkbeck knew that public sentiment was usually swayed by appeals to self-interest rather than to moral duty. Antislavery opinions were simply easier to hold in a region where people were building a society without the laws, customs, fears, and adjustments which accompanied slavery.

The Northeastern Methodists, too, were fortunate in being tempted neither by association nor interest to vindicate slavery. In fact, New England preachers actually took a few hesitating steps toward an open antislavery position before 1830. Their hesitation resulted naturally from the admitted failure of former Methodist attacks upon slavery. Their channel of expression was *Zion's Herald* of Boston, which backed the American Colonization Society and reported emancipations together with disclosures of the evils of slavery.[50] The editor, G. V. H. Forbes, was careful not "to accuse falsely or to kindle provocation" on slavery, yet he warned against the "moral degradation" which it created. Forbes suggested backing the Colonization Society because its program would demonstrate the Negro's ability to govern himself, thereby removing the greatest objections of proslavery men, as he thought, and create "an irresistible moral feeling on this subject. . . ." Within a year, the editor despaired of gaining any direct results through the society, but he still hoped that its moral power would help to achieve gradual emancipation with "proper remuneration" for the owners. When Benjamin Lundy came to Boston in 1828 looking for allies in his fight against slavery, Forbes assured

[49] Morris Birkbeck, *An Appeal to the People of Illinois on the Question of a Convention,* Shawneetown, Illinois, 1823.

[50] *Zion's Herald*, February 4, 1824, p. 2; June 2, 1824, p. 2; November 10, 1824, p. 4; April 20, 1825, p. 1; October 5, 1825, p. 2; October 12, 1825, p. 2; October 19, 1825, p. 1; November 16, 1825, p. 2; November 30, 1825, p. 3; February 8, 1826, p. 2; May 17, 1826, p. 1; July 19, 1826, p. 1.

the Quaker that he might "always calculate upon the cooperation of Boston." And when Lundy asked the ministers of the New England Conference if he could in fact count on such cooperation they replied unanimously that they viewed "with much pleasure the success that had attended the emancipation of the Slave population, and [did] earnestly desire that a system so degrading as that of Slave-holding [might] soon be extirpated from our nation."[51]

In thus repeating the all but dead Section on Slavery in the Methodist *Discipline,* the language of the New England Conference was very little more than vague sentiment. Although Methodists who professed to dislike slavery were freer to express their opinions in the North than in the South, they did so with caution. They tacitly accepted the compromise with slavery, and their foremost spokesman, Nathan Bangs, could earnestly vindicate this adjustment. Born in 1778, this learned blacksmith's son emerged from the frontier of western New York to become one of the most influential and powerful men in the entire Methodist Episcopal Church. Self-educated and often self-important, Bangs served as editor of church periodicals, chief Methodist apologist, secretary of the Methodist missionary society, and perennial New York delegate to the General Conference.[52] Early in his public career he had appealed for sympathy with the Negroes who were "in many places groaning under the cruelty of their unfeeling masters." There was some hope for them, he noted, because the Methodists had done much "to raise [the slaves] to the rank of rational beings." Yet the slaves were not his primary concern. After the Missouri controversy, Bangs was anxious for national peace and harmony. He anticipated the solution to the "great evil"

[51] *Ibid.,* October 11, 1829, p. 3; also May 9, 1827, p. 2; June, 27, 1828, p. 2; April 2, 1826, p. 2; August 13, 1828, p. 2.

[52] Abel Stevens, *Life and Times of Nathan Bangs,* New York, 1863, pp. 15–46, 51–65, 165, 182, 222, 227.

of slavery in the designs of the American Colonization Society, warning Northerners that they had done as much as Southerners to make the Negroes into slaves.[53]

When he became editor of the *Christian Advocate and Journal,* Bangs continued his cautious course. Founded in 1826, the *Advocate* by 1830 had become one of the largest weekly periodicals in the United States, and the official newspaper of the Methodist Episcopal Church.[54] The editor believed without question the warnings from South Carolina that the South was extremely "jealous of any attempt to interfere with slavery, even the preaching missions to the slaves."[55] When, therefore, a woman wrote to him in September 1830 about the problem of slavery, he replied, "We are not sufficiently acquainted with local circumstances, and other peculiarities in this case, to enable us to judge for another. All we can say is, in the language of the apostle, 'If thou mayest be free use it rather.' "[56] This answer was anathematized by the watchful and perceptive Benjamin Lundy; he wrote that many "honest and pious" Methodists, unlike Bangs, were " 'Sufficiently acquainted' with both general and 'local circumstances,' connected with the system of slavery, to set their faces decidedly against it, and readily answer 'questions' relating to it. In short, it is a *doubtful*

[53] Nathan Bangs, *The Substance of a Sermon Preached on opening the Methodist Church in John Street . . . 4th January, 1818,* New York, 1818, p. 17. *Christian Advocate and Journal,* July 20, 1827, p. 181.

[54] The *Advocate* had about 15,000 circulation. See Barclay, *Missionary Motivation and Expansion,* p. 218. Also Frank Luther Mott, *American Journalism,* New York, 1941, pp. 202–203. Mott, *A History of American Magazines, 1741–1850,* New York, 1930, I, 513–516. A survey of the *Advocate* for two years preceding Bangs' editorship will reveal the bias that it had in favor of the cautious course of the American Colonization Society.

[55] James O. Andrew, "Rise and Progress of Methodism in Charleston, South Carolina," *Methodist Magazine and Quarterly Review,* XII (January, 1830), 19–21.

[56] *Christian Advocate and Journal,* September 24, 1830, p. 14.

Christianity that [would] shut its eyes to the abominations of this 'supreme curse,' and refuse its extinction."[57]

The caution and hesitancy so scorned by Lundy were, of course, the result of many factors—individual, social, political, geographic. These, along with the ideals, goals, and growth of the Church, and the fears entailed upon men through no doing of their own, combined to muffle Methodist antislavery voices. As ordinary people who had created no special community apart from the world, Methodists shared the political and economic beliefs of all Americans whose attitudes on slavery were determined largely by where they lived. The acceptance of slavery by the Methodist ministry, however, was not spawned in the 1820's. It began with the first compromise on slavery years before, which had been defended as facilitating the conversion of both whites and Negroes.

The preachers' apologetic for their compromise was complemented by Methodist piety. That piety emphasized not only a life of prayer, Bible reading, and church attendance, but also a strict personal discipline of sobriety in food, drink, and raiment. Methodists also required an honesty in personal and economic relationships which precluded gambling and criminal indebtedness. When ministers like William Winans acquired slaves and still lived an exemplary life, those accustomed to accepting the moral validity of exemplary lives could accept slaveholding too. The major responsibility of a good man who owned slaves would be to see that they also "knew Christ" and adopted the "goodness" of their master—sobriety, integrity, piety, and an unstinting devotion to their work. Such personal piety could certainly not shatter social institutions, especially when it was linked with a popular movement—the Methodists doubled their membership between 1816 and 1830. As they did so they became more sectional. A Protestant church is essentially local rather than universal, and it is quite easy for local institutions to value

[57] *Genius of Universal Emancipation,* December 1830, pp. 132f.

an individual ethic of personal goodness without disturbing the peace and structure of society. Thus the Southern Methodists could help the Negro only through their own circumscribed understanding of the Christian life.

Ministers from all sections of the nation still toyed with the question of what to do for the benefit of the Negro. They wrestled with slavery in moral terms, and then accepted its inevitability. But they need not have yielded as much as they did. They could at the very least have passed rules to demand good treatment of the slaves. They could have maintained some distinct, rigid reminder of the tension between local social structures and transcendent ethics by not becoming connected with slavery. Self-vindication too easily extends into a vindication of institutions. The ministers had not, however, meant to leave the Negro to his fate. They continued to believe that their preaching could make him a free man in spirit even if their former exhortations had not made him a free man in body. If they affirmed the compromise with slavery, they yet hoped to help the slave in other ways.

CHAPTER III

THE SOUTHERN COMPROMISE OF CONSCIENCE:
The Mission to the Slaves
1824–1844

THE essence of compromise to men of principle is tinged with defeat, and the Methodist ministry as men of principle could never admit that they had wholly compromised their primary responsibility to the Negroes. Between 1824 and 1844, therefore, the more alert and dedicated Southern preachers fashioned their labors for the slaves into a great moral cause. Their message to white men had in part urged freedom for the slaves, and it had failed. They were determined that their message of Christian freedom would not be silenced, for if the Negro had lost one hope, he should not be deprived of ultimate consolation. Circumscribed by their own mentality, prejudices, and social context, Methodist preachers did "convert" many Negroes, caring for them in local churches paternally controlled by whites. The institutional symbol of the Methodists' special concern, however, was the Mission to the Slaves. While not taken seriously by some historians and only casually mentioned by most, the Mission was the Church's conscientious alternative to antislavery activity—its peculiar work within the peculiar institution. And although a survey of the Mission demonstrates the extent of Methodist subservience to slavery, it also reveals how the Christian churches were the only institutions in the South which could and did speak for the Negro.

The Mission was partially the result of continuous interest

in the Negro's spiritual welfare. Before the Baptist and Methodist revivals of the revolutionary generation, Negroes had had very little religious instruction. Although Anglican priests, Moravian missionaries, and Quakers now and then dedicated themselves to preaching to them in the face of opposition, slaves were even more "unchurched" than whites in early America.[1] In 1780, Bishop Asbury had urged the preachers to work carefully with the Negroes and by 1787 they constituted 15 per cent of Methodist membership. Constant evangelization had increased their rolls by 1800 to 20 per cent, or 13,500, and the General Conference voted to allow the bishops to ordain local deacons of "African brethren" if they had been recommended by white ministers and two-thirds of the men in their society.[2] But this half-step toward constitutional equality within the Methodist Episcopal Church was never fulfilled.

Methodist ministers, like most Americans, could never really accept Negroes on the same basis as whites. They shared misgivings about equality based not on science, or fear, or hatred, but upon environmentally conditioned experience. That experience was usually interpreted not through reflective perception of the effects of enforced caste distinctions, but through unregenerate common sense. Thus, they tended to allow less independence even to Northern free Negroes than the latter thought they deserved. Finally after years of patience spiced by conflict with Methodist leaders,

---

[1] Marcus W. Jernegan, "Slavery and Conversion in the American Colonies," *American Historical Review*, XXI (April, 1916), 514–520. Earnest, *Religious Development of the Negro in Virginia*, pp. 30–49.

[2] *Minutes of Annual Conferences*, I, 12, 28. *Jounals of the General Conference*, I, 44: "The bishops have obtained leave, by the suffrages of this General Conference, to ordain local deacons of our African brethren, in places where they have built a house or houses for the worship of God: *Provided*, they have a person among them qualified for that office, and he can obtain an election of two-thirds of the male members of the society to which he belongs, and a recommendation from the minister who has the charge, and his fellow-laborers in the city or circuit."

Daniel Coker and Richard Allen led a secession to form the African Methodist Episcopal Church. Other Negro Methodists joined them, objecting not only to certain articles of the *Discipline*, but also to their unequal treatment at the hands of whites. By 1822 the independent church movement among Wesleyan Negroes extended from New York to Charleston.[3] In reaction to the schisms, and to petitions from other Negroes requesting their own conferences under the bishops, the General Conference of 1824 decided to employ Negroes as itinerants wherever necessary. They also were prepared to allow Negro preachers and members to have "all the privileges in the district and quarterly conferences which the usages of the country in different sections [would] justify."[4]

Although the "usages of the country" differed greatly and often prevented independent action, Negroes exercised ministerial functions throughout the nation and particularly in the South. Most Negro pastors were lay preachers who, although unable to celebrate the sacraments, did preach and administer discipline among their people. Usually responsible to the quarterly conferences of local churches, they sometimes worked as colleagues of white circuit riders even when it was illegal to do so.[5] A few of these Negro pastors attained

[3] Robert Emory, *The Life of the Rev. John Emory, D.D.*, New York, 1841, pp. 70ff. Aptheker, *A Documentary History of the Negro People in the United States*, pp. 67ff. Carter G. Woodson, *The History of the Negro Church*, Washington, D.C., 1921, pp. 78–85, 91. Joshua Soule to William McKendree, undated letter; McKendree to Enoch George, April 23, 1821; Thomas Sargent to McKendree, June 28, 1818, McKendree Papers.

[4] *Journals of the General Conference*, I, 294. See also William McKendree to Enoch George, April 23, 1821, McKendree Papers.

[5] See for example Wightman, *Life of Capers*, p. 139. Capers recalled that he and the other Charleston preachers had sent out eight Negroes to work with the slaves in 1811. Although the ministers could not "exactly square it" with civil or ecclesiastical law, they believed their action necessary. See also William Winans to Ebenezer Hearn, June 6, 1822. William Winans, Diary, March 20, 1842, Winans Collection. LeRoy Beaty, *The Work of the South Carolina Methodists Among the Slaves*, Columbia, S.C., 1901, pp. 20–23.

widespread reputation, especially Henry Evans, a free local preacher who founded the Methodist Episcopal Church in Fayetteville, North Carolina. Although the number of Negro local preachers is unknown, they were certainly the vast majority of the Negro ministry. Local elders and deacon's orders were conferred upon a few Negro ministers in the Virginia, Holston, and Baltimore conferences. The last-named reflected its peculiar relationship to slavery by ordaining the largest number of Negro ministers, at least 15 between 1818 and 1841, also appointing a Negro to travel among the members of his race in the Baltimore district in 1830.[6] Furthermore, wherever laws and custom curtailed activities of Negro preachers, the Methodists could bend the law by licensing "exhorters," who formally assisted the white minister, but who could assume the role of pastor. Since the pastoral relationship is more a personal than an institutional creation, the more wise, mature, and saintly of these Negroes could become "spiritual" leaders of their people.[7]

Carter G. Woodson, *The Education of the Negro Prior to 1816,* Washington, D.C., 1919, pp. 72–73. Also John S. Field to the Reverend Mr. Moore, March 21, 1833, South Carolina Conference Papers. Trent Circuit, Virginia, Recording Stewards Book, Randolph-Macon College. William Compton to Peter Doub, July 4, 1821, William C. Doub Papers, Duke University. Edenton Methodist Church Record Book, pp. 84–87, Southern Historical Collection, the University of North Carolina. Carroll Circuit, Georgia Records May 21, 1831, Methodist Episcopal Church Papers, Duke University.

[6] *Ibid.,* pp. 124–127. Also Virginia Conference Journals, 1826. "Holston Conference Minutes," October 10, 1835. Baltimore Conference Journals, II, 28, 160, 175, 203, 216, 235, 264, 295, 317, 327, 337, 390 (1818–1834); III, 79, 100, 156, 157 (1837–1841). Local deacons and elders were ordained, but, unlike the itinerants, were confined to one locality. Below the ordained men were the local preachers who did not celebrate the sacraments.

[7] In 1832 both Alabama and Virginia passed laws to make preaching by Negroes so difficult as to be almost impossible. It was also against the law in South Carolina: the missionary on the Black River had to stop the Negroes from preaching because of it. *Christian*

The Negro's secondary position was reflected in the life of the local church as well. To be sure, some preachers fought to protect the Negro's dignity; one even claimed that slaves had "an equality of rights and privileges with their masters."[8] Before the War of 1812, the Philadelphia and Baltimore Conferences accepted the testimony of Negroes against white ministers. But these and other instances of equality were exceptions to the general acceptance of the caste system of slavery. Negroes and whites met together in prayer meetings, revivals, Sunday School, and preaching services, but not on an equal basis. During the sermon Negroes often sat in the gallery at the back and sometimes stood outside listening at the window. They often received the Lord's Supper after the whites and sometimes left the church by a separate door.[9] The Christian ideal of the equality of all believers was abrogated by the social and historical fact of Negro servitude.

However subordinate their role, the number of Negro Methodists continued to grow. By 1844 they numbered 145,000 or about 13 per cent of all Methodists. One-third of all Southern Negro Christians, or nearly 121,000, were

---

Advocate and Journal, June 26, 1835, p. 174. Hurd, *Law of Bondage,* II, 9, 151. For a discussion of the police, see Henry, *Police Control of Slaves,* pp. 133ff. Also Kenneth M. Stampp, *The Peculiar Institution,* New York, 1956, pp. 192ff.

[8] *Exposition of the Causes and Character of the Difficulties in the Church in Charleston in the year 1833,* Charleston, 1833, pp. 4–11. Also *Report of the Committee of the South Carolina Conference of the Methodist Episcopal Church, on the Subject of the Schism in Charleston with the accompanying Documents,* Charleston, 1835, pp. 3–8. Also William Winans to Moses Groves, March 31, 1834, Winans Collection.

[9] Virginia Conference Journals, 1826. Baltimore Conference Journals, II, 28, 175, 203, 216, and *passim. Minutes of Annual Conferences,* I, 25, 28. Asbury, *Journals,* II, 584. *Exposition of the Cause and Character of the Difficulties in the Church in Charleston in the year 1833, passim.* Woodson, *History of the Negro Church,* pp. 78–91. Colbert, "A Journal of the Travels of William Colbert . . . ," March 12, 1820.

Methodists.[10] These sharp statistical reminders of human endeavor represent the results of Methodist interest in the slaves, but do not reveal the peculiar work which institutionalized that interest into a proud, romantic, moral cause—the Mission to the Slaves.

To many of its supporters the Mission was more an idea than an organization. It was the result not only of the Church's natural interest in converting all men, but also of the peculiar reverence for missions which issued from the revivals before the War of 1812. Congregationalists in New England and Presbyterian synods further inland began to organize missionary societies before the war; the American Board of Commissioners for Foreign Missions sent out their first emissaries in 1812; and in 1814 the Baptists organized a convention for foreign missions. Supporters of the American Colonization Society continually emphasized the value of their colonies in West Africa as posts for "Christianization" and civilizing of the "dark" continent. The best thing an enlightened nineteenth century Christian could do for people less fortunate than he, was to send missionaries who would preach, teach, and heal. Thus, like other Christian denominations, the Methodists in April 1819 organized their own Missionary Society and prepared to send missionaries to the Indians throughout the United States.[11]

The enthusiasm for missions seeped into the South, although hardly with the same impact as the enthusiasm for cotton. In 1824, the South Carolina Conference announced that it hoped to create "a separate department which should exclusively be directed towards [the Negro's] spiritual welfare." Through publication of a weekly periodical, a committee of Carolina ministers hoped to popularize missionary activity, especially that to the slaves.[12] Praising English

---

[10] *Minutes of Annual Conferences,* III, 477.

[11] Barclay, *To Reform the Nation,* pp. 112–117.

[12] "Extracts from the Third annual Report of the South Carolina Conference Missionary Society," *Methodist Magazine,* VII (May, 1824), 198. Thomas Leonard Williams, "The Methodist Mission

Methodist missions to West Indian slaves, they agreed with the preacher who deprecated "that pitiful philosophy which would degrade blacks below the standard of men." Such statements, however, failed to attract many missionary enthusiasts, and the Reverend James O. Andrew accused the Church of negligence. He pointed out that present Negro Methodists exemplified how many more would be capable of living a Christian life.[13] Forty per cent of Carolina and Georgia Methodists were Negroes in 1826. But because they found that many slaves on the larger plantations were still not under care of the Church, Andrew and some of his colleagues understood these statistics as a challenge to further action. The major problems were how to calm suspicion aroused by the early Methodist antislavery activity and the Denmark Vesey conspiracy, and how to arouse interest despite their own enervating caution.

In spite of their solicitude for the slaves, the Methodist clergy were prompted to act by the decisions of others. Impressed by Methodist influence upon the Negroes of a neighboring plantation, Charles Cotesworth Pinckney, later lieutenant-governor of South Carolina, asked the South Carolina Conference in 1829 to send special preachers to his slaves. Other planters sent similar petitions—one congregation of masters even offered to support a missionary from their own purses if the conference would send him. The circuit riders had not paid enough attention to the slaves, they said, and the slaveholders could do little since the "relationship between *Master* and *slave*" made "void the best efforts of the most pious owners in Christianizing them."[14] Thus encouraged, the South Carolina Conference sent two

---

to the Slaves," unpublished Ph.D. thesis, Yale University, 1943, p. 27.

[13] *Wesleyan Journal*, October 8, 1825, p. 3; October 22, 1825, p. 2; July 1, 1826, p. 2; November 16, p. 3.

[14] L. H. de Yampert to the South Carolina Conference, January 10, 1829, South Carolina Conference Papers. See also Wightman, *Life of Capers*, p. 291.

missionaries to the "low country" plantations on the Ashley and Santee rivers. The superintendent of missions, William Capers, now had to convince enough reputable planters of the value of his "experiment."[15]

Capers was a slaveholder of Huguenot descent who had rejected Blackstone for the Bible, entered the Methodist ministry, and become a pastor to Negroes and a missionary to Indians. A dignified, thoughtful, and moderate man who served the Church far better than most of his fellow Southerners, he was a lifelong "apostle" to the Negroes. One of his first churches was in the Negro district of Wilmington, North Carolina; as a minister in Charleston he had sent out Negro preachers to the slaves despite the illegality of his action. Later as a prominent pastor he fought a hard and bitter fight with cynical whites in his congregation who wished to degrade and segregate the free Negro members. To him the slave was a soul to be valued, a human being ultimately equal to his master, even if "uncontrollable circumstances" effaced that equality in society.

When Pinckney asked the Methodists for a missionary, Capers was president of the South Carolina Conference Missionary Society, a position he usually held and one which enabled him to build and direct the slave missions in South Carolina and Georgia. In 1840 he became Secretary of the new Southern Department of Missionary Work of the Methodist Episcopal Church, a post which greatly increased his authority and responsibility. His influence, however, had never been entirely localized. As editor of the *Southern Christian Advocate,* he publicized missionary reports and encouraged the extension of preaching to Negroes on plantations too far from the reach of established circuits. As the South Carolina example encouraged first Georgia and then the other Southern conferences to adopt Capers' suggestions,

[15] *Christian Advocate and Journal,* September 25, 1829, p. 14. W. P. Harrison, *The Gospel Among the Slaves,* Nashville, 1905, p. 155.

the idea of the Mission grew. From Texas to Kentucky to Virginia to South Carolina, he applauded valiant efforts, lamented flagging zeal, and secured general financial support.[16]

Capers' letters, appeals, and instructions were complemented by the actions of James O. Andrew. A rough-hewn Southern frontiersman and one of the early proponents of the Mission in the South Carolina Conference, his paternal interest in the Negro race was in part the result of his fervent belief that all men must know the consolation of the Gospel. He himself was not a slaveholder when the missions were first established, and consequently he was elected a bishop in 1832 as the only nonslaveholding Southern candidate. "Careless and almost blunt in manner," Andrew continually appealed for the support of the missions to the slaves through addresses and letters to church periodicals. By 1844 Capers and Andrew, together with missionaries, planters, and Methodist journals in New York, Richmond, Nashville, Charleston, and Cincinnati had established the Mission throughout the South. Eighty Methodist missionaries working in every Southern state cared for over 22,000 slave members and preached to thousands more.[17] Success, however, had not come easily.

Although opposition diminished as the Mission grew, it never entirely disappeared. Masters often considered preaching to their Negroes an imposition, a nuisance, and even a danger. They claimed that the Negroes were already con-

---

[16] See Wightman, *Life of Capers*, pp. 11–12, 37, 69, 118, 124, 133ff. *Exposition of the Causes and Character of the Difficulties in the Church in Charleston in the year 1833*, pp. 4–11. *Southern Christian Advocate*, February 9, 1838, p. 134; May 28, 1841, p. 198; June 4, 1841, p. 202; July 23, 1841, p. 21; October 1, 1841, p. 62; October 15, 1841, p. 71; November 19, 1841, p. 90; November 26, 1841, p. 94; January 7, 1842, p. 118; January 28, 1842, p. 130; March 25, 1842, p. 162; February 17, 1843, p. 140; June 23, 1843, pp. 6–7; August 18, 1843, p. 138.

[17] Smith, *Life of Andrew*, pp. 24–31, 46, 106. Harrison, *Gospel Among the Slaves*, pp. 189–196.

verted, or that they could never understand Christianity; that they would not respond to preaching, or that they would respond too much. Some slaveholders grumbled about losing working time during religious instruction and others feared that the converted slaves would be more difficult to manage.[18] One of the most pervasive fears, however, was that somehow Methodist missionaries would loosen the bonds of slavery. The national Church still officially recorded that it was "as much as ever convinced of the great evil of slavery," and Methodists in Maryland and Tennessee had not long ago preached against it. Many times Southerners equated the Mission with "antislavery tendencies." Some even demanded that Methodist missionaries quit preaching because they feared that religious instruction would induce a thirst for general education. If satisfied, that thirst would lead to emancipation, for, they said, "Intelligence and slavery have no affinity for each other." Missions to the slaves would "ultimately revolutionize [the] civil institutions" of the South.[19] If the preachers wished to enforce their moral idealism and help the Negro, they would have to be trusted.

Faced with such opposition, the Methodists' response was a combination of assurance and challenge. They learned much from listening to friendly planters. Charles Cotesworth Pinckney, for example, told the Agricultural Society of South Carolina in August 1829 that religion could take the place of emancipation. "Nothing is better calculated to render man satisfied with his destiny in this world," he said, "than a conviction that its hardships and trials are as transitory as

[18] Charles Colcock Jones, *The Religious Instruction of the Negroes in the United States,* Savannah, 1842, pp. 175ff., 193ff. Charles Cotesworth Pinckney to William Capers, January 23, 1835, South Carolina Conference Papers. *Southern Christian Advocate,* November 19, 1841, p. 90; September 15, 1843, p. 54. *Christian Advocate and Journal,* September 25, 1829, p. 14. Charles Sydnor, *Slavery in Mississippi,* New York, 1933, p. 253.

[19] *Anti-Slavery Lecturer,* March, 1839, p. 3. See also *Southern Christian Advocate,* October 5, 1838, p. 62. *Christian Advocate and Journal,* November 20, 1835, p. 50.

its honors and enjoyments." By improving the slaves' morality, the missions would improve slavery, giving the South the "advantage in argument over . . . our Northern Brethren."[20] In defending the Mission, therefore, William Capers already had some arguments available, not only because Pinckney had outlined them, but also because most Methodists agreed that religion was a moral discipline for this life and a hope for the next. Furthermore, Capers' experience as a pastor suggested that, "backsliders" notwithstanding, the Christian gospel could make Negroes better people. They would be less susceptible to incendiary leadership, more trustworthy, and more willing to work. The superintendent could always assure detractors that the "fruits" of the mission were "the superior contentment, the improved morals, the more principled and worthy obedience of the . . . negroes."[21] It seemed obvious to supporters of the missions that their moral responsibility to the Negroes was irrefutably based upon experience as well as principle.

While pragmatic results may have been foremost in the planters' minds, they were not in the Methodists'. Their chief concern had never been merely to make the Negro behave, but to allow him to realize his full manhood as a child of God—to convert him. Methodists pointed out that since the master had assumed complete control over the slaves, he was completely and morally responsible for their care, including religious instruction. The latter was especially important because "no poverty of outward condition, no degradation of *caste,* no ignorance or debasement of manners [could] strip the immortal soul of its value." And precisely

---

[20] Charles Cotesworth Pinckney, *An Address delivered in Charleston before the Agricultural Society of South Carolina at its Anniversary Meeting,* Charleston, 1829, pp. 4–5, 10–14, 16–18.

[21] *Southern Christian Advocate,* February 8, 1838, p. 134. *Minutes of the South Carolina Conference of the Methodist Episcopal Church for the year 1832,* Charleston, 1832, p. 10. Also the *Minutes* of 1836, pp. 30f. *Southwestern Christian Advocate,* March 20, 1841, p. 78.

because of their value to God, argued the missionaries, Negroes had the right to religious instruction. Bishop Andrew urged his men to convince Christian slaveholders that "their negroes [were] fellow heirs of immortality, *and that [they] must care for their souls as well as their bodies.*"[22] No amount of opposition ever made the Methodists retreat from this principle of the Negro's moral claim. And in emphasizing his humanity, they were chipping away almost unconsciously at the legal conception of the slave as property, and therefore blunting the logical extension of the law.[23]

As the Church appealed to idealism and duty as well as to self-interest, its apologetic was always limited by the need to clarify the Southern Methodist position on slavery. With each challenge, the position became more conservative. In 1824 the South Carolina Conference reacted to the Vesey conspiracy by applauding the lot of the slave; in 1826 when a New York newspaper attributed an antislavery petition to them, Carolina Methodists objected that they would no more pass laws against slavery than would the South Carolina legislature.[24] With the rise of abolitionist activity in the 1830's, Southern Methodists felt called upon once again to explain themselves. Although claiming that "the question of the abolition of slavery" was not religious, they continued to go beyond "matters of piety" in order to display their social orthodoxy. "We believe," they announced, "that the Holy Scriptures, so far from giving any countenance to [the]

[22] *Ibid.*, July 23, 1841, p. 21; November 19, 1841, p. 90; December 30, 1842, p. 112; May 12, 1843, p. 188. See also the *Christian Advocate and Journal,* September 25, 1829, p. 14. South Carolina Conference *Minutes* for 1831, pp. 15–16; for 1832, pp. 11–13; for 1833, p. 12; for 1839, pp. 15, 16.

[23] See Charles G. Sellers, "The Travail of Slavery," in the collection of essays which he edited, *The Southerner as American,* Chapel Hill, 1960, pp. 40–71.

[24] *Wesleyan Journal,* April 15, 1826, p. 3; May 13, 1826, p. 2. The actual petition came from Maryland, see the *Genius of Universal Emancipation and Baltimore Courier,* April 8, 1826, p. 252.

delusion [of abolitionism], do unequivocally authorize the relation of master and slave."[25] Missionaries who claimed to believe such exegesis could certainly be trusted by anxious masters; but trust would not necessarily imply enthusiasm.

Capers worked hard to gain the basic evidence of institutional success—financial backing and an increase in numbers, but the problems were great. Since the national missionary society made the conferences responsible for work with the slaves, financial resources were limited. Consequently, Capers at first welcomed the patronage of well-to-do planters such as William Aiken, Robert Barnwell Rhett, and Joel R. Poinsett.[26] When depression curtailed large donations, however, the superintendent requested, urged, and shamed preachers throughout the South to form local missionary societies, giving the program a popular base. Negroes, preachers, children, and farmers donated their pennies and dollars, but by 1844 Southern Methodists were spending only one dollar per slave each year. This figure of $22,000 compared favorably with the national society's receipts of $35,000 in 1843, but neither figure approached the $200,000 which the Church needed for all its missions.[27] Furthermore, in spite of the increase in the number of slaves served by the Mission, the ratio of black to white Methodists in the South remained the same. No one realized more than the indefatigable Capers that much of the progress was illusory. He complained that most people did nothing for the slaves, and often " 'something' when done was but a

[25] South Carolina Conference *Minutes* for 1836, p. 30; see also those for 1839, p. 14.

[26] *Ibid.,* for 1833, p. 16; for 1834, p. 21; for 1838, p. 17; for 1839, p. 18; for 1841, p. 18; for 1843, p. 13.

[27] *Southern Christian Advocate,* May 28, 1841, p. 198. June 8, 1841, p. 202; October 1, 1841, p. 62; October 15, 1841, p. 71; January 7, 1842, p. 118; February 11, 1842, pp. 138–139; February 17, 1843, p. 140; June 23, 1843, pp. 6–7; June 30, 1843, p. 10; August 18, 1843, p. 38. Also *Christian Advocate and Journal,* December 12, 1843, p. 75.

substitute for nothing"—a plaint which echoed throughout the South.[28]

There were other problems as well. The laws, customs, and peculiar problems of slavery delimited the missionaries' freedom—their preaching and teaching, hours of work, and methods of administration. Slaves could meet only at certain times, and often Negroes could not legally exercise major pastoral functions; instruction could never be supplemented by reading; and there was no legal sanction for slave marriages to stabilize families. Furthermore, no numbers of stars in a minister's "crown" could make it very pleasant to risk health and life in miasmic swamps for the honor of being called a "nigger preacher." Capers wrote a friend that few men could "be a servant of slaves literally—treated as inferior by the proprietors, as hardly equal to the overseers, half starved sometimes, suffocated with smoke, sick with the stench of dirty cabins & as-dirty negroes, sleepless from the stings of . . . musquitoes [sic] and all in the very centre . . . of the kingdom of disease. . . ."[29]

Some men, however, could endure these complaints because the slaves did, and because somehow their ministry could be fulfilled only in preaching to the Negroes. These missionaries were Southerners, members of annual conferences to whom they answered. Their purpose was not emancipation, but conversion, and pastoral care. Their constant repetition of the masters' duty to his slaves might in rare instances influence a few to preach equality of white and black before God. And being men of strong and untutored emotions they would express their conception of the Mission in sentimental terms, revelling in the look of wonder in the children's faces, the gratitude of the adults,

[28] *Ibid.*, February 3, 1843, p. 132; also January 18, 1844, p. 126. *Christian Advocate and Journal,* January 10, 1844, p. 87; January 17, 1844, p. 89.
[29] William Capers to Willbur Fisk, September 12, 1833, Willbur Fisk Papers, Wesleyan University.

the prayers of confidence from a dying grandfather.[30] Theirs was not a pleasant task, as Capers had said, and certainly not cynically undertaken to degrade the Negroes, but to help them in the only way they knew how. For a pittance they would cover broad circuits, perhaps tending 23 congregations in three weeks, always straining to explain their message in plain language and short sentences. After the exhaustion of their patience they might complain of the slaves' "depraved ignorance, blind superstition, and extreme stupidity"—and turn back once again to do their work.[31]

The missionaries faced ethical and religious problems as well as personal hardship. They would nurse the slaves through a probationary period only to have them "backslide," perhaps, as Capers said, because "the prevalent conceit that sin is sin for white men not negroes . . . [held] a fond control over them."[32] Sometimes the Negroes would react favorably to the instruction—and then wander off into religious aberrations or the Baptist church. Such behavior would naturally make the missionaries suspect an increase in "conversions" during a cholera epidemic.[33] These problems, however, could hardly defeat ministers who had dealt with similar situations among white people and received fewer thanks. Thus, together with their Negro assistants, the missionaries wended their way through the masters' laws and the slaves' mores to preach the gospel.

[30] *Southern Christian Advocate,* July 3, 1840, p. 11. See also *Christian Advocate and Journal,* October 31, 1834, p. 38. Also the latter for July 17, 1835, p. 186; August 18, 1837, p. 206; September 29, 1837, p. 22. *Zion's Herald,* August 18, 1824, p. 2.

[31] *Ibid.,* September 2, 1837, p. 43; November 3, 1837, p. 78; May 24, 1839, p. 194. *Christian Advocate and Journal,* May 15, 1835, p. 150. Wightman, *Life of Capers,* p. 344. South Carolina Conference *Minutes* for 1833, p. 17; for 1834, pp. 17–18.

[32] William Capers to Willbur Fisk, September 12, 1833, Fisk Papers.

[33] *Christian Advocate and Journal,* October 31, 1834, p. 38. See also *Southern Christian Advocate,* September 2, 1837, p. 43; May 11, 1838, p. 2; July 2, 1841, p. 10; July 28, 1843, p. 26.

The content of that gospel was outlined in a special catechism. Since the Negroes initially knew too little about Christianity to understand the sermons, oral instruction was initially far more important than preaching. Either after Sunday morning worship or at stated times during the week, the missionary would gather the slaves' children in the front row, and have them repeat their lessons after him phrase by phrase.[34] He probably used an Episcopal catechism before 1833, when Capers published *A Catechism for little Children and for Use on the Missions to the Slaves in South Carolina*.[35] By 1844 Methodists throughout the South were using this booklet as a supplement to the Apostle's Creed and selected Biblical verses.

Much less sophisticated and detailed than Charles Colcock Jones' catechism for Presbyterian slaves, the simplicity of Capers' work made its message easier to memorize if not to understand. Its purpose was to teach the basic tenets of orthodox Protestant Christianity "without the encumbrance of metaphysical refinements on Decrees, Foreknowledge, and Predestination."[36] The Methodists followed the basic outlines of the gospel story, emphasizing the love of God who sent His Son into a sinful world to preach repentance and to offer a new life. This "new life" had two aspects: the present and the future. After conversion men loved God, did their duty, and preserved the integrity of personal relationships with wife, family, and master. They therefore could hope that they would be accounted righteous at the last judgment and merit eternal life. Righteousness

---

[34] *Ibid.*, July 6, 1838, p. 132; January 1, 1830, p. 70. *Southern Christian Advocate*, May 24, 1839, p. 129; December 24, 1841, p. 110; April 1, 1842, p. 166; September 15, 1843, p. 54. *Southwestern Christian Advocate*, June 19, 1841, p. 238. Harrison, *Gospel Among the Slaves*, p. 217.

[35] Williams, "Methodist Missions to the Slaves," p. 41, B. M. Palmer's *A Plain and Easy Catechism, Designed Chiefly for the Benefit of the Colored Persons with suitable prayers and Hymns attached*.

[36] See *Southern Christian Advocate*, October 28, 1837, p. 2.

—or the raising of moral standards—had, after all, been offered the masters by the Church. And although the traditional Protestant emphasis on God's grace was replaced with a naive "works righteousness," such an ethic was not too different from that of the average white Methodist. The Ten Commandments and selected passages of scripture enforced the eternal necessity of being "good." Slaves were warned to love their enemies, keep their marriage vows (Matthew 5:27, 28, 39, 44; 18:15–17), never to lie, steal (Zechariah 5:3), swear (James 5:2), or break the Sabbath (Numbers 5:32, 35–36).[37]

The Negroes were also forcefully reminded that they were slaves. As one missionary reported, "The Gospel . . . teaches [the Negro] obedience to God, and faithfulness to the interests of his earthly master."[38] The catechism instructed the slaves to memorize the famous injunction to obey in Paul's letters to the Ephesians and to Timothy.[39] But unlike either the Presbyterians or the Episcopalians, the Methodists left out the apostle's statement about the equality of men before God to whom masters were also accountable.[40] Why Capers shortened the scriptural passage

[37] All the references to Capers' catechism are from a copy which was printed in the *Southern Christian Advocate,* October 21, 1837, pp. 69–70. See also Charles Colcock Jones, *Catechism of Scripture doctrine and Practice, for families and Sabbath School Designed also for the oral instruction of colored persons,* Savannah, 1844. John F. Hoff, *A Manual of Religious Instruction specially Intended for the oral teaching of colored persons,* Philadelphia, 1852.
[38] *Christian Advocate and Journal,* February 12, 1836, p. 98.
[39] Ephesians 6:5–6. "Servants be obedient to them that are your masters according to the flesh, with fear and trembling, in singleness of your heart, as unto Christ; not with eye service, as men pleasers, but as servants of Christ, doing the will of God from the heart." I Timothy 6:1–2. "Let as many servants as are under the yoke count their own masters worthy of all honors, that the name of God and his doctrine be not blasphemed. And they that have believing masters, let them not despise them, rather do them service, because they are faithful and beloved, partakers of the benefit. These things teach and exhort." KJV.
[40] Hoff, *Manual of Instruction,* p. 136. Jones, *Catechism,* p. 93:

is not clear. Perhaps he unconsciously suffered from the Methodists' earlier disrepute among the older, more respectable denominations, and also hoped to atone for past anti-slavery "sins" by being beyond reproach on the subject. In any event, the Methodists were living up to their promise to teach obedience. Furthermore, since analogy is a common way to teach theological concepts, the relationship of master and slave was enforced even more by comparing God to the former. The South Carolina Conference reported in 1837 that the Negroes were "pointed from earliest infancy to a MASTER in heaven, whose eye sees in darkness as in light."[41]

The clergy found the results they sought. The slaves' understanding of life was changed in enforcing moral standards and preaching God's love. Missionaries reported that slaves were more clean and honest, less thieving and adulterous than ever before. One preacher was particularly pleased that they no longer sang "Massa Hab de Grog Bottle," but rather "Free Grace and a Dying Lamb." Many slaves were quite grateful for the preachers' obvious concern, and gratitude as much as theology may account for the moral improvement. But gratitude did not guarantee that they would always hang on every word which cautioned obedience to masters. Ethics were secondary to hope and consolation. At one prayer meeting a slave testified: "Brethren, I have my hard bone to chaw and my bitter pill to swallow, but religion make de bone turn to marrow and de bitter to sweet." The slaves hoped that God would make things right in the next life. Jesus rose; they would also, and there would be

---

"Q. Does [God] favor the Master more than the Servant *because* he is the Master? A. No. Eph. 6:9." Ephesians 6:8–9. "Knowing that whatsoever good things any man doeth the same shall he receive of the Lord, whether he be bond or free. And ye masters, do the same things unto them, forebearing threatening; knowing that your Master also is in heaven, neither is there respect of persons with him." KJV.

[41] South Carolina Conference *Minutes* for 1837, pp. 18–19.

no more toil, nor tears, nor blood. The gospel which the Methodists preached gave some slaves purpose, hope, and love in a purposeless, hopeless, loveless world—much as it had to some whites.[42] Thus, the Methodist preachers were doing what they were ordained to do, and their successes gave substance to their claims that the Mission was the best and most moral way to help the Negroes.

The laws of slavery, however, did not allow conversion to be informed by literacy. This situation necessitated an appeal to the Negroes' conscience, hopes, and fears, and resulted in great religious excitement.[43] The impact of an emotion-packed, evangelical Protestantism upon an uneducated people might result in excesses, and for obvious reasons. The Negroes' religious and emotional spontaneity was informed in part by the behavior of white Methodists. A Yankee school teacher in Virginia reported that the Negroes in a leaky meeting house "exhorted, prayed, sang, shouted, cried, grunted & growled. Poor Souls! they knew no better, for I found that when the other services began, the sounds were similar [to those] which the white folks made; and the negroes only imitated them and shouted a little louder."[44] Although the slave's Christianity freed him from the bondage of his hopes, it was as bound by environment and slavery as he. And the symbol of that bondage was the certificate which planters issued to missionaries, allowing them to establish their missions. Without the

[42] *Southern Christian Advocate,* May 15, 1840, p. 190; July 3, 1840, p. 11; December 29, 1843, p. 114; January 19, 1844, p. 126. See also Benjamin E. Mays, *The Negro's Idea of God as Reflected in His Literature,* Boston, 1938, pp. 21–53. Lunsford Lane, *Narrative of Lunsford Lane,* Boston, 1840, p. 21. *Ninth Annual Report of the Association for the Religious Instruction of the Negroes in Liberty County, Georgia,* Savannah, 1844, p. 25. For a discussion of the slave's adaptability to slavery upon which some of the above is based, see Bertram Wilbur Doyle, *The Etiquette of Race Relations in the South,* Chicago, 1937, p. 80.

[43] *Ibid.,* September 13, 1844, p. 54.

[44] J. Milton Emerson, Journal, September 26, 1841, Methodist Episcopal Church Papers.

master's support the preachers could do nothing.[45] The Christianity of the Mission was not wilfully distorted—the essential message of God's love was always preached—but it was almost obsequiously adapted to the white man's law and fears and the Negro's experience.

Although many slaveholders had yet to be convinced of the value of the Mission by 1844, those who had supported it were pleased. Planters were particularly impressed by the raising of moral standards which meant that the slaves were more "devoted to their owners' interests." One master was quite gratified that his barn had not been broken into since his slaves "got religion."[46] The conversion of his slaves would obviously please a Christian slaveholder who was concerned with the state of their souls, and who might even have had some secret misgivings about owning them. If Negroes could not be trusted with the gospel, Christianity might be "at war" with slavery, but if they became true Christians within the structures of Southern society, they would be living proof of God's favor, and conscience might be satisfied.[47] After all, the Church had said that the master's first duty was to provide for the salvation of his servants.

The extent to which the Methodist Episcopal Church could outline and enforce a master's duty, however, was

[45] Harrison, *Gospel Among the Slaves*, p. 211.

[46] *Southern Christian Advocate*, April 13, 1838, p. 2; January 11, 1839, p. 2. *Proceedings of the Meeting in Charleston, S.C. May, 13–15, 1845 on the Religious Instruction of the Negroes together with the Report of the Committee and the Address to the Public*, Charleston, 1845, pp. 22, 34. The Mission to the Slaves is, of course, one instance of the use of religion as social control. The ambiguous purposes and results described above are similar to those reported for 19th century England and the 20th century American South. See, for example, Charles I. Foster, *An Errand of Mercy: The Evangelical United Front, 1790–1837*, Chapel Hill, 1960, *passim*, but especially pp. 49–55, 89. Liston Pope, *Millhands and Preachers: A Study of Gastonia*, New Haven, 1942, *passim*, but especially pp. 29–31.

[47] See Capers' argument to this effect in *Southern Christian Advocate*, February 8, 1838, p. 134. Also May 12, 1843, p. 188.

curtailed and made quite difficult. The American doctrine of the separation of Church and State had bound the Church over to the "people," upon whom it depended for its existence and often its ethics. In spite of this impediment, the Methodists and other denominations did try to exert moral power on behalf of the slave. Once the Church's right to evangelize him was recognized, no one could easily forbid it to speak on his behalf. Preachers lectured slaveholders on their duty to provide protection and care, and the *Southern Christian Advocate* dutifully printed such admonitions in its role as tribune for the slaves. "They are . . . human beings, and have the feelings too, with many of them as delicate and sensitive as your own, and which demand to be respected, and carefully preserved from outrage."[48] A particular champion was Bishop Andrew, who braved accusations of abolitionism to denounce repeatedly the irresponsible treatment of those who could not speak for or defend themselves.[49] But as usual in matters of moral coercion the Church had no rules or powerful leverage to enforce what its ministers believed was right; it could only reply upon preaching and exhortation—a subtler and slower influence than force and law.

This preaching was certainly not prophetic enough to bring justice to the slaves. To be sure, the growth of the Mission subjected more people to a continuous reiteration of the doctrine that the Negro's humanity limited the rights of property. Although this acknowledgment was thus enlarged into a general appeal to moral action, there was little evidence to indicate that the Mission would lead to abolition without pressure from economic necessity and political institutions. Even if Southern Christians had increased in numbers significantly, they would still have dealt with slavery according to preconceptions not formed entirely by their

[48] *Ibid.*, March 16, 1838, p. 2.
[49] *Ibid.*, July 23, 1841, p. 21; November 19, 1841, p. 90; November 26, 1841, p. 94; December 30, 1842, p. 112.

religion. Thus if the missions—Methodist and others—were subversive of slavery they were not at all destructive. The preachers proposed to humanize the peculiar institution—to reform it and perfect it, and perhaps with centuries of time they could have eased it out of existence—but slavery was too much involved in economic and political aspirations to be shuffled off painlessly. The Methodists, furthermore, did not continue the moral antagonism against slavery which had tortured Bishop Francis Asbury. They were becoming respectable. In 1839 Methodist preachers could shamelessly boast that the Mission had "thrown a new element into the moral circulation—planted fresh props beneath the established order of things, and reared up additional securities around the charities of home and household affections."[50]

Obviously the Methodists were quite proud of their work and had some reason to be. In comparison with other denominations their efforts were by far the most developed and widespread in 1844. Although the Baptists apparently had more Negro members because of the independence of their congregations, they did not send out missionaries. Protestant Episcopalians did a small amount of work with the slaves, and Presbyterians were spurred into widely publicized action by the able and dedicated Charles Colcock Jones. While a student at Princeton, Jones had decided to work with the Negroes since "all souls [were] equally precious" to God, and when he returned to Georgia he established missions and wrote in favor of general religious instruction. Great as Jones' work was, it could not match that of the Methodists. When a nondenominational convention of mission enthusiasts met in Charleston in 1845, it could agree that the Methodists' spontaneity and organization "had advanced [them] beyond all others' in direct and well sustained efforts in the colored field."[51]

[50] South Carolina Conference *Minutes* for 1839, pp. 15–16.
[51] *Proceedings . . . in Charleston . . . on Religious Instruction,* p. 69.

83

Pride in these efforts tempted the missionaries to idealize them beyond all contact with organization, sweat, and disappointment. To some, the puzzling slaves became pious, easily contented "sable sons and daughters of Africa"; missionaries who had never been in Africa, or in the North, or in servitude proclaimed that the missions had made the lot of the slaves far superior to that of native Africans or Northern free Negroes.[52] The idealization of the missions unified them into one "cause." Never organized under one board, only loosely responsible to Capers after 1840, and encompassing only one-fourth of the Negroes in the Church, they were a special symbol of the Christian Crusade—not missions, but *The Mission*. This cause, like abolitionism, was warmly and morally supported by a few dedicated men who created the basis of a moral mythology for their section of the United States. The Mission gave Methodist ministers a sense of joyful daring; for although not universally proscribed, it was at least opposed by enough people to stimulate self-conceit, yet supported by enough people to guarantee success. There is a bit of Saint George in every man if the dragon is not too large.

The Mission was not only a "great" work, but also a beneficial one for the Methodists who, through it, became special representatives of the South in the fight with the rejuvenated activity of Northern abolitionists. In ecclesiastical newspapers, correspondence, and meetings, Southern Methodists demanded that Northern conservatives help them to destroy abolitionism, arguing that it made Southerners apprehensive of the Mission. Antislavery preaching had endangered preaching to the slaves before: it must not be allowed to do so again![53] In response, conservative Northern

---

[52] *Southern Christian Advocate*, July 3, 1840, p. 11. Also December 25, 1840, p. 110; June 11, 1841, p. 206; March 11, 1842, p. 154; September 1, 1843, p. 46.

[53] This argument was always calculated to move some Northerners to sympathize with the South and Capers used it to good effect in the General Conference of 1840. See *Christian Advocate and Journal*, May 29, 1840, pp. 161–163.

churchmen helped denounce abolitionism and praised the Mission as the South's way of helping the slave. They believed from past experience that the Mission was all that the Church could give the slave, only vaguely adding that one day, perhaps, he would be freed after he had realized his manhood.[54]

The abolitionists were not convinced. They all agreed that it was "perfect nonsense to think of making *men* out of *slaves* 'till you abolish that which destroys their mankind—slavery."[55] Educated in the Biblicism of American evangelical Protestantism, they could not understand how a religion uninformed by reading the Bible could "teach Christ" to the slaves. What they did see was the attempt to "engraft upon [slavery] the holy purity of Religion." With William Lloyd Garrison they refused to join their Northern brethren in endorsing slaveholding piety.[56] There was something "diabolical" in making a "mutilated" gospel the "instrument of bondage and degradation." The leader of Methodist abolitionists, vibrant Orange Scott, despaired of a Christianity which made a "*good slave,* not a bold soldier of Jesus Christ. . . ." The abolitionists could sometimes admit that the Methodist Misssion was charitable, but they insisted that the slave needed justice first and charity second.[57]

[54] *Exposition of the Object and Plans of the American Union for the Improvement of the Colored Race,* Boston, 1835, pp. 9, 11, 14–15. *Colonizationist and Journal of Freedom,* June, 1833, pp. 80–81. *Christian Register,* March 9, 1844, p. 38. *Christian Advocate and Journal,* February 21, 1834, p. 103. *Western Christian Advocate,* September 29, 1843, p. 94. *Emancipator,* July 21, 1836, p. 46.

[55] *Philanthropist,* April 23, 1839, pp. 2–3.

[56] *Liberator,* June 29, 1833, p. 103; December 6, 1839, p. 195. Also *Zion's Watchman,* September 28, 1836, p. 155.

[57] *Philanthropist,* August 4, 1841, p. 2. Also *National Anti-Slavery Standard,* April 15, 1841, p. 177. *Anti-Slavery Examiner,* I, No. 3, New York, 1837, "A Letter of Gerrit Smith to Reverend James Smylie of the State of Mississippi." *Herald of Freedom,* October 8, 1836, p. 126. *Emancipator,* August 13, 1840, p. 62. *Anti-Slavery Lecturer,* February, 1839, p. 1. *Anti-Slavery Reporter,* November, 1840, p. 70.

Southerners replied in righteous indignation that demands for justice hurt the Mission—which in part they did. The Methodists' history often made them subject to suspicion, and when their ministers received unsolicited antislavery propaganda, their loyalty to Southern institutions was further cast into doubt.[58] Indeed missionaries were sometimes kept from preaching, but generally the abolitionists helped them in a rather ironic way. After all, not until Charles Cotesworth Pinckney had convinced the planters that religion was a good substitute for emancipation had Methodist appeals for a Mission been answered. And as Southerners sought a way of meeting their critics on moral ground, the Church, for its own reasons, provided the answer in the Mission. Upon the selfless moral dedication of the few missionaries, many planters could build a self-righteous vindication of their status. The Mission would have grown without the abolitionists, for pious slaveholders, the indefatigable Capers, and the blunt Andrew would eventually have cooperated in special efforts for the slaves. But the abolitionists made the matter urgent; their threat gave Methodists an opportunity to offer the South security and moral superiority. The acceptance of the offer allowed the Church finally to condemn the opponents of the Mission as enemies of Southern institutions.[59]

Thus, the Mission was a paradox: as a moral crusade and as a conscientious moral alternative to compromise of principle and to emancipation. Motivated by Christian concern, practicality, and self-interest, its growth was stimulated by necessity, fear, and compassion. Representing only a part of the South's Negro Christians, it symbolized the plight of their enslavement and the hope of their release. Adapted

[58] *Christian Register*, December 23, 1837, p. 202. *Emancipator,* October 20, 1835, pp. 2–4; July 21, 1836, p. 46. *Southern Christian Advocate,* October 3, 1838, p. 62; November 2, 1838, p. 79. *Southwestern Christian Advocate,* March 20, 1841, p. 78.

[59] See for example *Southern Christian Advocate,* February 8, 1838, p. 134.

as it was to the "peculiar institution" under attack from the North, it underwrote the status quo. But as the peculiar work of Southern Methodist Christianity there can be little doubt that it also changed conceptions and attitudes. Once scorned, it became a celebrated moral cause, evaluated correctly by abolitionists and partisans alike. The former had accused it of social control, of distortion, of neglecting justice. The missionaries, believing piety more important than emancipation, claimed that the Mission gave Negroes a Christian life, stabilized the relations of master and slave, and extended Christian and moral concern to the bondsman. Both sides were right.

Perhaps the paradox can be revealed in an interchange between a missionary and his people. The preacher was a devoted man who served his eternal Lord by risking health and reputation to serve the Negroes; his congregation were slaves who knew better than he what their temporal lord wanted. The result was a revelation of the grotesque mixture of ethics and exploitation. The missionary asked: "What did God make you for?" The answer: "To make a crop." He asked again, "What is the meaning of 'Thou shalt not commit adultery?'" The answer: "To serve our heavenly Father, and our earthly master, obey our overseer, and not steal anything."[60] As a great moral cause the Mission was a noble effort to give men new life; but it also reenforced an ignoble effort to keep men in bondage.

[60] Reported in Anson West, *A History of Methodism in Alabama,* Nashville, 1893, p. 605.

CHAPTER IV

THE GENTEEL COMPROMISE OF CONSCIENCE:
Methodists and Colonization
1824–1844

METHODISTS who valued the ideal of emancipation as well as that of the Mission sought still another conscientious alternative to an ultimate compromise of their antislavery principles, the American Society for Colonizing the Free People of Color of the United States. More a state of mind than a plan of action, the colonization cause enticed men to placate their consciences, conciliate the slave-holders, and shed tears over the plight of the Negroes whom they hoped to ship to Africa. Initially recommended to the Church as a part of the rising interest in missions, the movement embraced enough moral sentiment against slavery to appeal to the Methodist antislavery inheritance. Highly respectable for its caution, its obliging statements, and its honored founders, colonization was sufficiently catholic in appeal and ambiguous in principle to commend itself to a large national church which included slaveholding as well as nonslaveholding members. Gradually, through abolitionist pressure and the involvement of the Church in the movement, bishops, editors, and other prominent Methodist spokesmen became agents and welcome apologists for the American Colonization Society. It did not counter white prejudices but honored them by acceptance, and preached not the wrath of justice but the genteel piousness of patronizing charity.

Methodists had no part in founding the American Colonization Society, which was created by a circle of prominent men. The most active of these was Robert Finley, a Presbyterian clergyman from New Jersey, who was determined to alleviate the low condition of the free Negroes in America by sending them away from the degrading effects of white prejudice. In December 1816, Finley and a group of eminent politicians met in Washington to form a society "to promote and execute a plan for colonizing (with their consent) the Free People of Colour residing in our Country, in Africa, or such place as Congress shall deem most expedient." Judge Bushrod Washington, slaveholding nephew of his country's first president, was named to the presidency of the Board of Managers. Among the other officials were William H. Crawford, Henry Clay, Andrew Jackson, Francis Scott Key, and that archpriest of Virginia agrarian conservatism, John Taylor of Caroline. Finley reasoned that his society would help Negroes to work out their own destiny as full-fledged citizens in Africa, carry the benefits of American religion and civilization to the "dark continent," relieve America of the dangers of "amalgamation," and perhaps eventually free all the slaves through expatriation.[1]

These high hopes were difficult to infuse in other minds even though the idea of colonization was not new. Thomas Jefferson had toyed intellectually with it, and Paul Cuffee, a Negro Quaker shipmaster, had carried 38 Negroes to Africa in 1815 to exemplify the idea. But support for the new organization was difficult to achieve. Free Negroes opposed the Colonization Society because they did not trust the

---

[1] Constitution of the American Society for Colonizing the Free People of Color of the United States, in Liber W.G.D.W., Colonization Society, I, American Colonization Society Papers. Also see Philip J. Staudenraus, *The African Colonization Movement, 1816–1865*. New York, 1961, pp. 12–22. Also Early Lee Fox, *The American Colonization Society, 1817–1840*, Baltimore, 1919 (Johns Hopkins University Studies in Historical and Political Science, Series 37, number 3), pp. 46–51.

practice of expatriation to remain voluntary or believe in its ultimate benevolence. Southerners often feared its adverse effect upon slavery. Friends of the Negro scorned it as a slaveholders' plot to increase the value of slaves; and many people simply claimed that it was hopelessly impracticable. Moreover, the society was weakened internally from the contradictory motives of its backers: some believed that removal to Africa was the only way in which Negroes could achieve dignity, while others hoped to rid themselves of a "social nuisance." Still other half-hearted supporters accepted the society with the hope that it would inadvertently exert some moral influence against slavery.[2] Nevertheless, so acute an observer as John Quincy Adams deplored the colonization movement because he thought he saw "exceedingly humane, weakminded" people speculating in "political popularity."[3]

The Methodists were at first equally wary of backing this unwieldy cause. Whereas, in 1819 the Presbyterian General Assembly approved the colonization society for its beneficence to the "colored people," the Methodist General Conference of the next year objected that the "objects, designs, and advantages" of the society were "not sufficiently developed" to justify official support.[4] The Methodists had good, practical reasons for withholding approbation, for the society was in the midst of an intensive flirtation with disaster. With the help of the federal government, the Board of Managers had sent an expedition to the west coast of Africa only to have it fail because of disease, mismanagement, ac-

[2] See *Zion's Herald,* May 9, 1827, p. 2; June 27, 1827, p. 2. Franklin, *From Slavery to Freedom,* p. 235. Staudenraus, *Colonization Movement,* pp. 9–11, 32–34, 104–105. Louis Filler, *The Crusade Against Slavery, 1830–1860,* New York, 1960, pp. 21–22. *First Annual Report of the American Society for Colonizing the Free People of Color of the United States,* Washington, 1818, pp. 10ff.

[3] Charles Francis Adams, ed., *The Memoirs of John Quincy Adams,* Philadelphia, 1875, IV, 293.

[4] [Ezekiel Cooper] to [Allen W. Lane] September 13, 1820, Cooper Papers. McGill, *American Slavery as viewed by the Presbyterian Church,* p. 15.

cident, and treachery. Thereafter, as the initial policy of achieving full federal support began to disintegrate, the managers were tempted to try the new tack of arousing popular support.[5] Appeals to the benevolence of the American people saved the society for a short time. And the Methodists, impressed by the crescendo of praise for the colonization idea, decided in 1824 to support it. This decision, like that to develop missions to the slaves, was a part of the general interest and faith in the missionary ideal. Before the General Conference met, the Secretary of the Missionary Society of the Methodist Episcopal Church, Nathan Bangs, was enthusiastically predicting that if the Colonization Society's hopes were fulfilled, "colonies [would] ere long be found established in abundance along the coast of Africa, and that through them civilization, science, and Christianity [would] pour their blessings over a suffering and degraded continent."[6] Colonizationists, who had finally established an African colony in that same year, again prodded this Methodist interest by asking for an official recommendation. The General Conference replied with a cautious referral of all appropriate action to the Missionary Society, and resolved to send a missionary to Africa when it could find sufficient funds.[7] Thus the Methodists became one of many institutions that began to approve of colonization. By 1826 they had been joined by Episcopalians, Baptists, Quakers, and

[5] Staudenraus, *Colonization Movement*, pp. 53ff., 69–74.

[6] [Nathan Bangs] "American Colonization Society," *Methodist Magazine*, VII (January, 1824), 29–30. See also "American Colonization Society," *Methodist Magazine*, VI (September, 1823), 347–350. "American Colonization Society," *Methodist Magazine*, VII (November, 1824), 417–420. See also Barclay, *Reform the Nation*, pp. 32, 37, 112–286, 404f., 407, and Barclay, *Missionary Motivation and Expansion*, pp. 280–305.

[7] *Journals of the General Conference*, I, 291. Report of the Committee to Consider the Address of the Acting Committee of the American Colonization Society and other Documents, Joshua Soule Papers, Drew University.

Presbyterians as well as legislatures from Southern, Western, and Northern states.[8]

During the next few years Methodist periodicals and annual conferences enlisted in the cause. The *Christian Advocate and Journal* printed mundane notices and high flights of oratory on behalf of the Society; *Zion's Herald* was less enthusiastic but still hopeful for the moral pressure which colonization could exert against slavery; and the *Methodist Magazine* never lost an opportunity to eulogize the beneficence of helping Negroes and "saving" Africa at the same time.[9] Methodists also became involved through other agencies. The Colonization Society commissioned a Methodist preacher, William McKenney of Maryland, as traveling agent for the area from Delaware to North Carolina, and allowed the indefatigable secretary, Ralph Randolph Gurley, to begin publishing the *African Repository and Colonial Journal*. McKenney persuaded other Methodists to back the Society while Gurley in his magazine described the "inestimable good" which would be accomplished through July Fourth collections in churches of all denominations. "The consciousness of having done a work so noble, would be a rich reward," he promised. Thus prodded, Methodist conferences began to stir into activity by 1827.[10]

[8] The legislatures were those of Virginia, Maryland, Tennessee, Ohio, New York, Connecticut, Rhode Island, and Indiana. See Fox, *Colonization Society,* pp. 78–79.

[9] *Christian Advocate and Journal,* September 30, 1826, pp. 2–3; October 14, 1826, p. 2; January 20, 1827, p. 79; January 27, 1827, p. 83; March 3, 1827, p. 102; March 10, 1827, p. 107; July 20, 1827, p. 181. "American Colonization Society," *Methodist Magazine,* VII (November, 1824), 417–420. "American Colonization Society," *Methodist Magazine,* IX (January, 1826), 31–35. Gabriel P. Disosway, "American Colonization Society," *Methodist Magazine,* IX (May, 1826), 178–185).

[10] *African Repository and Colonial Journal,* II (June, 1826), 126. R. R. Gurley to the Baltimore Conference, April 9, 1827, Baltimore Conference Papers. Staudenraus, *Colonization Movement,* pp. 100, 104–105.

The results of popular appeal were mild and aspiring rather than spectacular. The first approvals came with great caution from the New York, Baltimore, Virginia, and Mississippi conferences. William Winans wrote Gurley that the Mississippi clergy would back colonization, but "from motives of prudence" would not allow anyone to publicize their resolutions.[11] The next year that conference found a little more courage and with at least eight others publicly announced approval of the American Colonization Society, thereby joining Methodists in every section of the country except South Carolina and Georgia.[12] The resolutions were not so indicative of the firm conviction in a great crusade as of a guileless belief in benevolence and charity uninformed by justice.

To support this charity, the ministers were called upon for funds. Thus, on every July Fourth Methodist ministers followed the advice of the annual conferences by joining other denominations in praising colonization and taking special collections. How much they collected would depend upon the persuasiveness of individual preachers, the gen-

[11] William Winans to R. R. Gurley, February 21, 1827, Winans Collection.

[12] Christian Advocate and Journal, May 19, 1827, p. 146; June 15, 1827, p. 162; May 28, 1830, p. 155. African Repository, II (February, 1827), 382; VII (June, 1831), 120; VIII (January, 1833), 342. Western Christian Advocate, October 16, 1835, p. 99. William Winans to R. R. Gurley, February 21, 1827; Winans to Nathan Bangs and John Emory, January 3, 1828, Winans Collection. Beverly Waugh to R. R. Gurley, April 21, 1827; Thomas Mason to Gurley, May 21, 1827; Moses M. Henkle to Gurley, June 20, 1827, American Colonization Papers. "Journals of the Genesee Annual Conference of the Methodist Episcopal Church, 1810–1848," typescript copy in Duke University Library, August 3, 1831. Minnie Spencer Grant, "The American Colonization Society in North Carolina," unpublished M.A. thesis, Duke University, 1930, p. 14. Jones, Mississippi Methodism, II, 140. Barclay, Missionary Motivation and Expansion, p. 327. Recommendations came from the Mississippi, Virginia, Baltimore, New York, Philadelphia, Kentucky, Holston, Genesee, and Missouri conferences, and local groups in Ohio, Maine, and North Carolina.

erosity of contributors, and the prosperity of the time. Winans sent at least $150 each year from 1826 to 1831 out of his collections in Mississippi. In New York City, the book agents of the Methodist Episcopal Church acted as collectors for Methodist donations in the Northeast and reported collecting rather sizable sums; individual pastors would send checks for $10 or sometimes $40. Methodist financial backing, however, was certainly no more extensive than that of the other major denominations.[13]

Numerical superiority did enable the Methodists to offer more manpower to the American Colonization Society than any other church. The New York, Baltimore, Kentucky, and Ohio clergy were especially favorable and encouraged support by delivering special sermons and lectures, as well as by providing agents for the Colonization Society. The General Conference by 1832 had shed its reluctance to support non-Methodist organizations actively and resolved to allow the bishops to appoint agents for the society, but they were merely legalizing what had already become acceptable practice. In 1829 the Pittsburgh Conference voted unanimously to permit the eloquent Henry Bidleman Bascom to become a general colonization agent, and in 1831 the Kentucky

[13] R. S. Smith to R. R. Gurley, March 19, 1828; M. D. Mathews to Gurley, July 6, 1829; Samuel A. Latta to Gurley May 4, 1832; Henry Slicer to Bushrod Washington, July 12, 1827, E. A. Davis to Gurley, July 17, 1827, Isaac Cox to Joseph Gales, August 31, 1836; William Winans to Gurley, May 15, 1830, August 13, 1830, August 21, 1831; M. Pearce to Richard Smith, September 14, 1830; John Clark to Richard Smith, September 15, 1830; William A. Smith to Joseph Gales, August 6, 1834; W. R. Stone to Gales, July 8, 1834, American Colonization Papers. William McKenney to Charles Howard, June 6, 1835, Maryland State Colonization Society Papers, Maryland Historical Society, Baltimore. *African Repository,* II (September, 1826), 225f.; III (July, August, September, 1827), 158, 159, 191–192, 223; IV (July, August, October, November, 1828; January, 1829), 159–160, 191–192, 253, 256, 352; V (March, May, August, 1829), 32, 96, 189, 190; VI (June, July, September, 1830), 126, 157, 215–224; VII (March, May, August, 1831), 31, 96, 187–192; VIII (July, September, 1832), 155–160, 217–224.

and Ohio conferences allowed George C. Light and Samuel A. Latta to become agents for their areas.[14]

Bascom had been interested in colonization for some time before he lent his great oratorical talent to the Society. More flamboyant in dress and elegant in manner than the average Methodist preacher, he was so popular in the West that the ever-watchful Gurley was delighted with the opportunity to hire him. Within eight months of his first lecture as an agent, the golden-throated Bascom had formed 19 auxiliary colonization societies thereby increasing the financial as well as moral support of the parent organization.[15] For over two years he stormed from easily agitated western New York through the middle states and finally down the Mississippi to blasé New Orleans. From there he went to Natchez, where he collected $500 and helped his friend William Winans establish a state society. Even though his ability to hypnotize crowds made him a popular speaker and an exceptionally valuable fund-raiser, Bascom finally returned to the security of the college campus whence he had come, resigning his position over Winans' protests.[16]

Bascom had been preceded in the West by a part-time agent, Moses M. Henkle. An Ohio clergyman who later became a leader of the Methodist Protestant Church, Henkle

[14] Barclay, *Missionary Motivation and Expansion,* p. 327. *African Repository,* VIII (July, 1832), 146. Also Nathan Bangs, *A History of the Methodist Episcopal Church,* New York, 1840, IV, 99–101. C. C. Harper to R. R. Gurley, July 9, 1827; Samuel A. Latta to Gurley, December 1, 1831, American Colonization Society Papers.

[15] Henry B. Bascom to R. R. Gurley, January 26, 1827; October 24, 1827; October 21, 1828; February 29 [sic], 1829; May 4, 1830; June 4, 1830, American Colonization Society Papers. Moses M. Henkle, *The Life of Henry Bidleman Bascom,* Louisville, 1854, pp. 110ff., 131ff., 204ff., 286ff.

[16] Henry B. Bascom to R. R. Gurley, September 18, 1829; March 5, 1833, American Colonization Society Papers. William Winans to William M. Goodrich, July 22, 1831; Winans to R. R. Gurley, August 21, 1831; Winans to John Armstrong, September 3, 1831; Winans to Henry B. Bascom, December 19, 1832; Bascom to Winans, March 5, 1833, Winans Collection. *African Repository,* VI (May, 1830), 82.

was responsible for converting many Ohio Methodists to colonization. Like most agents, he would announce a meeting in a church or Masonic hall, address the much harangued throng about the plans and ideals of the American Colonization Society, and urge them to form an auxiliary society. If successful, he would handily produce a printed constitution and take a collection. One of his major feats was the creation of an Ohio state auxiliary after having exhorted the governor and fellow officials for one and one-half hours. The intrepid agent hoped that enlistment of public men would command "a moral influence which [was] not to be computed in *dollars* & Cents!"[17] With these enterprising beginnings, the successors to Henkle and Bascom continued to increase the number of Methodists who supported colonization in Kentucky, Missouri, and the Old Northwest.[18]

In the East, the New York Conference became an auxiliary of the Colonization Society in everything but name. The conference annually passed resolutions supporting, encouraging, and vindicating the organization. Some of its most distinguished men combined their interest in missions with their support of colonization; two of the chief officers of the Methodist Young Men's Missionary Society of New York, David M. Reese and Gabriel P. Disosway, were ardent colonizationists.[19] Impressed with Methodist support and organization, the enterprising Gurley asked the New York

[17] Moses M. Henkle to R. R. Gurley, May 8, 1827. Also January 4, 1827 and October 14, 1826, American Colonization Society Papers.

[18] Porter Clay to Samuel Wilkeson, January 22, 1839; R. R. Gurley to Wilkeson, February, 21, 1839 and April 3, 1839; M. M. Henkle to Wilkeson, April 27, 1839 and October 17, 1839; Samuel A. Latta to Gurley, December 1, 1831; Edmund W. Sehon to Messrs. Ewing, Morris *et al.,* December 27, 1834; George Peck to Wilkeson, January 17, 1839, American Colonization Society Papers. *Western Christian Advocate,* July 30, 1841, p. 59.

[19] Disosway was also a member of a merchant family which carried on a profitable trade with the African colonies. See Gabriel P. Disosway to R. R. Gurley, September 5, 1834, and also for May 6, 1829, June 23, 1831, and January 14, 1834, American Colonization Society Papers. *African Repository,* III (May, 1827), 90–91; x (June, 1834), 127; xiv (June, 1838), 168.

Conference to transform its circuits into actual auxiliaries of the American Colonization Society. In 1832 through his agent in New York, Laban Clark, Gurley sent out a feeler on the subject, only to be refused. Clark, a Methodist clergyman, reported that his colleagues did not wish to become too intimately connected with a "secular" agency which would merely add burdens to some already overworked clergymen; but the New York clergy had by no means renounced colonization.[20]

To the south, Methodists in the Baltimore, Virginia, and Mississippi conferences allied themselves with Episcopalians in backing the scheme. Bishop William Meade of the Episcopal diocese of Virginia was a leading colonizationist and Charles Wesley Andrews, an Episcopal rector, was a most effective agent. They were joined by the ubiquitous Methodist, William McKenney, who stumped Maryland, Virginia, and North Carolina for over fifteen years.[21] William Winans of Mississippi, although never an official agent, popularized colonization while denying vehemently that it had "originated with some *long headed* Yankee."[22] Winans, McKenney, Clark, Bascom, and Henkle were but a few of the hundreds

[20] James Boyd to R. R. Gurley, March 23, 1827; C. C. Harper to Gurley, July 9, 1827 and February 26, 1828; J. P. Durbin to Gurley, August 6, 1832; Laban Clark to Gurley, January 30, February 20, 1832, American Colonization Society Papers. Also *African Repository*, III (May, 1827), 91. Staudenraus intimates that the plan which Gurley proposed included only Maryland Methodism, but the secretary actually hoped to include the whole church if he could. John H. B. Latrobe apparently proposed a similar arrangement for the Masonic lodges in Maryland and the Maryland State Colonization Society, but all he got was scattered financial support. See Staudenraus, *Colonization Movement*, p. 111.

[21] See Charles Wesley Andrews Papers at Duke University. Also reports of William McKenney for 1832 and 1833 in the Maryland State Colonization Society Papers, Maryland Historical Society. William McKenney to Samuel Wilkeson, March 18, 1840, April 15, 1840, May 23, 1840, American Colonization Society Papers.

[22] William Winans to R. R. Gurley, February 21, 1827; also March 30, 1827, July 26, 1827, September 11, 1829, August 13, 1830. Gurley to Winans, December 15, 1826 and June 18, 1827, Winans Collection. Charles Sydnor, *Slavery in Mississippi*, pp. 203, 207–209.

97

of Methodist preachers who became colonization agents and supporters.[23] Methodism and colonization were for many devotees of both, complementary to each other.

Appeals for support of the Colonization Society were linked from the first with the Christian missionary impulse. Methodists believed that new colonies in Africa would provide a toehold for expanded missionary activity on that continent, but they had a very difficult time in sending their first missionary. As early as 1825 the missionary society proudly told the bishops that it had enough funds to establish a mission. In spite of this news and the example of a Baptist mission founded in 1826, the bishops strangely refused to appoint a missionary. They presumably had an opportunity to do so, for one Methodist preacher in a flash of zeal dedicated himself and his Negroes to Africa that same year.[24] Such interest, however, was quite rare. Liberian Methodists were guided by able Negro local preachers and faithfully encouraged by Nathan Bangs of the missionary society, but they needed more help.

Finally in 1831 the Young Men's Missionary Society of New York City and the parent body persuaded the bishops to act. In 1833 they sent one Melville B. Cox to Africa, but he was so weakened by tuberculosis that he died of a fever, a fate shared by two of his colleagues.[25]

[23] See for example I. A. Easter to J. H. Latrobe, March 28, 1836, Maryland State Colonization Society Papers. Henry B. Bascom to R. R. Gurley, March 23, 1837, July 3, 1832; Martin Ruter to Henry Clay, February 20, 1837; George Cookman to Gurley, July 4, 1827; Thomas Clinton to Gurley, May 7, 1827, American Colonization Society Papers.

[24] Charles Dresser to R. R. Gurley, September 16, 1826; Alexander Talley to Gurley, May 14, 1827, American Colonization Society Papers. "Liberia," *Baptist Missionary Magazine*, (March, 1826), 92–93. Barclay, *Missionary Motivation and Expansion*, pp. 327–329.

[25] Barclay, *Missionary Motivation and Expansion*, pp. 329ff. *African Repository*, VII (June, 1831), 116. Nathan Bangs to R. R. Gurley, October 16, 1827. John McPhail to Gurley, December 13, 1827; Gurley to the Board of Managers of the American Colonization Society, May 3, 1835 and May 5, 1835, American Colonization Society Papers.

In 1834 capable and determined John Seys managed to escape the martyrdom of his predecessors and began to organize 200 Methodist colonists into a conference. The missionary ideal now had concrete form, and Methodist periodicals in Maine, New York, Ohio, and Virginia praised it in words much like those sung by enthusiastic New Englanders just before the first missionaries sailed:

> But soon the light of God its way
> Shall mark and shine on mount and dale,
> While millions greet the welcome day
> That breaks the captives' galling chains.[26]

Some Methodists hoped that colonization would ultimately break the "galling chains" of American Negro slavery as well. This optimistic belief was held in the surcharged atmosphere of a growing controversy over the nature of the movement. Colonizationists fended off attacks from the South, and found their movement under serious condemnation in the North. Easily excited Southerners feared that the moral influence of the national and state colonization societies would eventually bring emancipation. The Georgia legislature, remembering the Missouri controversy, actually called Northern support of colonization an interference "ruinous to the prosperity, importance and political strength of the southern states."[27] Colonizationists found themselves extremely uncomfortable in certain parts of the South in an

[26] "New England Mission to Africa," *Colonizationist and Journal of Freedom*, I (October, 1833), 186. See also *Maine Wesleyan Journal*, August 2, 1833, p. 134 and October 31, 1833, p. 169. *Christian Advocate and Journal*, June 26, 1835, p. 174. *Western Christian Advocate*, July 29, 1836, p. 53. *Christian Sentinel*, November 15, 1833, p. 93.

[27] Charles Sydnor, *Development of Southern Sectionalism*, pp. 185–186. South Carolina, Georgia, Louisiana, Alabama, Missouri, and Mississippi legislators joined in attacking Northern interference in Southern domestic concerns, Staudenraus, *Colonization Movement*, p. 170. See also T. P. Hunt to R. R. Gurley, October 5, 1826; John French to Gurley, December 9, 1826; Unidentified Colonizationist to Gurley July 4, 1827, American Colonization Society Papers.

atmosphere in which writers promised to defend "the fairest portion of the Union" from a Northern onslaught upon slavery.[28] Henry Clay tried to calm these opponents of freedom by pointing out that the desire for liberty was universal and destroyed only where "universal darkness and despair prevail." And in 1832 R. R. Gurley tried to convince South Carolinians that his society was pacific, benevolent, and consistent with Southern interests. Those interests, he pointed out, demanded that slavery be seen as evil and eventually abolished.[29] Such statements could only convince hypersensitive Southerners that their gravest fears were correct.

There were a few Northerners, however, who attacked the Colonization Society as a singularly anti-Negro and pro-slavery institution. These proponents of "emancipation without expatriation" found the best articulation of their views in the words of William Lloyd Garrison. In 1832 Garrison, a former associate of Benjamin Lundy and then editor of the struggling *Liberator,* extended his violent and valid criticism of the Colonization Society into a booklet, *Thoughts on African Colonization.* Garrison accused even the most purely motivated colonizationists of tending "to perpetuate slavery, to encourage persecution, and to invigorate prejudice." Instead of fighting racial prejudice, he pointed out, the American Colonization Society nourished it by denying the possibility of elevating Negroes in this country. Furthermore, colonizationists accepted slavery by recognizing slaves as property, by apologizing for slavery in the South, and by increasing the value of slaves. Aside from the immorality and impracticability of the colonization scheme, Garrison found its proponents inconsistent. They proposed to take what they believed were "miserable outcasts" and make them

[28] *Controversy between Caius Gracchus and Opimius in reference to the American Society for colonizing the Free People of Colour of the United States,* Georgetown, D.C., 1827, pp. 5–12, 13–18, 21–29; also 40–49 for reply. See also B. M. Palmer to R. R. Gurley, June 8, 1827; D. I. Burr to Gurley, January 1, 1827, American Colonization Society Papers.
[29] *African Repository,* VI (September, 1830), 193–209.

into "missionaries of salvation" and civilization. "I believe," said the editor, "that neither a sea voyage nor an African climate have any miraculous influence upon the brain. . . . I believe also, that they who are capable of doing so well surrounded by barbarians, may do better among a civilized and christian people."[30] These and other anticolonizationist arguments were repeated and polished by the growing abolitionist movement which soon began to win energetic and volatile Methodist preachers. The colonizationists in the Church found themselves on the defensive, and their apology became that colonization was the only proper way to abolish slavery.[31]

To be sure, some Methodists had always believed that colonization was a moral alternative to a total acceptance of Negro servitude. They had suffered the failure of antislavery preaching early in their lives and had continued some of their concern for the Negro in supporting colonization. Of course there were many preachers like William Winans who emphasized the Negro's removal more than his emancipation. And although some undoubtedly agreed with the planter who welcomed a way to get rid of "idle and rougish free negroes," many Northern and Western and some Southern Methodists believed that the Colonization Society would "extirpate slavery from the land."[32] Abolitionists, therefore, shocked many articulate colonizationists into protestations

[30] William Lloyd Garrison, *Thoughts on African Colonization,* Boston, 1832, pp. 155–156 and *passim.*
[31] For an example of Methodist abolitionist attacks on colonization, see *Zion's Watchman,* April 22, 1837, p. 61; May 13, 1837, p. 73; November 10, 1838, p. 178; November 24, 1838, p. 185. At the 1833 meeting of the New England Conference abolitionists succeeded in permanently postponing procolonization resolutions by a decisive vote, *Liberator,* June 22, 1833, p. 99.
[32] For anti-Negro bias of the ministers see for example, William Winans to R. R. Gurley, June 20, 1826 and February 21, 1827; William Winans to Benjamin Drake, May 16, 1831; William Winans to Hugh McCollum, September 25, 1833, Winans Collection. See also J. G. Flournoy to R. R. Gurley, March 29, 1838 for the comment on the Negroes; also Arch Smith to Gurley, March 3, 1838, American Colonization Society Papers.

of their own antislavery purity and denunciations of their opponents' revolutionary ideas.

One of many early encounters between colonizationist and abolitionist involved a heated exchange between Nathan Bangs and the undaunted Garrison. Bangs fancied himself somewhat of a professional apologist, having earned that reputation for his part in a pamphlet war with Calvinists some years before. In January 1833 he haughtily reviewed Garrison's *Thoughts on African Colonization* in the *Methodist Magazine and Quarterly Review* which he edited. "We have frequently sustained, by our feeble means," he wrote, "every *humane and judicious* project aiming at the abolition of the slave trade and of mitigating the evils of slavery itself." He added that he was against slavery in the "abstract," but had no love for "wild enthusiasts" who raised a "popular clamor" against Southerners for having had the great evil of slavery "entailed upon them by the act of others." He sneered at Garrison's references to his own fight with slavery as revelations of an egotist, and scored the abolitionist's malevolence towards so honorable an organization as the American Colonization Society. He accused Garrison of extracting quotations from context (which he had done) and of using bad tactics and language. Then Bangs revealed the character of his own tactics by abusing Garrison as a proponent of racial amalgamation. The Methodist was so pleased with his article that he had it printed for free distribution. He had thrown down the gauntlet and Garrison was only too happy to pick it up.[33]

The abolitionist was furious. He referred to the "gross misrepresentations, Billingsgate epithets, and scandalous fictions" which had been written about him by a certain Methodist minister. The man was either a "liar" or an "ignoramus," he said, and finally concluded that Bangs was an

---

[33] [Nathan Bangs] "The American Colonization Society," *Methodist Magazine and Quarterly Review,* xv (January, 1833), 111–116. *Liberator,* February 16, 1833, p. 27.

"ambitious, meddlesome, domineering" liar and a "painted hypocrite." Unfortunately the adjectives were very close to the truth. Garrison went on to refute the claim that slavery had been guiltlessly entailed upon Southerners. "Vile refuge," "excellent nonsense!—a capital nostrum to quiet the consciences of Southern kidnappers" who indulged in cruelty, lust, and hate "with as much alacrity, zeal, and unanimity as did ever the inhabitants of Sodom and Gommorah." As for the charge of advocating amalgamation, Garrison denied it categorically. He pointed out that he neither advocated nor opposed marriage between races. Totally irrelevant to the issues at hand, the charge, he claimed, was leveled merely to "exploit hostility to us and our cause," a "wicked subterfuge, worthy of fiends, but utterly disgraceful to human beings."[34]

The battle between leading Methodists and abolitionists had only begun. Bangs was joined in defending what he considered to be his church's true position by David M. Reese, a physician, colonizationist, and a leading supporter of missions. With the benefit of neither meekness nor brotherly love, he roundly condemned the abolitionists on evidence selected from the first report of the American Anti-Slavery Society. Curiously prefacing his remarks with a quotation of Pontius Pilate's, he shamed the abolitionists for being un-American and revolutionary in declaring "the legally constituted right of slaveholding" to be a *"heinous crime in the sight of God."* Reese also echoed Bang' accusation that abolitionists were amalgamationists, evidenced by their desire to have children educated *"without regard to complexion!"* Reese shrieked, "Such a proposition from any source entitles its authors to the execration of their species."[35] Within a year the colonizationist enlarged his contri-

[34] *Liberator,* February 16, 1833, p. 27; March 16, 1833, p. 43.
[35] David M. Reese, *A Brief Review of the First Annual Report of the American Anti-Slavery Society,* New York, 1834, pp. 5, 11–14, 43–45. Reese headed his pamphlet with Pilate's "What I have written, I have written."

bution to American literary life by attacking William Jay's clear and convincing *Inquiry into the Character and Tendency of the American Colonization and American Anti-Slavery Societies.* Jay, a distinguished attorney and son of the former Chief Justice of the United States, had badly damaged the colonization cause with arguments very much like Garrison's.[36] In reply, Reese failed to meet any of the abolitionist's arguments and relied upon countercharge and bold denial in a very poor refutation. The Methodist—whom Garrison called a "vindictive, selfish, and loathsome . . . creature"—played upon the theme that colonizationists were better antislavery people than abolitionists since the former did not antagonize the South.[37]

By 1835 every major Methodist publication except *Zion's Herald* of Boston was enlisting in the colonization ranks. The colonization society was peaceful in its benevolence, and respectful of the Union in its national backing, said the *Christian Advocate and Journal* and the *Northern Christian Advocate* of New York. It offered the only apolitical plan for ridding the nation of the moral wrong of slavery, claimed Ethelbert Drake of the Virginia *Christian Sentinel;* in these sentiments he was joined by the editor of the *Western Christian Advocate,* Thomas Morris.[38] A prominent Ohio preacher and an active colonizationist, Morris carried with his large girth a caution on slavery which he had learned as a young minister in Kentucky. He agreed thoroughly

[36] R. R. Gurley to the Board of Managers of the American Colonization Society, May 1, 1835, American Colonization Society Papers. William Jay, *An Inquiry into the Character and Tendency of the American Colonization and American Anti-Slavery Societies,* New York, 1835, *passim.*

[37] David M. Reese, *Letters to the Hon. William Jay, being a Reply to his Inquiry into the American Colonization and American Anti-Slavery Societies,* New York, 1835, p. 116. *Liberator,* January 16, 1836, p. 11.

[38] *Christian Advocate and Journal,* August 15, 1834, p. 202; June 26, 1835, p. 174; April 3, 1844, p. 133. *Christian Sentinel,* February 22, 1833, p. 151; November 15, 1833, p. 94.

with the statement penned by Henry Bidleman Bascom for the Kentucky Conference in 1835. Slavery, said Bascom, was "an evil in all its tendencies . . . even in its most tolerable aspects"; it ought to be removed "wherever such exertions and influence [could] be brought to bear without infringing the right of others, constitutionally secured in the construction of the federal government." Therefore, the abolition of slavery should be gradual and not exceed the "disposition" and "ability" of the country to transport freedmen to a place where they could share equally in the "rights and privileges with the rest of mankind."[39]

Reflective and ethically acute colonizationists were thus entrapped by their ideals as well as by their respect for the inviolability of the political and social order. On the one hand, their ethics made them condemn slavery as a moral blot on the escutcheon of American freedom, but on the other, sectional political controversy, devotion to the Union, and the failure of past antislavery preaching made them eschew the "radical" idea of emancipation in America. Furthermore, they were prisoners of their own antipathy towards the Negroes. They believed that circumstances and history had degraded the American free Negro, but they would not attempt to change those circumstances or divert history.

In spite of their self-conscious Arminian devotion to the freedom of the will, Methodist colonizationists did not presume to pit themselves against society. If history were to be adjudicated on behalf of the black man, let it be done in Africa! As members of the master class, they could extend charity but not dispense justice. Their fear and prejudice erupted in their arguments concerning racial amalgamation. Their reading of history told them that two different races had never existed together in equality: either one subjected

[39] *Western Christian Advocate,* October 23, 1835, p. 103; May 30, 1834, p. 19; November 21, 1834, p. 117; August 14, 1835, p. 63; July 8, 1836, p. 42.

the other to itself, which was immoral; or the lesser died out, which was tragic; or the two formed a third race, which was horrible. Thus, enlightened people who valued social stability, abhorred violence, and feared Negro equality would unite to return the slaves to Africa whence they had come.[40] At every turn colonizationists exercised that respect for order and propriety, that dislike of the "lower" classes which characterizes gentility. Colonizationists, when faced with what they considered a social evil, were more likely to murmur, "Tch, tch," than to proclaim "Thou shalt not . . . ."

The most respected and outstanding colonizationist in the Methodist Episcopal Church was Willbur Fisk, president of Wesleyan University. A graduate of Brown College and a proponent of education in a denomination that was just beginning to value learning, Fisk was an "easy, affable, and ingratiating" New England gentleman of lean and narrow build. When he was invited to lead the new Methodist college at Middletown, Connecticut in 1830, he was already a disciple of colonization, a devotee of national union, and a partisan of Methodist solidarity. Sensitive to social problems, Fisk was a leader of the Temperance Reformation in New England Methodism, a supporter of the African Education Society, and an apologist for the ill-fated American Union for the Relief and Improvement of the Colored Race. By temperament, health and position he was allergic to any idea which would erupt into mental, physical, or psychological violence. And he despaired of what he called the "ultraism" of his day. "We can scarcely engage in any enterprise, in spite of the devil," he told a colonization meeting in New York, "but what he himself will turn character and ruin by intemperate and furious zeal, a cause he cannot resist."[41]

[40] *Western Christian Advocate*, November 27, 1835, p. 121; December 4, 1835, p. 125; September 11, 1835, p. 77.

[41] *Ibid.*, July 31, 1835, p. 53. Also Joseph Holdich, *The Life of Willbur Fisk, D.D.*, New York, 1842, *passim*. *Zion's Herald*, June 24, 1835, p. 97; June 3, 1835, p. 86. Circular Letter of Isaac Orr, Secretary of the African Education Society to Willbur Fisk, April 4, 1832, Fisk Papers.

Fisk conceived of himself as a responsible reformer who accepted what he could not change and within those bounds changed what he could not accept.

Since 1826 when he was manager of the auxiliary society in Vermont, Fisk had worked hard to promote and to defend colonization as a nonrevolutionary, sensible reform. He often introduced procolonization resolutions into the annual meetings of the New England Conference and, when the abolitionists defeated his motions and generally succeeded in undermining his reform, he was much taken aback. They did not know how sensitive the South was on the subject of slavery, or worse—they did not care, he thought. They did not worry about the harm that they would do to the delicate relations between North and South; they did not value the solidarity of the Church; they did not really know how to help the Negroes. They opposed the only true reform—the American Colonization Society, "a Society," wrote Fisk in 1835, "that has indirectly liberated more slaves, probably, than all the antislavery societies in our country from the beginning until now! A Society which the unprincipled slaveholder hates and dreads, because it leads to abolition; and the ultra-abolitionist opposes because it stands in the way of his dangerous high-pressure engine. A Society which, by a successful experiment, makes fair promise of giving to the world a convincing and extended exhibition of negro elevation, moral, intellectual, and social."[42]

Such remarks from so respected a person as President Fisk naturally pleased the hard-pressed colonization leaders, and when Fisk went to Europe for his health later in 1835 he acted also as the official representative of the New York and Pennsylvania colonizationists to the British African Colonization Society.[43] Upon his return, he continued to hold a high position as a defender of the cause of order,

---

[42] *Zion's Herald,* March 11, 1835, p. 37.

[43] Letters of Certification by John Breckinridge, President of the Young Men's Colonization Society of Pennsylvania. See also Elliott Cresson to Willbur Fisk, August 26, 1835, Fisk Papers.

benevolence, and responsibility—the cause of the Methodist Episcopal Church.

Most high ranking Methodist spokesmen agreed with Fisk. Bishop William McKendree, Francis Asbury's colleague and successor, personified the continuity between the antislavery preaching of the 1790's and the colonization movement of the 1830's. Once he had signed the antislavery rules of the Western Conference, and then he had urged caution, and in his old age rather than compromise completely with slavery, he had become one of the vice presidents of the American Colonization Society. By 1840 he was joined by Bishops James O. Andrew, Beverly Waugh, and Thomas Morris, as well as William Winans, Willbur Fisk, and President John Durbin of Dickinson College. Bishops Enoch George, Joshua Soule, and Elijah Hedding were also quite friendly to the movement, although Hedding preferred to aid the American Union for the Improvement of the Colored Race, a short-lived organization that aspired to educate Negroes. Thomas E. Bond, Sr., editor of the *Christian Advocate and Journal* after 1840, had been perennial vice president of the Maryland State Colonization Society, and William Capers believed the colonization idea a good one. Annual conferences in every part of the United States except the Southeast had by 1836 passed resolutions favoring colonization, and in 1840 the General Conference warmly commended the American Colonization Society for its "benevolence to the souls and bodies of people of colour both in our country and in Africa."[44] No prominent American Methodist ecclesiastic disagreed with those sentiments.

[44] C. C. Harper to R. R. Gurley, July 9, 1827; I. A. Easter to Gurley, January 10, 1839, American Colonization Society Papers. Enoch George to John H. Kennard, March 28, 1842, Maryland State Colonization Society Papers. William Capers to George Coles, July 3, 1840, George Coles Letters, Drew University. *Western Christian Advocate,* October 31, 1834, p. 106. *Friend of Man,* March 13, 1839, p. 358. *Emancipator,* July 21, 1836, p. 46. *Exposition of the American Union for the Improvement of the Colored Race,* Boston, 1835.

Indeed, there was no religious denomination more closely connected with colonization than the Methodist Episcopal Church. This was true in spite of a rather bad episode which began in 1839. John Seys, the chief Methodist missionary in Liberia, was not only extremely energetic and efficient, but also jealous of rights and privileges which he claimed had been breached by the petulant governor, Thomas Buchanan. The Methodists accused Buchanan of tyrannical confiscation of goods and hostility to the Mission. Buchanan accused Seys of ecclesiastical domination and independence subversive of good order and economic success. The mission actually had acted as a government within a government with little attention to the legitimate authorities, but Buchanan dealt with the problem inexpertly and incurred the displeasure of the Methodists' missionary society. Nathan Bangs warned the executive committee of the American Colonization Society that his church had always spoken of it with "affection and respect" and would regret "weakening the influence of the Methodists in the colonization scheme." With this threat, the officials of the Society scurried into action and after 18 months of discussion, the matter was settled.[45] Hard-pressed by the abolitionists and suspected by Southerners, colonizationists could not afford the displeasure of the largest Protestant denomination in the United States.

There was, however, little danger that Methodist leaders would turn against colonization because it was their conscientious alternative to compromising completely with slavery. Although some, like David Reese, were excited by anti-Negro bias, others like Willbur Fisk were motivated by a genuine concern for Negroes uncomplicated by conscious prejudice. They could all agree that history had created a grave social problem which had thwarted outright antislav-

[45] Nathan Bangs to American Colonization Society Executive Committee, October 21, 1840. Thomas Buchanan Dispatches, July 21, 1840, September 6, 1840, American Colonization Society Papers.

ery preaching previously. Many believed that the moral influence of the American Colonization Society would one day dissolve the bonds of slavery—but this was a silent, often inarticulated hope. The silence was enforced by the sectional tension which had increased greatly since the first orations were delivered on the Missouri controversy. Slave conspiracies and abolitionist literature had helped to increase the hostility that reasonable men deplored. Identifying with values that perpetuate political and social institutions, influential and powerful Methodists were profoundly suspicious of those who identified with values that emphasized human freedom and implied racial equality. Colonization was created to meet the needs of minds overwhelmed by a complex moral problem; it became a gentle, wistful hope of readjusting social dislocation painlessly. It was also, however, the very essence of inaction because it lacked even the power of moral suasion after a short time. That moral power was grasped more firmly by fervent, outspoken men unawed by history and scornful of the genteel compromise of conscience.

PART II

THE CHURCH AND ABOLITION

CHAPTER V

THE RADICAL ALTERNATIVE TO COMPROMISE:

The Rise of Methodist Abolitionism
1832–1836

ABOLITIONISTS sharpened to a keen edge the latent hostility against Negro slavery which had been blunted by toleration, accommodation, and reverence for political stability. They carved away at the moral, mental, and institutional adjustments behind which Americans had hidden, and preached a gospel of immediate freedom for the slaves. As soldiers in this general crusade against slavery, Methodist evangelical abolitionists helped to intensify the tumultuous evaluation of American institutions, customs, and ideals which began after the War of 1812. In this era of reform which valued peace, women's rights, education, community virtue, and social responsibility, abolitionists were social revolutionaries. In their moral urgency they denounced accepted norms of goodness as pious masks for the depravity and sinfulness of slavery. They condemned as bulwarks of evil those institutions which refused to turn their authority against slavery. They attacked as anti-Negro the American Colonization Society which refused to fight slavery directly. The Southern Mission to the Slaves they rejected since it accepted the existence of slavery as normal. Because of such behavior, abolitionists appeared to be wild enthusiasts, agitators, and radicals rather than genteel reformers, and consequently they were opposed by government, newspapers, mobs, and churches.

Since most of the radical antislavery men were connected

with Christian denominations, they tried to force ecclesiastical leaders to issue clear and unreserved antislavery statements. This attempt was most vividly dramatized in the Methodist Episcopal Church with its antislavery precedents, evangelical ethos, large Southern and slave membership, and ecclesiastical authoritarianism. Furthermore, this church was one of the largest national institutions in the United States and representative of a great many Americans.

By 1832 Methodists had relegated the slavery issue to the periphery of moral and institutional concern. Church leaders wished neither to condemn nor explicitly to condone Negro servitude, partially because of previous experiences with antislavery preaching and partially because of their dedication to the American Colonization Society and the missions to the slaves. Furthermore, the Methodist ministry, except for men like William G. Brownlow, Peter Cartwright, and William Winans, wished to avoid political matters as John Wesley had demanded. Since slavery had, with the Missouri controversy, become involved in political conflict, Methodist ministers feared that statements about it would be construed as meddling in politics—quite an un-American action for men of the cloth in Jacksonian America.[1] For the most part, therefore, delegates to the General Conference of 1832 thought that the question of slavery was settled insofar as church action and responsibility was concerned. They had other problems: the secession of Methodist Protestants who had insisted upon lay representation in conferences and the restriction of episcopal powers; methods

---

[1] Brownlow was a Whig publicist as well as a Methodist minister; Winans was a devoted Mississippi Whig; and Cartwright was an active Democratic campaigner in Illinois. Nevertheless, Methodist ministers were not supposed to take active part in politics. Asbury had never approved of it, and although there had never been any rules on the subject, Methodist tradition simply did not support it. Alexis de Tocqueville found the American ministers of all denominations anxious to avoid being thought politically minded. See Alexis de Tocqueville, *Democracy in America* (Henry Reeves, translator), New York, 1945, I, 309.

of ecclesiastical procedure; and religious instruction of the young.[2]

Slavery nevertheless intruded upon the business of the conference through petitions and the election of a new bishop. Stephen G. Roszel, who had led the Baltimore Conference in curtailing a slaveholding ministry, persuaded the chair to appoint a committee on slavery; the committee report, however, was "tabled" into oblivion. The conference also quietly ignored a memorial from colored Methodists who asked their coreligionists to petition state legislatures for the repeal of laws that denied Negroes freedom of worship and education. The memorialists also questioned the Christian morality of Methodist preachers who held slaves, and were thus guilty of "administering to all the evils arising from" slavery, including insurrections. Referring to charismatic Nat Turner's insurrection in Southampton County, Virginia, the previous year, they suggested that without slaves there would be no danger of servile rebellion. In reply, the committee on slavery reported that it was "inexpedient" to act upon the memorial at that time, and the conference agreed.[3] This refusal to deal with a delicate subject, revealing as it was, was not however the delegates' most important action concerning slavery.

Far more important than the timid reaction to the Negroes' petition, the election of a new bishop reflected lingering sensitivity to antislavery opinion and portended grave difficulties between the North and South. William Winans, the Mississippi colonizationist, was one of the delegates who had pondered the problem of electing another man to aid the four active bishops in superintending a half-million Methodists. He thought that William Capers and a Georgian, Lovick Pierce, were the most obvious candidates, but he remembered that there had been opposition to a slaveholding

[2] *Christian Advocate and Journal,* May 11, 1832, p. 146.
[3] *Journals of the General Conference,* I, 367, 413, 415. *Liberator,* July 28, 1832, p. 118.

115

clergy in the East, West, and North. He might also have recalled that in 1826, Bishops Elijah Hedding and Enoch George had refused to allow a slaveholder to represent the American church at the conference of English Methodists.[4] William Capers himself knew of this Northern sensitivity and so declined to be a candidate for the episcopacy. But just how great opposition to a slaveholding bishop was is uncertain because the Methodists concealed much information in secret caucuses at the conference. It is certain, however, that Northerners believed the new bishop should be from the South, that the South's most illustrious candidate (Capers) had withdrawn, and that some Northern delegates opposed a slaveholding bishop. Finally, after adept maneuvering by Stephen G. Roszel and Capers, James O. Andrew of Georgia was elected because he was a Southerner who did not own slaves.[5]

Andrew's biographer lamely denied that the qualification affected the election, claiming that "it was the merit of his life and the greatness of his mind that gained for him his Episcopal office." Any number of men, however, were certainly as good as Andrew, and he was scarcely better fitted for his new office than Capers, an educator and the superintendent of missions to the slaves. Capers had clearly stated why he had refused to accept the episcopacy; Roszel, delegate of a conference which refused to ordain slaveholders,

[4] William Winans to Beverly Waugh, December 17, 1831, Winans Collection. *Christian Advocate and Journal,* November 4, 1826, p. 1. D. W. Clark, *Life and Times of Rev. Elijah Hedding, D.D.,* New York, 1855, pp. 325–326.

[5] William Winans, Diary, May 22, 1832, Winans Collection. Capers recalled in the General Conference of 1844 how he had rejected any advances made to him because of his "circumstances with regard to slavery." Robert Athow West, *Report of Debates in the General Conference of the Methodist Episcopal Church, held in the City of New York, 1844,* New York, 1844, p. 99. See also William Capers to his wife, May 12, 1832, in Wightman, *Life of Capers,* p. 327. John Emory of Maryland was also raised to the episcopacy at the same time, *Journals of the General Conference,* I, 401.

was one of the leading supporters of Andrew. Andrew himself exclaimed to Lovick Pierce with tears in his eyes: "It is not my merit that has made me a Bishop, but my poverty"—his having no slaves. Winans was sure of it. He wrote in his diary: "Why was he chosen? Because he belonged to the South and because he had no slaves and because W. Capers and S. G. Rozzle [sic] were adroit in the arts of electioneering. . . . [A]s a southern man I must detest the principle on which this election was conducted and as a man I must abhor the manner in which it was managed. I fear for the consequences in time to come."[6] Before those consequences became apparent, however, much more had to happen, and most of what occurred was linked with the abolitionists.

These men and women became a vital force in American history out of a myriad of diverse personal and social pressures and ideals. They translated Americans' experience of creating their own history into the language of voluntarism that was sophisticated in New England and simplified in many a revivalist church. American history had emphasized the ability of men to free themselves of the degradation of poverty by seizing opportunities in land, trade, and politics. The great revivals of the nineteenth century were urging men to free themselves of the degradation of sin by deciding to become true Christians. And Americans were to find that the moral fervor of revivalism could very easily affect material as well as spiritual development. To a few who were unencumbered by responsibility in a slaveholding society and who were convinced that race prejudice and slavery were moral evils, the abolition of slavery became the true test of America's control of its destiny and salvation.

Abolitionists became prominent in the era of reform that was Jacksonian America. The attempted reformation of society was an American tradition—Americans had often

---

[6] Smith, *Life of Andrew*, p. 233. William Winans, Diary, May 22, 1832, Winans Collection.

thought of their land as a great experiment in solving the problems of society. For some it was the creation of a new and better England in the wilderness; for others, the building of a Quaker city of love; for still others the construction of a new nation after a Hamiltonian or a Jeffersonian dream. The Methodists and other evangelicals, too, had combined religion and the reformation of society in their peculiar way. But not until the greatest American reform—the independent federal union—had been inaugurated and its politics democratized did reforming activity begin seriously to affect the structure of all American society. True, antislavery prophets had tried to extend the American Revolution and the Christian religion into a kind of reform, but they chose a period when the most urgent business had been to create a nation. When the Union had been set upon its wobbly course, those adventurous souls who were not extending it could then intensify its advantages.

The flagging American antislavery tradition was spurred into action by a conjunction of events. After 1831 a few people began to follow William Lloyd Garrison who had served his antislavery apprenticeship with Benjamin Lundy on the *Genius of Universal Emancipation,* and had ardently explained to Boston the "guilt of the nation in permitting slavery to continue." Some Bostonians had already been impressed with the Quaker petition to Congress in 1829 asking for the abolition of the slave trade in the District of Columbia; they became even more interested in Negro servitude as British reformers increased their demands for the abolition of West Indian slavery. Elsewhere the young revivalist, Theodore Dwight Weld, was also imbibing British antislavery principles, along with his benefactors, Lewis and Arthur Tappan.[7] The combination of Garrison, Weld, the Tappans,

---

[7] See *Christian Register,* October 23, 1830, p. 170, December 4, 1830, pp. 194–195 for report of Garrison's remarks. Also a book review of James Stephens' *The Slavery of the British West India Colonies delineated . . .* in the *Christian Examiner and General*

the British example, and the evangelical revivals revived a moribund antislavery sentiment and transformed it into the abolitionist crusade.

The crusade was given urgency not only by revivalistic preaching, but also by the frustrating ineffectiveness of plans for gradual emancipation. The Missouri controversy and its aftermath had made many people avoid criticizing slavery, but in January 1831 Garrison began to publish the *Liberator* which was devoted to immediate emancipation. Educated in the political newspaper oratory of the day, Garrison denied that he would retard "the cause of emancipation by the coarseness of [his] invective, and the precipitancy of [his] measures." He wrote, "Posterity will bring testimony that I was right. I desire to thank God, that he enables me to disregard 'the fear of man which bringeth a snare,' and to speak his truth in its simplicity and power."[8] Garrison believed that the slaves should be freed, placed under the protection of law and "a benevolent and disinterested supervision, which [should] secure to them the right to obtain secular and religious knowledge, to worship God, according to the dictates of their consciences, to accumulate wealth, &c." Benjamin Lundy, who had been an emancipationist for years, agreed: "Christianity *requires,* and Justice demands the prompt advocacy and IMMEDIATE ADOPTION of measures, that shall break the fetters of the slave, and *prepare him* for the enjoyment of perfect freedom."[9] Thus the rise

---

Review, ns XVI (September, 1831), 109–138. The clearest study of the early abolitionist movement is still Gilbert H. Barnes, *The Anti-Slavery Impulse, 1830–1844,* New York, 1933. Benjamin P. Thomas has written the biography of the great antislavery evangelist in *Theodore Weld, Crusader for Freedom,* New Brunswick, 1950; John L. Thomas' Bancroft prize-winning biography of William Lloyd Garrison, *The Liberator: William Lloyd Garrison, a Biography,* Boston, 1963, is the best on that controversial figure.

[8] *Liberator,* January 1, 1831, p. 1.

[9] Printed in *Genius of Universal Emancipation,* December, 1832, p. 26.

of abolitionism was the culmination of one period of anti-slavery activity and the beginning of another.[10]

Methodist abolitionism began first in New England under the influence of the *Liberator* and its irrepressible editor. One of the first converts to Garrisonian ideas in 1831 was La Roy Sunderland, the Methodist minister at Andover, Massachusetts, whose great oratorical power swept his entire congregation along with him. Sunderland, a small dynamo of a man, hoped to identify the upsurge in abolitionist activity with the Methodist antislavery heritage, and later warned Garrison that he had printed a letter filled with erroneous accusations of Methodism. "Indeed," he wrote, "I do not believe that the Methodist Episcopal Church would suffer in a comparison with any other people, except the Quakers, in relation to the subject of slavery; and hence, I regret exceedingly that you should have admitted into the *Liberator,* statements so manifestly incorrect, and which will but tend to prejudice very many of your friends against *Anti-Slavery Principles.*"[11] Consistent with his old and new faiths, as he understood them, the vigorous Sunderland helped to organize the American Anti-Slavery Society in December of 1833. He had already helped to defeat pro-colonizationist resolutions in the New England Conference; and soon his and his successor's activities led to the creation of a local antislavery society in Andover.[12]

[10] See Alice Adams, *The Neglected Period of Antislavery,* pp. 249–252. See also David Brion Davis, "The Emergence of Immediatism in British and American Antislavery Thought," *Mississippi Valley Historical Review,* XLIX (September, 1962) 209–230.

[11] *Liberator,* June 15, 1833, p. 94. Also William Lloyd Garrison to La Roy Sunderland, September 8, 1831, William Lloyd Garrison Papers, Boston Public Library. David Kimball, Jr. to Elizur Wright, August 21, 1833, Elizur Wright Papers, Library of Congress. All manuscripts in the Boston Public Library are cited here by courtesy of the trustees of that institution.

[12] P. Knapp to Isaac Knapp, February 10, 1834; Arnold Buffum to William Lloyd Garrison, October 23, 1832, Garrison Papers. *Liberator,* June 22, 1833, p. 99. *Abolitionist,* December, 1833, p. 177.

Sunderland was soon joined by other Methodist ministers whose revivalism became scandalously particular in attacking slavery and preaching repentance for supporting it. The most exasperating and energetic of these men was George Storrs, a native of New Hampshire and a Methodist minister since 1824. A voracious worker and vigorous speaker, he enraged his detractors and worried his gentle mother with violent sarcasm and personal attacks. His great energy was expended in lecturing against slavery, organizing antislavery societies, and in distributing pamphlets. He joined the American Anti-Slavery Society in its drive to win Methodists by circulating hundreds of copies of John Wesley's *Thoughts Upon Slavery;* by 1834 he had become a member of the executive committee of the New Hampshire Anti-Slavery Society and a vice president of the national body.[13] Storrs and Sunderland and the anonymous few who formed a Methodist antislavery society in October of 1834 were gradually enlisting their coreligionists in the cause of Wesley and the early Methodist antislavery preachers who had called slaveholders "horsethieves and hogstealers" and who believed that slavery was a moral evil.[14]

The most fortunate Methodist addition to radical antislavery activity was Orange Scott—the man who more than any other came to symbolize Methodist abolitionism. The eldest son of a poverty stricken Vermont day-laborer, Scott was barely able to read and write when at the age of twenty he was converted to Christianity at a Methodist campmeeting. He soon discovered gifts of organization, oratory, and concentration which led to his ordination as a Methodist

[13] Receipt for printing, January 31, 1835; Lucinda Storrs to George Storrs, April 18, 1835, George Storrs Papers, New York Public Library. Elizur Wright to Amos A. Phelps, December 6, 1834, Wright Papers. *Christian Register,* December 6, 1834, p. 66. *Second Annual Report of the American Anti-Slavery Society,* New York, 1835, p. 25.

[14] See Lucius C. Matlack, *The History of American Slavery and Methodism from 1780 to 1849,* New York, 1849, p. 98.

minister in 1826 and to his appointment in 1830 as a presiding elder over all the preachers in the area near Springfield, Massachusetts. Two years later he was elected a delegate to the General Conference; at the age of thirty-two he was following a pattern of advancement which had led less talented men to the episcopacy. Preaching the gospel—not emancipation—was his primary concern. He had been unmoved when Benjamin Lundy had appealed to his conference in 1828 for help even though he had joined in expressing the sentiment that slavery should be abolished. Nor had he been enraged by the refusal of the General Conference of 1832 to heed the prayer of their Negro petitioners. But these experiences, plus the debate over a slaveholding bishop and a familiarity with the Section on Slavery in the *Discipline* undoubtedly made him receptive to abolitionist ideas.[15]

Scott's conversion to abolitionism resulted in part from the antislavery pamphlet campaign of 1834. Although at first interested in the American Colonization Society, he yielded to the influence of some of his abolitionist colleagues and subscribed to Garrison's fascinating *Liberator*. He then read the editor's *Thoughts on African Colonization,* and devoured the tracts written by Lydia Maria Child, George Bourne, and Amos A. Phelps. Mrs. Child's *Appeal in Favor of that Class of Americans called Africans* gave Scott a general understanding of the moral character of slavery; Bourne's *Picture of Slavery* impressed upon him Wesley's antislavery ideas; and Phelps' *Lectures on Slavery* warned him that the clergy's silence would enable Negro servitude to endure. Garrison's appeal to conscience, Bourne's appeal to John Wesley, and Phelps' appeal to the ministry somehow stirred Scott to become an abolitionist.[16]

[15] Lucius C. Matlack, *The Life of Rev. Orange Scott,* New York, 1851, pp. 5–28, 299.
[16] *Ibid.,* pp. 31–33, 69–70.

Immediately after his decision he began to "abolitionize" the New England Conference. He helped defeat a resolution supporting colonization and spent $100 of his own money to send the *Liberator* to all conference members.[17] He then initiated the first extended discussion of slavery in a Methodist periodical. Since the official church paper, the *Christian Advocate and Journal,* as well as *Zion's Herald* of Boston, refused to print abolitionist writings, Scott induced camp-meeting congregations to petition the *Herald* to publish a discussion of slavery. He was assisted in his efforts by the publishers' fear that the independent publication of the *Wesleyan Anti-Slavery Herald* in Concord, New Hampshire, would "rend" New England Methodism. Consequently, in January 1835, the Boston journal began to carry a series of articles that Scott had prepared to win popular Methodist support for the immediate abolition of slavery.[18]

Scott derived the intellectual content of his articles from the ideas of Phelps and Garrison, but the power behind them was his own. "I propose to deal in *facts* and *arguments,"* he wrote in a typical disclaimer, "and if such a course shall at times appear somewhat severe, it will not be owing to any fault in the *weapons,* but in the system which they oppose." The plan of the American Colonization Society was, he said, impracticable, unjust, and morally "blind" to slaveholding as it really was: "falsehood in theory, tyranny in practice, a violation of God's law, and the parent of all abominations." Scott scored the personal cruelties of slavery, but found its evil to be essentially in its "unjust assumption over the rights of man." In giving themselves absolute control over other men, slaveholders had simply usurped the place of God. Therefore, he preached repentance

[17] Orange Scott to William Lloyd Garrison, December 30, 1834, Garrison Papers.

[18] Benjamin Kingsbury, Jr., to Willbur Fisk, January 5, 1835, Fisk Papers. Matlack, *Life of Scott,* pp. 38ff. The *Wesleyan Anti-Slavery Herald* was published only a few times in 1835.

for supporting this sin as he had preached repentance of other sins at campmeetings and in revivals.

Scott's transformation into an antislavery revivalist required no change in method, for the "antislavery impulse" came out of evangelical preaching that demanded a willful rejection of sin. Abolition revivalists did not have a *plan* for emancipation, for in their world of Jacksonian oratory and evangelism they knew that men's minds were not changed by purely rational appeals. Radical change would come, they thought, when men decided to destroy slavery. And what then? As a seasoned revivalist, Scott had a *vision* if not a plan—a vision of the immediate emancipation of the slaves, the immediate provision for their education, the immediate passage of laws to guarantee them civil and legal rights so that "at the *earliest possible period, consistent with the best good of the slaves,* they should be FULLY EMANCIPATED."[19] Scott and his colleagues were convinced that with preaching would come repentance. The repentant would then put democratic pressure upon legislatures that would result in appropriate laws to liberate Negroes everywhere. Although this vision was sometimes vague, it was also simple and essentially easy to understand.

High Methodist officials, however, were not prepared to accept the morally explosive vision which abolitionists preached. They were dedicated to their own vague philanthropy—the colonization cause—as well as to the Church's national unity. To publicize this dedication they had a variety of talent. Their primary spokesmen at first were the editors of the *Christian Advocate and Journal* and President Willbur Fisk, who were followed by men such as the editors of the *Maine Wesleyan Journal* and the *Christian Sentinel* of Richmond, Virginia.[20] The editor of the *Advocate,* schol-

[19] *Zion's Herald,* January 7, 1835, p. 2; January 21, 1835, p. 10; January 28, 1835, p. 14; February 11, 1835, p. 22.

[20] *Maine Wesleyan Journal,* February 28, 1833, p. 94; July 18, 1833, p. 109. *Christian Sentinel,* September 7, 1832, p. 53; November 9, 1832, p. 89; November 15, 1833, p. 94.

arly John Durbin, had acquired his post in 1832 with Southern support, a fact which attested to his moderation and partially accounted for his reaction to radical antislavery ideas. His first statement on abolitionism came only nine days after a mob had driven the founders of the New York City Anti-Slavery Society from Clinton Hall on October 2, 1833. Instead of condemning mob rule, he warned Methodists that the "intentions of *recent* antislavery societies and some of the means they use [were] at variance with the vested interests, and constitutional rights and obligations of the country" because they hoped to "create great excitement and alarm and then force the [slavery] question under the action of congress." Methodists should respect law lest the Union be divided, he warned; Ethelbert Drake of the *Christian Sentinel* agreed and cautioned Christians to regulate "their own private conduct" and not engage in "political controversies" over slavery.[21]

When Durbin resigned as editor to become president of Dickinson College in July of 1834, Nathan Bangs succeeded him. An arch-enemy of both abolition and William Lloyd Garrison, Bangs had already smarted under the sting of Garrison's whip-like pen for his unfair review of *Thoughts on African Colonization*. He began his conduct of the *Advocate* with an editorial, "Abolitionists no friends to Slaves," in which he condemned the "insurrectionary" practices of radical antislavery men who preached doctrines that raised up mobs, albeit against themselves. Believing that time and the slow and gracious effects of Christianity would destroy slavery, Bangs went on to deplore those who endangered the Union by appeals for a plan that could be effected only with "cannon" and "bayonet." He never once called into question the responsibility of the slaveholders except to mumble something about being against slavery "in the abstract." What worried Bangs was not the injustice done

[21] *Christian Sentinel,* November 15, 1833, p. 94. *Christian Advocate and Journal,* October 11, 1833, p. 27.

the slaves, but the hostile reaction of the masters, and he maintained that the North would not help the slaves by "inflammatory harangues, but by deeds of charity."[22] Since Bangs believed that Methodists through colonization and domestic missions were actually helping the slaves, it is not surprising that he thought abolitionists un-Methodist and therefore refused to allow them a voice in the *Advocate*.

There were generally two stumblingblocks to following the abolitionists' path as far as their more reflective opponents were concerned: the immediacy of emancipation and Southern reaction. Professor D. D. Whedon of Wesleyan University, who had been selected by Fisk to answer Orange Scott, discussed both problems in *Zion's Herald*. Whereas Scott had been enflamed with the knowledge that something had to be done, Whedon was afraid that that "something" could mean anything. The professor was not put at ease by Scott's statement that immediate emancipation meant that the slaves should be freed from the masters' control and protected by adequate legislation. He accused the abolitionist of "facetious equivoque" and of merely offering emancipation gradually accomplished. Yet the boldness of even beginning gradual emancipation at once conjured up a demonic vision of amalgamation and social upheaval for which he was not prepared. Like many Northern antiabolitionists, Whedon considered himself to be opposed to slavery and in favor of some kind of emancipation someday; but his own confusion concerning when and where to free the slaves revealed that he could not consistently condemn abolitionists for having no definite plans. His reaction to the generally vivid and energetic attacks upon slavery, however, was not to hear or read their words of freedom, but to gasp at their tone of condemnation. Could Scott and his antislavery

[22] *Christian Advocate and Journal,* August 15, 1834, p. 202; also July 25, 1834, p. 190. Nathan Bangs, *The Life of the Rev. Freeborn Garrettson,* New York, 1832, p. 66n. John A. Roche, *The Life of John Price Durbin, D.D., LL.D.,* New York, 1890, p. 103.

brethren not see that the sectional feeling in the United States doomed demands for emancipation merely to "solidifying the South into a compact body of opposition" and of "firmer pressure on the slave?" He concluded: "That may be an honest, but it is an ill-directed benevolence, that takes measures to defeat its own purposes, by ruining the object it would benefit."[23]

Official opposition to abolitionists, especially that of the *Christian Advocate and Journal,* challenged them to greater efforts in popularizing their cause. On February 4, 1835 *Zion's Herald* published an "extra" edition: "An Appeal on the Subject of Slavery Addressed to the members of the New England and New Hampshire Conferences . . . ." signed by five Methodist ministers. Sunderland, who had resigned from his pulpit but not his ordination, was the principal author, but he was joined by a colleague from Dover, New Hampshire, Jared Perkins; a preacher at Lowell, Abram D. Merrill, who had signed the subscription list for Amos A. Phelps' *Lectures on Slavery;* Shipley Willson, former editor of *Zion's Herald* and of the *Methodist Preacher;* and the indefatigable George Storrs. They proclaimed that "No man has, or can have, a right to hold a fellowman as a piece of merchantable property," or to deny him his liberty or "means of social, moral, and intellectual improvement." Whoever presumed to do so they held to be "guilty of a *crime* which [could not] be reconciled with the spirit of the Christian religion." They reprinted John Wesley's condemnation of slavery, and reminded their readers that the *Discipline* of the Church actually opposed slavery even though the General Conference had allowed slaveholders to become Methodists. Furthermore, they charged that the *Christian Advocate and Journal* did "apologize for the crimes of the enslavers of the human species and attempt to justify the system." They concluded by asking all Meth-

[23] *Zion's Herald,* February 11, 1835, p. 27; also March 25, 1835, p. 46; April 29, 1835, p. 58; May 13, 1835, p. 75.

odist ministers to study slavery and to urge its immediate abolition along the lines that Scott had already outlined.[24]

This open attack upon the *Advocate* and the bold appeal to uphold the Methodist antislavery inheritance brought vigorous denials and countercharges. Bangs repudiated the calumny that he had justified slavery, and explained that he hated the "disease" but could not approve of "the prescriptions of the physicians."[25] The symbol of a joined battle, however, was a "Counter-Appeal" signed by a group of ministers led by President Fisk and supported by Bishop Elijah Hedding. They objected to the "Appeal's" proposed "revolutionizing" of society and its implied "unchristianizing" of fellow Methodists, but they did not mention thousands of their coreligionists who were in bonds. Although they admitted that slavery was a "sin," Fisk and his friends believed that it could be removed only by a slow and scarcely perceived process; in a faulty recollection of history, they denied that Methodists had ever meant to forbid slaveholding. Furthermore, they attempted to prove that the "Appeal" was thoroughly unscriptural and much too extreme in its demands to achieve its ends. What antiabolitionists wanted more than anything else was peace, but their opponents continued to point out that for millions there could be no peace without freedom.[26]

The discussion between spokesmen for the two sides was futile almost from the beginning because antiabolitionists, motivated by fear, pitted themselves against men who were

[24] Shipley W. Willson, *et al.*, *An Appeal on the Subject of Slavery Addressed to the Members of the New England and New Hampshire Conferences of the Methodist Episcopal Church, Together with a Defense of Said Appeal in which is Shown the Sin of Holding Property in Man*, Boston, 1835, *passim*, but especially pp. 3–23.

[25] *Christian Advocate and Journal*, February 20, 1835, p. 102.

[26] Willbur Fisk, *et al.*, "A Counter-Appeal" in the *Maine Wesleyan Journal*, April 30, 1835, pp. 69, 72. The "Counter-Appeal" was orginally published in a special edition of *Zion's Herald*, April 8, 1835. See also *Christian Advocate and Journal*, February 20, 1835, p. 102.

motivated by hope. They were not speaking the same language. The antiabolitionists feared "ultraism" and fanaticism which Fisk believed were aberrations that made abolitionists strike out "injuriously against all who oppose" them. The disease, however, was epidemic. The President of Wesleyan could never really accept his opponents as rational men because they did not value the stability of institutions; they did not worry about consequences, the fears of the South, the unity of the Church, the peace of the nation.[27] In reaction to pleas for weighing consequences, Orange Scott replied, "I am of the opinion that we should ascertain our duty from the Bible, and from the laws of *equity* and justice."[28] The abolitionists did not fear consequences because they did not bear responsibility for the national unity of the Church. Their values were not set by extant institutions but by a vision of righteousness that did not necessarily blind them to their problems. The more enlightened abolitionists explained that "northern men would be southern men in their circumstances; and . . . southern men would be northern men in ours, where moral principle was equally felt." But they insisted that even though lack of direct implication in slavery allowed abolitionists to be emphatically opposed to slavery, their principles were right. Even if the masters were "good, kind, benevolent, and useful" Christians—as abolitionists could admit they were—they were still slaveholders and therefore involved in a grave crime.[29] Even "good" men, they insisted, could be and were implicated with evil.

The necessary discussion between the two sides never took place because the defenders of institutions condemned abolitionists as "fanatics" and the apostles of freedom condemned their opponents as servants of slavery. When the

[27] *Zion's Herald,* March 11, 1835, p. 37. See also some of Fisk's notes on fanaticism in the Fisk Papers.
[28] *Ibid.,* February 24, 1836, p. 30.
[29] *Ibid.,* May 6, 1835, p. 71. Also June 17, 1835, p. 93; October 21, 1835, p. 165. *Zion's Watchman,* January 27, 1836, pp. 14–15.

antiabolitionists lost sight of their own bearings and became involved in a scriptural exegesis that tried to show that slaveholding was moral in certain circumstances, the abolitionists seemed to be vindicated in their charges. The *Christian Advocate and Journal* even printed a series of articles by a colonizationist who believed that the slaves were happy, contented, and protected.[30] Essentially, however, the issue was simply formulated differently: to most Northern antiabolitionists it was abolitionism and its effect upon society and the lot of the slave, whereas for most abolitionists it was slavery and the future of the Negro. And if the abolitionists were guilty of moral simplicity in their assault upon slavery as has been charged, their opponents were equally guilty of a simplicity which could not see that revolutionary activities such as those undertaken by the abolitionists were legitimate signs of embedded social evil. To nineteenth century American Methodist ministers, the moral urgency of "practical Christianity" could give the simplicity of both sides the dignity of eternal verity if fallible men were convinced that they acted from principles alone. A test of strength at the annual conference could be, in this electric atmosphere, a rather exciting affair. The "antislavery vanguard" would see to it that such a confrontation occurred.

The abolitionists were preparing to assault the majesty of the General Conference and to do so they would have to go through the annual conferences. Thus, in May 1835 Orange Scott called a meeting of "true abolitionists" at Lynn, Massachusetts, to prepare for action that would "set an example to other conferences and to the nation." He confidently suggested that the meeting form an abolition society to coordinate antislavery action, discuss the passage of antislavery resolutions at the annual conference, and decide upon the election of abolitionist delegates to the General

[30] *Christian Advocate and Journal*, April 24, 1835, p. 137; June 12, 1835, p. 165; July 3, 1835, p. 177; September 4, 1835, p. 5; October 2, 1835, p. 21. See also *Zion's Herald*, May 4, 1836, p. 70.

Conference. He also suggested that they invite George Thompson, a Scottish antislavery orator, to speak to them as fit preparation for going into battle at the annual conference.[31] At the meeting, Methodist abolitionist preachers formed the New England Wesleyan Anti-Slavery Society under the presidency of Shipley Willson, one of the authors of the "Appeal." Assuming that every intelligent being could "do right" and that no one could be legally compelled to "do wrong," the members of the new society maintained that anyone who believed that the slaveholders could not free their slaves was *"non compos mentis."* All slaves, they repeated, so as to make themselves clear, should "be IMMEDIATELY brought under the protection of suitable laws."[32]

The formation of the new abolition society was actually a part of the general growth of the antislavery crusade. By the summer of 1835 abolitionists had acquired the talents of James G. Birney, former agent of the flagging colonization cause, and would-be publisher of an antislavery paper in Kentucky. They had also acquired a college, Oberlin, when abolitionist students at Lane Seminary left Cincinnati for a more favorable administration and faculty. That same year Theodore Dwight Weld, leader of the Lane Rebels, began to evangelize the West with the Gospel of "immediate abolition, gradually accomplished."[33] And in New England George Thompson was arousing tempers among conservatives and finding much of his favorable response among Methodists at Lowell, Andover, and at the Bennett Street Church in Boston. The fiery Scot bitterly antagonized many Americans who, like Nathan Bangs, thrashed out at "officious intermeddling of foreigners," but he sparked en-

[31] Orange Scott to J. A. Merrill, May 7, 1835, New England Methodist Historical Society Papers, Boston University School of Theology.
[32] *Zion's Herald,* June 17, 1835, p. 94; August 26, 1835, p. 136; September 2, 1835, p. 140.
[33] Barnes, *Anti-Slavery Impulse,* pp. 65–67, 69ff.

thusiasm among Methodist abolitionists who faced a difficult task at the annual meeting of the New England Conference.[34] When the conference members met in Boston on June 3, 1835, Bishop John Emory of Maryland warned them to be "jealous" of themselves "rather than of *others,* watching [their] own *spirits* and *words.*" The abolitionists answered by beginning a discussion of slavery, but the presiding bishop, Elijah Hedding, refused to put the resulting antislavery resolutions to a vote. His action, said the *Liberator,* revealed the "spirit of aristocracy, which had *enslaved* the clergy of all denominations . . . by opposing almost every great and good movement." Following Hedding's example, President Fisk tried to get the conference to censure La Roy Sunderland for his participation in writing the "Appeal," and he also tried to have the conference sever relations with *Zion's Herald* because it had encouraged abolition. Fisk failed in both instances, as well as when the abolitionists won six seats of the seven man delegation to the General Conference on Sunderland's adept electioneering. The seventh man, Fisk, resigned in a fury. He unleashed his anger upon Sunderland, for whom he had the most unsanctimonious disgust, by accusing him of political maneuvering; Sunderland returned the attention with casual insolence. The *Christian Advocate and Journal* praised Fisk's actions, but both had been defeated.[35]

Abolitionists also claimed the New Hampshire Conference

[34] *Mr. Thompson's Journal,* January, 1835; Henry E. Benson to George W. Benson, February 2, 1835, Garrison Papers. *Christian Advocate and Journal,* October 24, 1834, p. 34 and January 23, 1835, p. 85. *Liberator,* September 12, 1835, p. 147.

[35] *Maine Wesleyan Journal,* September 17, 1835, p. 145. James Mudge, *History of the New England Conference of the Methodist Episcopal Church, 1790–1810,* Boston, 1910, p. 279. "Minutes of the New England Conference of the Methodist Episcopal Church," typescript copy prepared in Boston in 1912, II, 167–169. Willbur Fisk to La Roy Sunderland, June 30, 1835, July 29, 1935, January 10, 1837; Sunderland to Fisk, June 15, 1835, July 24, 1835, January 2, 1837, Fisk Papers. *Liberator,* June 13, 1835, p. 95.

in August. The conference investigated a charge by the *Christian Advocate and Journal* that George Storrs was guilty of "reviling" and reported not only that the *Advocate* was wrong in its accusations but also in its presumption to publicize them even had they been true. Storrs had been arrested at an abolition meeting in March on charges of being an "idler, a vagrant, a brawler," but the court had discharged him and the conference affirmed his innocence. The preachers also elected seven abolitionists to go to the General Conference and published a report on why they should oppose slavery. As ministers they were obliged to condemn sin and idolatry wherever it existed; as Methodists they had to remember their fellow Wesleyans in bondage; as Americans they were concerned so long as "this nation, *as* a nation, [held] in bonds a single slave"; as Northerners they were compelled to fight the "slaveholding principle" wherever it prevailed outside the South.[36] Abolitionists had now captured two conferences, but their first victories went no further.

Bishops John Emory and Elijah Hedding led a general ecclesiastical countercharge against the abolitionist gains. In September they publicly addressed the ministers of the two abolitionist conferences emphasizing the constitutional impossibility of Americans' controlling the "internal and domestic affairs" of states of which they were not citizens. Furthermore, they accused the abolitionists of unjustly and unkindly attacking fellow Christians and of compounding the "perplexing" problem of slavery by "arbitrary denunciations."[37] The same intermixture of political allusions and caution echoed in conferences from the Bay of Fundy to the plains of Kansas. The Ohio, Maine, Holston, Tennessee, Missouri, Baltimore, and Kentucky conferences at once re-

---

[36] *Zion's Herald*, September 30, 1835, p. 153; also August 12, 1835, p. 127. *Christian Advocate and Journal*, August 21, 1835, p. 206. For Storrs' account of his adventure, see his *Mob under Pretence of Law or, the Arrest & Trial of Rev. George Storrs at Northfield, N.H.*, Concord, N.H., 1835, pp. 1–20.

[37] *Christian Advocate and Journal*, September 25, 1835, p. 17.

jected abolitionist ideas, arguing that Americans would never accept the abolitionist amalgamation of the races. Nevertheless most of the resolutions were prefaced with a prefunctory statement of opposition to slavery.[38] The Ohio resolutions, which became a model for others, most noticeably appealed for maintenance of social order. The abolitionists' activities would lead to civil war between the North and South, they warned: "Their appeal has not been to the judgments, sympathies, or benevolent feelings of the south, but to their jealousies, fears, and violent passions. They destroy confidence, engender strife, and cause the reins of domestic government, in slave districts, to be drawn with more severity, to keep the slaves in subjection under circumstances so alarming." The true friends of the slaves, they concluded, would oppose abolitionism.[39]

South of Tennessee and the Potomac the tone of reaction was more openly and decidedly defensive of slavery. The South Carolina Conference, surrounded by a tense white population and carrying the burden of past pronouncements on slavery, assured Carolinians that the question of slavery was nonreligious. Nevertheless, they thought they knew whence abolitionism had come: not from "money speculation" as businessmen might think, or from *"party electioneering* purposes" as politicians believed, but from an heretical *"vain conceit of a higher refinement"* which rejected Biblical authority. The Bible authorized the "relation of master and slave" by teaching that both were loved equally by God, and by enjoining duties on each in regard to the other. They added in all artlessness that "Masters could never have had their duties enforced by the consideration, 'your

---

[38] *Western Christian Advocate,* September 11, 1835, p. 77; October 16, 1835, p. 99; October 23, 1835, p. 103; December 4, 1835, p. 126. See also *Maine Wesleyan Journal,* July 16, 1835, p. 110. "Holston Conference Minutes," October 12, 1835. Baltimore Conference Journals, III, 67–68 (1836). Baltimore Conference Papers for 1836. William Warren Sweet, *Circuit-Rider Days in Indiana,* Indianapolis, 1916, pp. 145, 209, 217.

[39] *Ibid.,* September 11, 1835, p. 77.

MASTER who *is in heaven*,' if barely being a master involved in itself anything immoral." In an obvious effort to protect their missionaries, the ministers concluded by emphasizing that they sent out men who taught the slaves submission, faithfulness, and obedience.[40] The ministers of the South Carolina Conference belied their disclaimer of authority to speak on the civil question of slavery; and in their reaction they were not alone.

The fire of abolitionism descended like a diabolical Pentecost on the citizens of the South. Already their dedication to slavery had been proved in the Missouri controversy, and they reacted to the new threat by making sure that all suspicious persons were "sound" on slavery, which Governor George McDuffie of South Carolina called the "cornerstone of our republican edifice." Knowing that fellow Southerners were capable of whipping anyone suspected of abolitionism—as they had Amos Dresser of Lane Seminary—Methodists were under a great deal of pressure because of their antislavery heritage. When in the summer of 1835 western Mississippians were terrorized by the rumor of a slave insurrection, they associated the supposed plot with abolitionists, and abolitionists with Methodists, much to William Winans' dismay.[41] Methodists in Wilcox County, Alabama, also found themselves under suspicion of being proabolitionist, and like their coreligionists in Guilford Circuit, North Carolina, passed resolutions to explain that they believed abolitionist measures "subversive of the public peace and tranquility, and well calculated to defeat the purposes

[40] South Carolinas Conference *Minutes* for 1836, pp. 30f.
[41] William Winans to Benjamin Drake, August 28, 1835; Winans to Matthew Winans, August 26, 1835, Winans Collection. Clement Eaton, *Freedom of Thought in the Old South*, Durham, 1940, pp. 96–97. Filler, *Crusade Against Slavery*, p. 75. Thomas A. Morris, an Ohio Methodist leader, noted that the "high handed course of Governor M'Duffie" was calculated to make more people into abolitionists. "We are Methodist, and Methodism has no fellowship with the principles of oppression on one hand, or those of political incendiaries on the other." *Western Christian Advocate*, December 25, 1835, p. 138.

of those engaged in the amelioration of the condition of the slaves."[42] Methodist ministers joined those of other churches in Richmond, Virginia, to assure the public that they were not abolitionists, and tried to convince the editor of the *Emancipator* as well. For when the American Anti-Slavery Society sent copies of its new paper to Southern Methodist preachers, the recipients were shunned as opponents of slavery, or as promoters of slave insurrections.[43] In reaction to pressure upon them to clarify their ideas on slavery, Methodists from Mississippi to Kentucky to Maryland anathematized abolitionism. And William Capers joined a colleague to appeal for support of a new Southern Methodist newspaper which would counteract "the mad and fanatical spirit of Abolitionism" and give more impetus to Methodism.[44]

The movement to establish a Methodist journal in the Southeast is not surprising, for most conference newspapers were reluctant to state openly that slavery was the substructure of a stable society. Only the Nashville *Western Methodist* published articles which could be interpreted as definite defenses of slavery; the Richmond *Christian Sentinel* was still under the direction of a moderate editor as was the *Maine Wesleyan Journal*. Nathan Bangs defended colonization and Christian slaveholders in the *Christian Advocate and Journal* but he was not a Southerner and professed to be opposed to slavery.[45] Thomas A. Morris of the *Western Christian Advocate* held that Methodism could never counte-

[42] *Christian Advocate and Journal,* November 6, 1835, p. 43. A Book of Record for Guilford Circuit, North Carolina, October 10. 1835, Methodist Episcopal Church Papers.

[43] *Emancipator,* October 20, 1835, pp. 2, 3, 4.

[44] Whitefoord Smith and William Capers circular letter, August 10, 1835. Whitefoord Smith Manuscripts, Duke University.

[45] *Christian Advocate and Journal,* April 24, 1835, pp. 135, 137; June 12, 1835, p. 165; June 26, 1835, p. 174; July 3, 1835, p. 177; September 4, 1835, p. 5. *Zion's Herald,* December 30, 1835, p. 206. *Christian Sentinel,* August 14, 1835, p. 251. *Maine Wesleyan Journal,* January 29, 1835, p. 14; February 26, 1835, p. 30; March 5, 1835, p. 34; March 19, 1835, p. 42; December 24, 1835, p. 202.

nance a defense of Negro servitude because the Church favored "gradual, peaceable, constitutional emancipation." He opposed the "incendiaries" of the antislavery movement as well as the "highhanded course of Gov. M'Duffie" of South Carolina. Morris also derided the flaunting of law and order evidenced in the mobs which attacked abolitionists and in the offer of a $50,000 reward for a well-known abolitionist.[46]

Other editors also tried to follow a moderate antislavery course. The learned and thoughtful Charles Elliott, editor of the *Pittsburgh Conference Journal* which had subscribers in slaveholding territory, pointed out that condemnation of abolitionists was being done in such a manner as to "condemn the principles of our common Discipline, and by this means give great countenance to the conduct of slaveholders." He added, "It is marvelous that our Southern brethren do not consider the extreme folly of charging the North with being incendiaries, when they only inform them that their slave system is dangerous, and they ought to do it away." Elliott, however, was a colonizationist rather than an abolitionist, and thus not so orthodox in his opinions as La Roy Sunderland thought he should be.[47] *Zion's Herald* was the paper most openly friendly to abolitionists, but it was subject to quasi-ecclesiastical jurisdiction and therefore not under their control. In such a collection of conservative journals the radical antislavery preachers could no more place their trust than could South Carolinians.

In January 1836, the abolitionist New York Wesleyan Association led by Shipley Willson began to publish *Zion's Watchman* under the editorial direction of La Roy Sunderland. Sunderland pointed out that his paper would do what the *Christian Advocate and Journal* would not do: "defend

---

[46] *Western Christian Advocate,* November 6, 1835, p. 111; November, 20, 1835, pp. 118–119; December 25, 1835, p. 138.

[47] Elliott was quoted in the *Philanthropist,* October 7, 1836, p. 2. See also *Zion's Herald,* February 17, 1836, p. 27. *Zion's Watchman,* January 27, 1836, pp. 14–15.

the discipline of the Methodist Episcopal Church against the SIN OF HOLDING AND TREATING THE HUMAN SPECIES AS PROPERTY." He also intended to demonstrate that immediate emancipation was not so "bloodthirsty" or "hairbrained" a scheme as opponents had charged, for it was a doctrine of morality rather than a plan of operation. "We have had too much experience of the perverseness and obstinacy of wicked men, to expect to accomplish our object immediately," he pointed out.[48] Having already published a catalogue of antislavery Biblical verses, and having participated in the work of the executive committee of the American Anti-Slavery Society, Sunderland was well prepared for his task. He attacked the *Christian Advocate and Journal* for using harsh words and epithets against the abolitionists; he derided the South Carolina Conference for its defense of slavery; and he questioned the soundness of abolitionists who did not agree with him or who failed to praise his activities.[49] With innuendo, sarcasm, and honest analysis, he vividly and earnestly slashed away at slavery. George Storrs helped Sunderland in his own inimitable style. He pointed out that 60,000 Methodists were "bought and sold in the market with *horses, mules,* and *swine!* yes denied the right to obey God, who said '*Keep thyself pure!*' for those church members are subject to the brutal lusts of *white* men. . . ."[50] Nothing escaped the new watchman on Zion's walls, and he soon had more than enough to do when the General Conference met in Cincinnati, Ohio, in May 1836.

The activities of Methodist abolitionists had been directed

[48] *Zion's Watchman,* January 1, 1836, p. 1; March 9, 1836, p. 38.
[49] *Ibid.,* February 3, 1836, pp. 18–19; March 9, 1836, p. 39; April 6, 1836, p. 54. To one man who criticized him, but claimed to be an "abolitionist to the core," Sunderland characteristically replied, "Your 'core!' we fear, is rotten, brother . . . ." March 2, 1836, p. 33. See also Sunderland's *The Testimony of God Against Slavery or a Collection of Passages from the Bible which show the Sin of Holding Property in Man,* Boston, 1835.
[50] *Ibid,,* May 11, 1836, p. 73.

in part towards assailing the General Conference with anti-slavery resolutions and petitions. The *Emancipator* of the American Anti-Slavery Society had helped to popularize antislavery ideas among Methodists by printing a special edition which contained the "Appeal," "Counter-Appeal," and a reply to the latter.[51] And while abolitionists everywhere in the North were petitioning Congress to abolish slavery in the District of Columbia, those among them who were Methodists circulated memorials praying the General Conference to return to the antislavery position of 1800. Orange Scott began another series of articles in *Zion's Herald* to support this effort, while George Storrs rampaged through New Hampshire "going where abolition never before trod."[52] Few in number, the abolitionists were determined to shake what they condemned as the moral complacency of the Methodist Episcopal Church. Wary of men like Storrs and Scott, the Missionary Society of the church forbade the latter to speak at its anniversary meeting in New York in April; the General Conference soon discovered, however, that the abolitionists were not silenced so easily.[53]

In Cincinnati in the late spring of 1836 almost 150 delegates met for the quadrennial discussion of church business. By horse, canal boat, and carriage they had come from the bleak coast of Maine and the humid, heavy air of Mississippi to meet for the first time west of the Ohio River. They had all been warned of abolitionism whether they owned slaves or whether they had never even seen a Negro. Ironically, the first discussion on slavery came from William Lord, the fraternal delegate of the Wesleyan Methodist Con-

[51] *Emancipator,* October 1, 1835.

[52] Mary Clarke to Francis Jackson, January 9, 1936, Garrison Papers. *Herald of Freedom,* March 19, 1836, p. 11; April 9, 1836, p. 20. *Zion's Watchman,* April 6, 1836, pp. 54–55. *Zion's Herald,* February 24, 1836, p. 30; March 16, 1836, p. 42; March 23, 1836, p. 46. Barnes, *Anti-Slavery Impulse,* p. 110. Mudge, *New England Conference,* p. 282.

[53] *Zion's Watchman,* April 27, 1836, p. 66.

ference in England. In the last part of his speech, Lord expressed his hope that "the prudence and wisdom" of the conference could devise plans for the termination of slavery as soon as possible.[54] The next day, Nathan Bangs read to the delegates the Wesleyans' formal address which must have made the editor somewhat uncomfortable. Rather pleased with their own part in the emancipation of British West Indian slaves, the English reminded the Americans that slavery was contrary to Christianity. Consequently, they believed that the General Conference would urge Methodists everywhere to lead public opinion towards "a unanimous rejection" of it and "its social mischiefs."[55]

The British address was an occasion for a discussion on slavery which would have erupted without it. The occasion was quite fortunate for American abolitionists because it revealed that they were not alone in condemning slavery, and because it made the conference explain its position on slaveholding. As one delegate observed. "The rub [would] be in constructing and passing such a reply as [would] be respectful to our British brethren and meet the views of our southern and northern members."[56] Nathan Bangs, William Capers, and Thomas A. Morris, ardent oppoents of abolitionism, were chosen to write the reply. The first draft aroused a storm over its reference to salvery, its discussion of the powers of government, and its harshness towards the British. One Southerner even objected to saying that Methodists would do all they possibly could for the Negro because such a statement could be interpreted to mean emancipation.[57] This sensitivity was almost epidemic, for the language of the toned down final draft was much sharper than the British address had warranted and bore the marks of sensitiv-

[54] *Christian Advocate and Journal*, June 24, 1836, p. 175.
[55] *Minutes of the Methodist Conference* [English], London 1838, VII, (1835), 616. *Journals of the General Conference*, I, 431.
[56] M. Hill, delegate of the Maine Conference, to Gershom Cox, May 3, 1836 in *Maine Wesleyan Journal*, May 21, 1836, p. 2.
[57] *Herald of Freedom*, May 28, 1836, p. 49.

ity to American abolitionists and Southern slaveholders. Had the British been more careful in their analysis, the Americans complained, their "tone of sympathy for us would have been deeper and more pathetic." They insisted that the Church was promoting the best interests of the slaves through its missionary program, and that any attempt to discredit slavery would cause unfavorable reactions.[58] Thus convinced, the Americans even refused to publish the address of their British coreligionists.

The General Conference was simply in no mood to condemn slavery, and tried futilely to prevent discussions on the matter from reaching the floor. When abolitionist memorials were introduced, they were quietly referred to the Committee on Slavery. The committee reported that it was "inexpedient" to change the Section on Slavery in the *Discipline,* and "improper" to "agitate" the subject in the General Conference.[59] But the subject became very much agitated when Stephen G. Roszel of the Baltimore Conference offered resolutions for the censure of two delegates from the New Hampshire Conference who had addressed an abolitionist meeting in Cincinnati. Samuel Norris and George Storrs were the culprits. Storrs, who could never resist a chance to speak against slavery, undoubtedly had been enflamed by his brief stop at Maysville, Kentucky, where on his way to the conference, he had seen some slaves.[60] His speech, however, was pleasing only to the antislavery society. The Northern antiabolitionists and the Southerners were determined that his incendiary morality should be condemned. Fat and pompous William A. Smith of Virginia thundered for the abolitionists' blood, and when Orange Scott arose

[58] *Minutes of the Methodist Conference* [English], London, 1841, VIII (1836), 114. *Journals of the General Conference,* I, 432, 434–435. *Debate on Modern Abolitionism in the General Conference of the Methodist Episcopal Church held in Cincinnati, May, 1836,* Cincinnati, 1836, pp. 84–85.
[59] *Journals of the General Conference,* I, 447, 448, 449.
[60] *Herald of Freedom,* May 21, 1836, pp. 46–47.

to answer him the Yankee was greeted with an uproar. The delegates already knew him, for on the boat from Pittsburgh to Cincinnati many of them had discussed nothing but abolition and slavery—Scott had characteristically proposed a formal debate on the subject. And as he waited for the bishop to protect his right to the floor, he was filled with ideas derived from writing articles and from conversing with slaveholders on his trip to Ohio.[61]

When he finally got his chance, he spoke calmly and carefully for two hours, denying that the abolitionists were firebrands for wishing the slaves to be freed "into law." He added that ministers ought not be condemned for opposing sin. Scott's opponents disregarded what he had said, and complained that abolitionism endangered the Union. William Winans told Scott, William Lord of England, and any interested Northerner that the South could manage its own affairs; he added that, after all, God had allowed slavery in the Old Testament, intimating that he must surely allow it still. Then, consistent with beliefs which he had held for over a decade, he proposed that ministers throughout the South acquire slaves as their Christian duty.[62] If Winans appeared too extreme for some delegates, Scott was too radical for most. Directed by fear and caution, the abolitionists' opponents soundly defeated by a vote of 120 to 15 the Yankee's sensible if sly proposal that the inevitable censure of abolitionists be prefaced by the traditional statement of Methodist opposition to "the great evil of slavery." They then overwhelmingly repudiated the actions of the two abolitionist delegates and disclaimed any "right, wish, or intention to interfere in the civil and political relation between master and slave as it exists in the slaveholding states of this union."[63]

[61] *Zion's Herald,* May 11, 1838, p. 74.

[62] *Debate on Modern Abolitionism in the General Conference,* pp. 6–14, 15ff. Orange Scott, *An Appeal to the Methodist Episcopal Church,* Boston, 1838, p. 52.

[63] *Journals of the General Conference,* I, 447.

The action of the General Conference might have ended the matter but for the irrepressible Orange Scott. In an anonymous pamphlet which he distributed to the conference, he accused his opponents of not taking cognizance of his arguments, and then proceeded to refute theirs. The antiabolitionists had accused the antislavery radicals of raising an "exciting" question. If abolitionists disturbed the peace of the Church in its "unholy alliance with slavery," Scott wrote, the peace ought to be disturbed. If "good" men held slaves, as some had pleaded, so much the worse for their goodness! If slavery were so divine an institution as William Winans had claimed, then how could there be any oppression of the slaves as a result of abolition doctrines? If missionaries suffered for Christ and the slave in the swamps of the Carolinas, how could their suffering possibly justify slavery?[64] Scott's pamphlet created a storm, especially in the mind of gruff, unbending William Winans. The Mississippi delegate offered a resolution declaring the broadside to contain "palpably false" and injurious statements which constituted an "outrage on the dignity of this body," and merited "unqualified reprehension." Winans forgot his own dignity, however, when he called Scott, who identified himself as the author, a "reckless incendiary or *non compos mentis.*" The debate turned into a long attack upon abolitionism and Scott, with Nathan Bangs thundering in "coarse, grating tones" against his foes. Finally, Winans' resolution passed 97 to 19.[65]

The all but complete victory of the ecclesiastical defenders of the status quo was summarized in the bishops' Pastoral Address. Written by the same three men who had penned the reply to the British Conference, the Address told Meth-

[64] Scott's pamphlet, *An Address to the Members of the General Conference of the M.E. Church (by a member of the body.),* was printed in *Zion's Watchman,* June 8, 1836, pp. 87–91.

[65] *Journals of the General Conference,* I, 486, 479. *Debate on Modern Abolitionism in the General Conference,* p. 79. G. W. D. Harris to William Winans, September 19, 1836, Winans Collection.

odists that the only scriptural way to deal with slavery was to refrain from discussing it. They should maintain social order in supporting the civil and religious institutions which they so justly valued as "freemen, as Christians, and as Methodists."[66] Whether 80,000 Methodist slaves valued all American civil and religious institutions only a very few of the delegates would have wondered.

In opposing abolitionism the General Conference was not alone. Although congregationally governed churches could not speak so authoritatively as the national assemblies of connexional churches could pretend to do, in 1836 leading churchmen of all denominations opposed antislavery agitation. New England Congregational ministers and representative Baptist bodies rejected abolitionism; Quakers tried to keep violence out of their antislavery work, suggesting in Baltimore, for example, that Friends avoid combinations with those whose "motives we do not understand."[67] Episcopalians and Methodist Protestants recoiled from a discussion of the problem, as did the Presbyterian Church, meeting in General Assembly at Pittsburgh while the Methodists were at Cincinnati. The abolitionist minority of the General Assembly recalled the words of a former meeting which had described slavery as a moral paradox and a sin, but they were put down in the same manner as their Methodist brethren.[68] The Roman Catholic clergy joined the Protestants in opposing Garrisonian abolitionism as dangerous to the United States and contrary to Christian morality.[69] Thus,

[66] *Christian Advocate and Journal*, June 17, 1836, p. 171.

[67] Drake, *Quakers and Slavery*, pp. 133–165. Mary B. Putnam, *The Baptists and Slavery, 1840–1845*, Ann Arbor, 1913, pp. 15f. Austin Willey, *The History of the Antislavery Cause in State and Nation*, Portland, Maine, 1886, pp. 3ff. Barnes, *Antislavery Impulse*, pp. 95–97.

[68] *Minutes of the General Assembly of the Presbyterian Church in the United States of America*, Philadelphia, 1836, pp. 247–248, 270–271, 293, 294. James Thayer Addison, *The Episcopal Church in the United States, 1789–1931*, p. 192. Drinkhouse, *History of Methodist Reform*, II, 390n.

[69] Madeleine H. Rice, *American Catholic Opinion in the Slavery Controversy*, New York. 1944, pp. 72–75, 85, 96.

denominational abolitionists faced a united ecclesiastical opposition.

Southerners found, however, that this antagonism to abolition did not necessarily imply an acceptance of slavery as a national institution—and Southern delegates to the Methodist General Conference of 1836 were forcefully reminded of this fact in the election of bishops. The conference chose President Fisk, Thomas A. Morris, and Beverly Waugh from the New England, Ohio, and New York conferences. Fisk was well known as an antiabolitionist; Morris had opposed both abolitionism and slavery in the *Western Christian Advocate;* and Waugh was originally from the Baltimore Conference which had condemned abolitionism but would not usually ordain slaveholders. All three were colonizationists; all were opposed to radical antislavery men; none was hostile to the South; and none held slaves. The South had nominated three men for the episcopacy: Morris and Fisk were elected, but William Capers was defeated by an almost unanimous vote of Northern delegates because he was a slaveholder. Chagrined and angry that one of their most notable men should be rejected for such a reason, Southern leaders accused Northerners of hiding their opposition to the South behind the secrecy of their ballots. Although they had elected two-thirds of their ticket, the Southerners smarted under what they inferred was a moral reprobation of slaveholders, slavery, and the South.[70] William Winans called it "proscription!" He wrote to a friend: "In the election for Bishops, Slaveholders were proscribed, which aroused a spirit of *protest,* if not of *nullification* and even *secession* in the breast of many a warm tempered Southerner."[71] The conference

---

[70] *Journals of the General Conference,* I, 478. George Lane to Willbur Fisk, December 13, 1837, Fisk Papers. When Fisk was elected to the episcopacy he was on a trip to Europe, trying to regain his health. He later refused to accept the office for reasons of health.

[71] William Winans to William Dowsing, June 17, 1836; Winans to Ebenezer Hearn, June 30, 1836, Winans Collection. See also George Peck to Willbur Fisk, February 21, 1838, Fisk Papers.

had decided not only that Methodists should not be abolitionists, but also that slaveholders could not be bishops.
Only a few years would reveal if either decision would continue in force.

The Methodist Episcopal Church, in the meanwhile, was
shaken: its compromise with slavery, and its genteel and
Southern accommodations with conscience were under embarrassing and persistent attack. Abolitionists offered a radical alternative to all compromise between conscience and
sin by insisting that Negroes had a right to their own persons
and destinies. They pointed out that the "slow influence"
of eighteen hundred years of Western Christianity had not
prevented slavery in a country which justified its existence
on the premise of human equality—and they, therefore,
urged the Church to speak against servitude as it had immediately after the American Revolution. Unlike their antislavery forebears, Methodist abolitionists did not come from
states where slavery existed, and this lack of complicity in
slavery, they claimed, helped them to see it for what it
was: morally evil. Therefore, as preachers and evangelical
Christians they demanded repentance. But in this demand
there was an internal paradox which thwarted them; for
they thought that those implicated in sin could willfully ex-
tricate themselves from it. If all men are sinners as they
believed, however, their wills are as sinful as any other
part of them. Those who would be converted must be
able to transcend sin or guilt either by accepting the evangelists' moral authority, or by being totally freed from a
guilty implication in the sin condemned. For those who accepted their moral authority, the abolitionists were prophets;
for the rest, they were meddlesome troublemakers.

To prominent Methodists they were troublemakers. Except in a few instances the responsible leaders of the Church
were so afraid of abolitionist agitation that they did not
stop to inquire what it was all about. They did know that
radical antislavery preaching had failed before 1800, and

they were convinced it would do nothing but harm in 1836. Furthermore, they considered the Negroes so alien to American society as to be subjects only for charity. Justice for the slaves made no sense to them, and they were, above all, sensible and conservative men. They wished to conserve the missions to the slaves, the Colonization Society, good will among sections, the unity of the Church, and the political Union. Their reverence for the peculiar character of American federal government became an appeal to its limitations as an excuse for moral inaction. The conservatives, however, did not conserve the antislavery heritage of the Church by clarifying Methodist opposition to slavery. They helped Southerners condemn abolitionism and disavowed any right to speak on slavery, consequently becoming untrue to their role as intelligent conservatives. Perhaps the political, religious, and sectional emotionalism of the time did warrant intelligent caution, but there is nothing to suggest that it justified an intransigent acceptance of slavery; the abolitionists would make that clear.

CHAPTER VI

CLASH OF ALTERNATIVES:
The Abolitionists and the North
1836–1839

T HE General Conference of 1836, far from securing peace for the Methodists, signaled the beginning of a great controversy. Northern antiabolitionists attempted to stop radical antislavery "agitation"; it resembled too closely the hopelessly ineffective efforts of an earlier generation. They feared that abolitionists would not only harm the proven philanthropies of colonization and the Mission to the Slaves, but also destroy the unity of the Methodist Episcopal Church and eventually that of the United States as well. The abolitionists, however, would not be put down. They resorted to extra-ecclesiastical newspapers and conventions, formed Wesleyan antislavery societies, and vigorously assailed ecclesiastical authoritarianism with good results. Through their difficulties and accomplishments, the abolitionists revealed what had happened to the tradition that Methodists always and everywhere were "as much as ever convinced of the great evil of slavery."

Abolitionist reactions to the General Conference of 1836 suggested what effects their antagonists could expect from the suggestion that no one "agitate" the question of slavery. William Lloyd Garrison lamented the "degeneracy" of a morality that sought the "praise of men more than the praise of God." He promised, "All genuine Methodists, after the primitive order, will loathe and abhor the pro-slavery doings of the Cincinnati Conference, and ascribe them to Satanic

148

influences."[1] Indeed, abolitionist newspapers were fond of reporting statements of just those "genuine" Methodists whom Garrison had described. They demanded to know if Wesley would have refrained from preaching against slavery, and repudiated the curtailment of abolitionist discussion as contrary to the principles of Protestantism.[2] Fearing that dissatisfaction would lead to secession, La Roy Sunderland reminded abolitionists that they need not leave the Church since the Pastoral Address of the General Conference was advisory rather than mandatory. This assumption that Methodists could still be abolitionists—and that good Methodists would be—led the New Hampshire and New England conferences to praise the actions of their delegates to the General Conference. And the New England Conference, faced with the implied condemnation of Orange Scott at Cincinnati, reported that his reputation for "truth and veracity [stood] fair and unimpeached."[3] The Methodist abolitionists reacted to their condemnation with moral indignation and buoyant confidence.

Hoping for international support, 89 New England abolitionists sent an address to the Wesleyans of England explaining the "present state" of American Methodism and slavery.[4]

[1] *Liberator,* August 13, 1836, p. 131; also June 11, 1836, p. 95 and November 12, 1836, p. 182.

[2] Such sentiments as these were shared as well by the conventions of the Ohio and the American Anti-Slavery Societies. See the *Genius of Universal Emancipation,* August, 1836, p. 129. *Friend of Man,* October 20, 1836, p. 70 and July 5, 1837, p. 11. *Zion's Watchman,* August 17, 1836, p. 129. *Emancipator,* June 23, 1836, p. 30. *Herald of Freedom,* October 8, 1836, p. 125. *Fourth Annual Report of the American Anti-Slavery Society,* New York, 1837, pp. 62–64.

[3] *Zion's Herald,* September 21, 1836, p. 150; also August 3, 1836, p. 122. *Christian Advocate and Journal,* August 26, 1836, p. 3.

[4] *Herald of Freedom,* July 23, 1836, p. 81. The address pointed out that the *Christian Advocate and Journal* had refused to discuss slavery, and complained that the prejudice against Negroes kept them from matriculating at Wesleyan University. The Americans suggested that foreign antislavery influence would have a salutary effect upon the United States. For further comment see also the *Emanci-*

Although they refused to accept this "unauthorized communication," the English Methodists did give the abolitionists what help propriety would allow. They were shocked at the unexpected reaction of the General Conference to their fraternal address, and disappointed by the refusal of Americans to reaffirm traditional antislavery principles. They hoped that Willbur Fisk could explain the actions of the General Conference. Since he was already traveling in Europe for his health, Fisk had been readily available as the American delegate to the English Methodist Conference. His presence at the Wesleyan meeting in Bristol was heralded by an English pamphlet which accused him of being a slaveholder as well as an apologist for slavery. In an attempt to vindicate himself and the General Conference, Fisk denounced the pamphlet, condemned slavery in terms reminiscent of Orange Scott, and vehemently denied that any American Methodist defended slavery. All that the General Conference had done, said Fisk, was to oppose those measures which tended to make conditions worse for the slaves.

Jabez Bunting, president of the English conference, graciously received Fisk's explanations, but was still puzzled as to why the General Conference had not delivered itself of the "moral" question of slavery—a point Scott also had raised. Bunting admitted that the various aspects of how slavery should be terminated were political matters, as Fisk had insisted, but the Englishman nevertheless thought that the Americans could have condemned slavery "so as not to be misunderstood."[5] The official reply to the American address went even further. Although English Methodists did not wish to expose their American coreligionists to "inconvenience, obloquy, or danger," they did believe that the American Methodists' proximity to slavery necessitated their moving against it. Christians, they pointed out, must

---

pator, September 29, 1836, p. 86 and *Zion's Watchman,* September 21, 1836, p. 150.
[5] *Christian Advocate and Journal,* October 7, 1836, p. 25.

not only "embody the principles of their holy religion in their formularies of doctrine and codes of discipline, but also . . . act upon them."[6] The English were alluding to the section in the Methodists' *Book of Discipline* which had for fifty years expressed opposition to slavery. The people whom President Fisk represented in England, however, could not be so easily dissuaded from the path suggested at the General Conference because the Church's institutional folklore confirmed their determination to muffle abolitionist propaganda. Open, unequivocal demands for emancipation had threatened the peace of the Church before—and to no avail. Thus, the bishops, the official periodicals, and all responsible "organization men" were pleased when the New York Conference demonstrated how respectable Methodists were expected to act. Immediately after the national meeting in Cincinnati, the clergy of eastern New York condemned *Zion's Watchman* for "sowing dissentions in the church," and voted to refuse the ordination of anyone who would not abjure abolitionism. "This is liberal indeed!" sneered Orange Scott, who pointed out that Methodist ministers were forbidden to speak out on what the *Discipline* considered a "crime." And the action of the New Yorkers earned for them a special place in abolitionist demonology.[7]

The proscription in New York did not preclude abolitionist activity elsewhere, however, for the annual meetings of Methodist ministers allowed many opportunities for florid oratory, appeals to justice, and brave resolutions. Although the presiding bishops had traditionally introduced business to be discussed, the procedure of the conferences had be-

[6] *Minutes of the Methodist Conferences* [English], London, 1841, VIII (1836), 117–119.

[7] *Christian Advocate and Journal,* July 1, 1836, p. 179. Also *Zion's Herald,* November 23, 1836, p. 186. For other comment, see *Friend of Man,* July 1, 1838, p. 227, *Zion's Watchman,* July 8, 1837, p. 108. *Fourth Annual Report of the American Anti-Slavery Society,* p. 64.

come democratic enough to allow the preachers to introduce and pass resolutions. But if a majority should try to do what the superior conference had warned against, then the question arose as to the responsibility of the presiding officer. Bishop Elijah Hedding believed that he should try to prevent that majority from disobeying the General Conference—and the New England Conference put him to the test.

When the conference members met just after their New York brethren in 1836, they appointed a Committee on Slavery and Abolition. In its report the committee suggested resolutions that condemned slavery as a sin, maintained the right of Northerners to fight a "calumny to the whole nation," and promised to continue discussing the moral question of Negro servitude. Hedding said that he would put the resolutions to a vote if they were consistent with Methodism—but somehow he never got around to mentioning them again. To cap his delaying tactics, Hedding removed Orange Scott from his post as presiding elder and assigned him to a Methodist church in Lowell, Massachusetts, evidently because he was an abolitionist.[8] At first, the abolitionists refrained from making an issue of Hedding's actions, hoping to win friends by their forebearance. But a month later, Scott demanded to know by what right Hedding and not the majority of the meeting had judged what was the proper business of the annual conferences. After the former presiding elder accused the bishop of showing "disdain" and "decided hostility to the anti-slavery brethren," a public controversy ensued between the two men. At last, Hedding prevailed upon Scott to retract his critical interpretations of the bishop's motives and attitudes, but not to withdraw his attack upon episcopal determination of conference business. In spite of Scott's continual lecturing and writing, some

---

[8] *Zion's Watchman,* July 24, 1836, p. 133. Clark, *Life of Hedding,* pp. 494–495. Mudge, *New England Conference,* p. 283. A presiding elder had charge of a district which was a subdivision of a conference.

antiabolitionists interpreted his partial retraction as a great victory and predicted peace.[9]

The abolitionists' antagonists were wrong. Prior to the next meeting of the New England Conference, J. A. Merrill, a presiding elder and an abolitionist, wrote to Bishop Beverly Waugh asking for a little time at the conference to introduce 65 memorials from 3,400 Methodist laymen who desired the ministry to take action against slavery. Merrill warned the hesitant bishop that there might not be any business done at all unless the petition were granted. Merrill's request was accompanied by a letter from La Roy Sunderland who demanded on the behalf of 90 preachers the right to refer the memorial to a committee. Waugh denied that the conference had any such *right,* although they might have a *privilege* to do so. But he agreed to accede to the abolitionists' wishes if they in turn would agree to limit themselves to a respectful petition of the General Conference and promised not to publish the proposed committee's report. When the abolitionists refused to be restrained, Waugh refused to honor their demands. For the moment his tactics seemed wise and effective enough for Bishop Hedding to follow them at the New Hampshire Conference.[10]

Orange Scott then raised the banner of "conference rights." He explained to Elizur Wright, editor of the *Emancipator:* "The discussion to which the course of our Bishop will give rise, will be of more service to the cause of God

[9] See *Maine Wesleyan Journal,* July 15, 1837, p. 2. *Zion's Watchman,* August 31, 1836, p. 139; December 7, 1836, p. 193; July 1, 1837, p. 101; July 22, 1837, p. 115; August 12, 1837, p. 127. *Zion's Herald,* June 21, 1837, p. 98. *Friend of Man,* August 11, 1836, p. 30. Also David M. Reese to Willbur Fisk, June 26, 1837, Fisk Papers: Referring to Scott, Reese wrote, "Bishop Hedding has killed him outright. . . . After signing a libel such as that you have seen in the [*Christian*] *Advocate,* it is impossible to believe that such a liar should ever again gain credence."
[10] Clark, *Life of Hedding,* p. 504. Matlack, *Slavery and Methodism,* pp. 45–57. Also *Maine Wesleyan Journal,* June 15, 1837, p. 2. *Zion's Watchman,* July 29, 1837, p. 117.

and the slave than any conference action could have been at the last session. A full discussion of the powers of the Bishops will create a public sentiment in the Methodist Church which they will not be able to resist. . . ."[11] The Methodist abolitionists could use the ecclesiastical imposition of silence as an issue to gain converts because it appeared to be a denial of Protestant and democratic rights. The situation in the Methodist Episcopal Church was analogous to that in the Congress of the United States. In order to avoid antislavery agitation as well as to protect the legislative machinery of the House of Representatives, that body, after 1836, refused to receive antislavery petitions. By charging the House and the South with denying Americans their constitutional right of petition, the abolitionists won new followers—or at least many sympathizers to their cause. The Methodist antislavery radicals intended the same strategem. Scott announced their intention "to discuss the subjects of the rights of Bishops and Conferences through the papers, *pretty freely.*" He added, "And we shall, perhaps, be better prepared to act understandingly by our next Conference, than we have been heretofore. If Bishop Waugh supposes he has *silenced* us, he is greatly mistaken."[12]

Thereupon Scott and George Storrs followed the bishops from conference to conference—Maine to Ohio—attempting to rally Methodists to the cause of abolitionism and conference rights. Storrs had resigned from the active ministry after his rough treatment at Cincinnati, and Scott had taken a leave of absence in order to be an agent of the American Anti-Slavery Society.[13] Bishop Hedding was especially irritated by his nemeses, their annoying ubiquity, and their charismatic denunications of slaveholding. As a partisan of ecclesiastical unity over a decade earlier he had so forcefully

[11] Orange Scott to Elizur Wright, June 26, 1837, Wright Papers.
[12] *Zion's Herald,* July 12, 1837, p. 110.
[13] Matlack, *Life of Scott,* pp. 119–121. *Herald of Freedom,* October 8, 1836, p. 125.

opposed the Methodist Protestant seceders that he had drawn libelous accusations from them. It was no surprise, therefore, when his anger was aroused by what he considered a new threat from another pack of schismatic super-moralists. Since he intended to be an apologist for peace, and nothing more, Hedding explained, "I hate slavery as I hate Hell, but I will not lift an axe and cut off a slave's head because I hate slavery." Consequently, he would allow the Genesee Conference of western New York to pass resolutions declaring slavery a great moral evil and condemning the slave trade; but he was quite pleased when they also deprecated intemperate and public controversy.[14]

Hedding tried to explain his position to the ministers of each conference over which he presided, and finally published a vindication of his position in the *Christian Advocate and Journal*. Because the bishops and the annual conferences were responsible to the General Conference, they could not countermand its direction, he insisted. Nor could the annual conferences determine what business they would do—they had never been able to do so. Furthermore, he pointed out, the question of conference rights had been raised only to facilitate antislavery agitation quite contrary to Methodist principles. "I believe," he went on, "such measures as have been proposed for conference action would injure the poor slaves. Instead of releasing them from bondage these measures would make their bondage worse than it now is, and deprive those poor children of Ham of many privileges which they now enjoy." He added: "The subject [of slavery] has been carried into quarterly conferences, class meetings, and other religious assemblies—exciting contention, unholy passions, and producing a loss of confidence and brotherly love." The bishop believed that if abolitionists

[14] Clark, *Life of Hedding*, pp. 69–79, 329, 393, 400, F. W. Conable, *History of the Genesee Annual Conference of the Methodist Episcopal Church*, New York, 1866, pp. 406–410. "Genesee Conference Journals," September 21, 1837. *Zion's Watchman*, August 26, 1837, p. 135.

were sincere in their hatred of slavery, they would preach the Gospel to both slave and master "until the rulers and the great body of the people of both colors [felt] its influence, and . . . the great jubilee [came]." Otherwise, emancipation would come only through *"war, blood,* and *revolution."* Hedding reminded the abolitionists that he could allow resolutions against slavery and the slavetrade, but not slaveholding and slaveholders because the Church had permitted its members to own slaves in states where emancipation was illegal or recently emancipated Negroes could not reside. The circumstances of law and custom curtailed freedom of action, he pointed out, although Methodists could not exercise the "cruel or oppressive rights" which the law might allow. That is, a Christian could own a slave without guilt only if he treated that slave as he himself would wish to be treated in a similar situation. Hedding then asserted in a very unfortunate choice of words: "The right to hold a slave is founded on . . . the Golden Rule."[15]

"DEFENSE OF SLAVEHOLDING IN THE M.E. CHURCH" was the headline which La Roy Sunderland put on his report of Hedding's remarks. The abolitionists would not let the bishop forget his "Golden Rule defense of slaveholding," as they assailed him in *Zion's Herald, Zion's Watchman,* and the *Maine Wesleyan Journal.* Although Charles Elliott, new editor of the *Western Christian Advocate,* deprecated the "horrible attack on a good man," neither he nor Hedding could retract what had already been said.[16] Quite openly and with the best of intentions, the bishop had defended the status quo and demonstrated that if the Methodist abolitionists wanted to discuss moral and public responsibility for the principles and existence of

[15] *Christian Advocate and Journal,* October 20, 1837, p. 33.

[16] *Zion's Watchman,* November 25, 1837, p. 185; also December 9, 1837, p. 193; December 23, 1837, p. 202. *Maine Wesleyan Journal,* January 20, 1838, p. 4; January 27, 1838, p. 1. *Zion's Herald,* January 31, 1838, p. 17. *Western Christian Advocate,* December 8, 1837, p. 131, February 9, 1838, p. 167.

slavery, they would have to go outside the usual ecclesiastical channels—which is what they did.

Abolitionists organized Methodist antislavery conventions. In August 1837, several small groups of Methodist laymen met in central New York to encourage more antislavery pressure upon the decision-makers in Congress and the Methodist Episcopal Church.[17] But the most outspoken and widely publicized convention was organized by Orange Scott at Lynn, Massachusetts, in October of the same year. "Brethren in the ministry, who believe that Annual Conferences have a right to express an opinion on a moral question," Scott beckoned, "rally to the Convention, and remonstrate against recent attempts to prevent Annual Conferences from bearing their testimony against slavery!" The resulting session said all that the bishops had hitherto kept official Methodist meetings from saying. The abolitionists condemned slaveholding as a "FLAGRANT SIN," and added: "We believe that the *professed* Christians of the South, together with their *apologists* in the North are the *main supporters* of slavery—and that all northern Christians, who neglect to lift up the warning voice, and *refuse to take sides* with God's suffering poor, *are scarcely less guilty.*" They concluded with a long list of resolutions appealing to the Methodist antislavery heritage, repudiating the bishops' imposition of silence, and pointing out that if circumstances could be used to vindicate the owning of slaves they could make any act innocent.[18] With the attack on Bishop Hedding and the meeting of the Lynn Convention, the battle was joined between the abolitionists and ecclesiastical authority.

Throughout the Northeast, Methodists discussed conference rights as partisans wrote letters to denominational pe-

[17] *Ibid.,* July 12, 1837, p. 127; December 16, 1837, p. 147. *Christian Advocate and Journal,* April 27, 1838, p. 141. Matlack, *Slavery and Methodism,* pp. 195–196.
[18] *Maine Wesleyan Journal,* November 25, 1837, p. 4; December 2, 1837, p. 4. *Zion's Herald,* November 22, 1837, p. 186; November 29, 1837, p. 189.

riodicals, passed resolutions at church meetings, and even pitted one Methodist paper against another. Prodded into action by Willbur Fisk, Dr. Samuel Luckey, editor of the *Christian Advocate and Journal,* wrote long and tedious editorials against the doctrine of "conference rights." Gershom Cox of the *Maine Wesleyan Journal* gently contradicted the *Advocate* and La Roy Sunderland continuously battered away at the authoritarianism of the Church's hierarchy.[19] Finally, Dr. Luckey asked President Fisk to help him out, whereupon the educator undertook to defend the prerogatives of the office he had just declined on account of ill health. The Methodist episcopacy and the procedures consequent to it were unique, he admitted, but they nevertheless gave American Wesleyans unity of faith, uniformity of administration, and a "bond of peace." After La Roy Sunderland charged that such an attitude was reminiscent of the Roman pontiffs and the Council of Trent, Fisk stopped discussing conference rights. Nathan Bangs explained to him that abolitionists might gain friends among many Methodists who thought that bishops had too much power.[20]

Fisk did not, however, stop writing against abolitionists, for he and his friends feared that antislavery preaching posed a threat to church unity. The "radicals" refusal to abide by the Pastoral Address of 1836, their attack upon the

[19] *Zion's Watchman,* September 30, p. 154; October 14, 1837, p. 161; December 30, 1837, p. 205; January 20, 1838, p. 9; February 10, 1838, p. 22; February 24, 1838, p. 28; March 3, 1838, p. 33; March 24, 1838, p. 45; March 31, 1838, p. 49. *Maine Wesleyan Journal,* August 19, 1837, p. 2; November 25, 1837, p. 2; December 9, 1837, p. 2; December 30, 1837, p. 2; February 3, 1838, p. 2. See also *Christian Advocate and Journal,* November 17, 1837, p. 50; November 24, 1837, pp. 54–55; December 1, 1837, p. 58. *Zion's Herald,* October 31, 1838, p. 174; January 23, 1839, p. 16. Willbur Fisk to Samuel Luckey, October 19, 1837; Samuel Luckey to Willbur Fisk, October 27, 1837, Fisk Papers.
[20] *Christian Advocate and Journal,* January 26, 1838, p. 91. See also *Zion's Watchman,* July 7, 1838, p. 106. Samuel Luckey to Willbur Fisk, October 27, 1837; Fisk to Luckey, December 18, 1837; Nathan Bangs to Fisk, January 12, 1838, Fisk Papers.

Southern slaveholders, their constant lecturing and writing, their abuse of Bishop Hedding, their newspapers, and their conventions—all were overwhelming evidence to Fisk that their activities would end in *"schism and in the dismemberment of the Church of Christ."* Much hatred, condemnation, and discord had resulted from the abolitionists' practice of "popular agitation" to change the rules of the "moral discipline of the Church." Such action was, he insisted, *"subversive of the essential principles of our ecclesiastical institutions."* Furthermore, Fisk was frustrated by the over-all evaluation of slaveholding as "under all circumstances sinful." Much as Bishop Hedding had done, Fisk tried to explain that the circumstances of many Southerners rendered abolitionist demands impossible and their condemnation unfair. If the radical antislavery men should persist in their course, Fisk predicted, they would either force the South to leave the Church or themselves secede.[21]

Fisk was answered not only by Orange Scott, but also by Luther Lee, a minister from western New York who explained his idea of social responsibility. Whereas Fisk believed men responsible *to* institutions, abolitionists believed men responsible *for* them. Slaveholders in a democracy could change the laws that "bound" them to slavery, Lee maintained; even if they could not do so, civil law could never transform something inherently evil into a good institution. If Fisk replied that Methodists were a minority, Lee would answer that so were all other denominations, but that fact could not excuse their refusal to act upon moral principles. If "circumstances" vindicated men of guilt, Lee went on, it would be easy "to reason away all responsibility from the slaveholding states, and the result [would] be, we [should] have a 'great evil' for which nobody [would] be held responsible." But such was not the nature of the abolitionists'

[21] *Ibid.*, February 9, 1838, p. 99; February 16, 1838, p. 101; March 2, 1838, p. 107; March 23, 1838, p. 121; March 30, 1838, pp. 125, 127.

understanding of human responsibility and evitability. They believed that men should act morally no matter how difficult it might be to do so. Methodists could, at the very least, petition for the repeal of slave laws as they once had, said Lee—but they did not! As for the common plea that some men treated their slaves well, the abolitionist replied that a man did not lose the right to freedom because he was owned by a good master. By defending "good masters," and complaining of vindication by "circumstances," Lee concluded, the Church "lends her influence to PERPETUATE the SYSTEM."[22]

The disputation over the proper moral responsibility of the Church and abolitionists was the primary issue of a warfare that included many minor skirmishes. Both sides asked, "What does the Bible say?" "What did Wesley say?" "What did Asbury do?" and both sides found the answers they wanted to find. Each side discovered that the other was "un-Methodistical"—perhaps even un-Christian; it was somehow contrary to the rules of the controversy to give the other side any benefit of a doubt, primarily because there was no doubt involved. Both parties were represented by rather imperious evangelical preachers who cheerfully twisted their opponents' words to suit their own purpose.

[22] *Zion's Watchman*, February 24, 1838, p. 30; April 14, 1838, p. 57 and thereafter every week for two months. The abolitionists could not admit that the circumstances might change the morality of a situation because they understood the possibilities of self-justification. A young abolitionist, James Floy, wrote to John McClintock, a college professor and a Methodist minister on November 19, 1839: "I can fancy when Drunkenness and Adultery would not be criminal: e.g, the man might get drunk to cure Rheumatism; or he might commit adultery by mistake, or to save the life of some female laboring under a complaint which nothing but his efforts in that way could cure. May I say therefore that adultery and getting drunk are not *always* criminal? God forbid. So precisely with the sin of slaveholding. If I swerve from the point and admit that circumstances may justify one man in holding another in involuntary bondage do you not see how readily every villain in the Church, or out of it, will plead that this is his case exactly?" John McClintock Papers, Emory University.

In 1837 the mob murder of Elijah Lovejoy, the Illinois abolitionist, provided an occasion for a typical fracas. Orange Scott confessed that despite his nonresistant principles, he had been taught by the killing of Lovejoy that abolitionists should be prepared to defend their rights and lives with "physical force." With masterful and eloquent irrelevancies, Nathan Bangs charged Scott with being unable to follow an argument, subject to "weakness of mind," and favoring the use of force to defend abolitionism.[23]

The typical charges, however, were those of misrepresentation, slanderous accusation, lack of Christian charity, and self-righteousness. Most of these charges were serious because they were incapable of proof and could be leveled at the annual session of the conference necessitating a trial before men whose judgment would depend upon their assumptions concerning abolition. Abolitionists in general and La Roy Sunderland in particular were the subjects of many trials. The New York Conference carried on a special battle with Sunderland who, although he was a member of the New England Conference, had charges preferred against him as a resident within the New York jurisdiction. Thereupon his home conference would be asked to sustain the accusations—usually for slander or misrepresentation—which it usually refused to do, presumably because the New England Conference did not believe that Sunderland's statements were untrue. On one such occasion, they disagreed with the New York Conference, and agreed with Sunderland that the *Christian Advocate and Journal* was "gagged by the slave power."[24] The New York clergy, however, assailed their own troublemakers with more assurance, suspending for "insub-

---

[23] *Christian Advocate and Journal,* January 26, 1838, p. 90; February 23, 1838, p. 105.

[24] *Zion's Watchman,* July 6, 1836, p. 106; also August 10, 1836, pp. 126–127; August 24, 1836, p. 135; July 21, 1838, p. 114; August 11, 1838, p. 126; August 18, 1838, p. 130; May 2, 1840, pp. 70–71. *Christian Advocate and Journal,* August 5, 1836, p. 198.

ordination" some whose only crime had been to attend an antislavery convention. Abolitionists in the Erie, Ohio, Michigan, and Philadelphia conferences could expect something of the same kind of treatment; and the friction at higher levels naturally filtered down to the local congregation where an abolitionist might create a controversy by lecturing in the church basement.[25]

Abolitionists could be rather obstreperous, too. George Storrs ridiculed Bishop Hedding by imaginatively describing him and his wife on a slave auction block. He consistently enraged his enemies with sarcasm, and sometimes stunned his friends with accusations that they were not "sound" abolitionists. Sunderland also parodied, sneered, and quibbled his way against slavery, slaveholders, and antiabolitionists.[26] Orange Scott, too, could be a very difficult man with whom to deal. When the editor of *Zion's Herald* refused to publish a much too lengthy article for him, Scott accused the man of denying freedom of discussion even though the *Herald* had been more than friendly with the antislavery crusaders.[27] Abolitionists and antiabolitionists alike were hypersensitive to any slight relaxation of either phrase or goal on the part of friend or foe, and quick to attack any soft spot.

Yet in the midst of controversy, friction, and war, some men hoped for a genuine and honorable peace. Gershom F. Cox, editor of the *Maine Wesleyan Journal* was a friend of Willbur Fisk and the son-in-law of Timothy Merritt, one

[25] Uncle Matthew Simpson to Matthew Simpson, June 17, 1837, Matthew Simpson Papers, Library of Congress. *Zion's Watchman*, June 2, 1838, p. 86; June 9, 1838, p. 90. J. N. Fradenburgh, *History of the Erie Conference,* Oil City, Pa., 1907, II, 500. "Minutes of the Michigan Annual Conference of the Methodist Episcopal Church," typescript copy in Duke University Library, September 11, 1838. Heman Bangs to Willbur Fisk, March 21, 1838; A. B. Snow to Fisk, February 27, 1838, Fisk Papers.

[26] *Zion's Watchman*, October 5, 1839, p. 57; October 18, 1838, p. 166; July 27, 1839, p. 117; November 9, 1836, p. 178; August 19, 1837, p. 130; December 29, 1838, p. 205.

[27] *Zion's Herald,* July 8, 1838, p. 126; August 22, 1838, p. 134; September 8, 1838, p. 141.

of the most respected ministers in the Methodist Episcopal Church and also an abolitionist. Cox was a pacific man who hated slavery but rejected indiscriminate denunciation and condemnation. He believed that individual Southerners were responsible for the sin of their society to the degree that they did not fight against slavery. A man's "guilt must be measured," he said, "in proportion to its enormity and by the law of God and the advantages the individual possesses, and the character of his intentions."[28] Encouraged by his association with kindly abolitionists like his mild-mannered father-in-law, by his own inclinations, and by a letter from the editor of the *Pittsburgh Conference Journal,* Cox developed a "Plan of Pacification" which he offered to the New England Conference of 1838 with the blessing of Bishop Joshua Soule. Cox's plan forbade Methodists to attack any of their brethren or to participate in activities which detracted from proper ministerial duties. Methodists could neither support a newspaper for the purposes of controversy, nor organize Wesleyan antislavery societies and conventions. They could, however, join non-Methodist anti-slavery societies which did not attack the Church; they could pray for the "abolishment" of slavery, explain Methodist antislavery rules, and petition the General Conference on slavery. In effect, antiabolitionists could use the plan to rid themselves of *Zion's Watchman* and the schismatic conventions, but Cox believed that antagonism to slavery would not be diminished. Both Timothy Merritt and Willbur Fisk supported the measures which the New England Conference accepted. Then Orange Scott reversed the decision with a new vote after he had explained to his fellows the error of their ways. Nevertheless, Fisk was optimistic about success when the Maine Conference adopted Cox's proposals, for he, like Scott, considered pacification harmful to abolitionism.[29]

[28] *Maine Wesleyan Journal,* May 19, 1838, p. 2. G. F. Cox to Willbur Fisk, May 16, 1837 and December 27, 1837, Fisk Papers.
[29] Willbur Fisk to Samuel Luckey, July 13, 1838; Fisk to his

Scott rushed to the rostrum of *Zion's Watchman* to warn Methodist abolitionists everywhere against accepting the plan. We can have no peace with oppression, he proclaimed, nor "can we destroy in a single hour, the labor and toil of years" by giving up the conventions. He pointed out, as Fisk obviously knew, that antiabolitionists lost nothing and that the plan bound no one to do anything for the slaves. Furthermore, it would not really allow Methodists to join the American Anti-Slavery Society because that organization could be legitimately accused of being "opposed" to the Church.[30] Although Scott at first thought Cox had offered pacification from pure motives, suspicion and misunderstanding of some of the editor's actions encouraged the abolitionist to attack him personally, intimating that Cox conspired against abolitionism. Other antislavery partisans chimed in to sing the refrain to Scott's verse and in October Timothy Merritt rejected the plan he had supported in June as contrary to the best interests of the slave.[31] In short, the pacification proposal provided not peace but warfare.

The reaction to pacification encouraged William Lloyd Garrison to write that the Methodists were "certainly taking the lead of all other religious denominations in efforts for the deliverance of the enslaved."[32] This remark was occasioned by the call for another Methodist antislavery convention at Lowell, Massachusetts, in November 1838. A show of strength and unity in the face of new antiabolitionist strategy, the Lowell meeting maintained the constitutional right of Methodists to oppose slavery. The delegates also

---

parents, July 16, 1838; Fisk to Daniel Fillmore, October 17, 1838, Fisk Papers. W. Hunter, editor of the *Pittsburgh Conference Journal,* to Matthew Simpson, March 10, 1838, Matthew Simpson Papers. *Maine Wesleyan Journal,* June 22, 1838, p. 2; August 13, 1838, p. 2.

[30] *Zion's Watchman,* July 7, 1838, pp. 106–107; September 1, 1838, p. 139.

[31] *Ibid.,* August 4, 1838, p. 121; November 3, 1838, p. 173. *Zion's Herald,* August 29, 1838, p. 137; September 5, 1838, p. 141; September 19, 1838, p. 149; October 31, 1838, p. 173.

[32] *Liberator,* November 16, 1838, p. 183.

scored proscriptions of abolitionists, attacked the "pernicious influence" of the *Christian Advocate and Journal* for its *"subserviency to the support of slavery,"* and passed resolutions favoring free discussion and opposing pacification. The fight continued in the local churches, and especially in the Maine Conference until in 1839 the ministers "down east" rejected the "peace proposals." Nevertheless, Cox still urged a dignified and reasonable course for antislavery men—eschewing epithets and employing petitions tempered by Christian understanding. His editorial policy was continued by his successor, but Orange Scott scorned and bitterly abused the temperate editors of the *Maine Wesleyan Journal*.[33]

Although most of the action in the abolitionist controversy occurred in the Northeast, its effects were far flung—from Maine to Michigan to Mississippi. Ten Methodist weekly periodicals with an estimated total circulation of 45,000 followed the fight over "conference rights" and pacification. Perhaps twice that many Methodists actually read those papers, suggesting that at the very least one church member in every ten knew something of the abolition controversies in the Methodist Episcopal Church merely from reading the denomination's newspapers.[34] This information would be supplemented by ministers returning from their annual conferences quite willing to tell their congregations what had been done to or for the abolitionists; if they did not

[33] *Maine Wesleyan Journal,* July 12, 1839, p. 2; also December 1, 1838, p. 2; December 8, 1838, p. 2; March 2, 1839, p. 1; April 27, 1839, p. 2. *Zion's Herald,* October 24, 1838, p. 170; November 14, 1838, p. 181; December 5, 1838, p. 193. *Zion's Watchman,* December 1, 1838, p. 190; February 25, 1839, p. 17; December 21, 1839, p. 201. *Liberator,* July 26, 1839, p. 120.

[34] Estimates based on various reports of circulation are as follows: *Maine Wesleyan Journal,* 3,500; *Zion's Herald,* 4,000; *Zion's Watchman,* 3,500; *Auburn Banner,* 3,000; *Christian Advocate and Journal,* 15,000; *Pittsburgh Conference Journal,* 3,000; *Western Christian Advocate,* 4,000; *Southwestern Christian Advocate,* 4,000; *Richmond Christian Advocate,* 4,000.

do so, a wandering Methodist abolitionist lecturer would. Orange Scott constantly toured New England and occasionally made excursions to Pennsylvania and New York. George Storrs harassed churchmen in New Hampshire and New York, and Guy Beckley traveled for the American Anti-Slavery Society in the Northeast before he went to Michigan. Daniel Wise and D. I. Robinson in New England and David Eastman in Ohio also spread the antislavery revival among their coreligionists, aided and abetted by willing laymen, pastors, and even presiding elders.[35]

Antislavery ideas were preached as if their bearers were conducting a revival. In fact, it is commonly assumed that much of the abolitionist crusade had revivalistic origins, either springing from the excitement aroused by Charles G. Finney and channeled by Theodore D. Weld against slavery, or arising from the moral earnestness left over from the "Second Great Awakening." But in the largest denomination of Protestant Christians in the United States, the abolitionist movement was not so much the result as the substance of a revival—perhaps a "Third Great Awakening" itself. After their conversion to abolitionist ideas, the powerful evangelists, Orange Scott, George Storrs, and La Roy Sunderland, had called for the Methodist Episcopal Church to repent of its subservience to the sin of slaveholding, and to return to the historic antislavery faith of Asbury and Wesley and Freeborn Garrettson.

They not only preached as itinerant antislavery revivalists and got others to do the same, but they also organized conventicles which kept the faith pure and unadulterated. These Wesleyan antislavery societies often followed promi-

[35] *Herald of Freedom*, July 7, 1838, p. 75. Daniel Wise to Amos A. Phelps, July 17, 1839, Amos A. Phelps Papers, Boston Public Library. Elizur Wright to James G. Birney, November 5, 1835; James G. Birney to Lewis Tappan, August 10, 1836; James G. Birney to Lewis Tappan, June 3, 1839, in Dwight L. Dumond, ed., *Letters of James G. Birney*, New York, 1938, I, 255–257; 349–352; 491–492. Also II, 698.

nent laymen whose abolitionist piety was greater than that of the ministers, revealing that the spiritually rather than the canonically eminent men were more to be trusted. Whoever preached, however, the message was always: "Repent and support the cause of the Slave!" This revivalistic immediacy and urgency was never wanting: the abolitionists demanded repentance *now*, decision *now*, the beginning of the new life *now*.[36] And as has been demonstrated elsewhere, revivalism emphasized that the new life involved society and the welfare of others—in this case the slave.[37] Although the kind of emotionalism usually associated with revivals was absent, the abolitionist revivals were developing a community of feeling that valued a certain way of looking at moral responsibility, society, and the Church—a community that valued the right moral decision over social sta bility and institutional unity.[38]

It is very difficult to determine just how large a radical

[36] For the most significant statement on revivalism and its effects upon abolitionism, see Barnes, *Anti-Slavery Impulse*. The references to the Methodists' antislavery past were numerous. In 1839, the American Anti-Slavery Society included in its report a six-page history of the Methodists' fall from grace on the slavery question. See *Sixth Annual Report of the Executive Committee of the American Anti-Slavery Society*, New York, 1839, pp. 68–73. Also *Friend of Man*, June 28, 1837, p. 6. *Zion's Watchman*, March 4, 1837, p. 34; February 3, 1838, p. 18; April 7, 1838, p. 54. The *Watchman* carried many references to the organization of local, district, conference, and national Wesleyan antislavery societies.

[37] See Timothy L. Smith's suggestive and influential *Revivalism and Social Reform*, New York, 1957, especially Chapters 2, 5, 12, 13. John L. Thomas emphasizes the perfectionist morality of the Second Great Awakening as a great influence upon abolitionism in his biography of William Lloyd Garrison, see *The Liberator*, pp. 228ff., 452ff.

[38] For a discussion of revivalism see, William Warren Sweet's outdated but pioneering *Revivalism in America*, New York, 1944. Other works on the subject are Bernard Weisberger, *They Gathered at the River*, Boston, 1958; William G. McLoughlin, *Modern Revivalism*, New York, 1959; Whitney R. Cross, *The Burned-Over District*, Ithaca, N. Y., 1950, Also Barclay, *Reform the Nation*, pp. 286–417.

antislavery community actually existed within the Methodist Episcopal Church. Abolitionist preaching certainly affected more people than it actually converted. In the quadrennium between 1836 and 1840, the membership of the entire church increased 12 per cent whereas there was a 22 per cent increase in those conferences most heavily bombarded by abolitionists. There were almost 302,000 Methodists in that region, one-third of whom were under the direct influence and preaching of abolitionist ministers. Most Methodist abolitionists lived in New England or in the repeatedly evangelized areas of New York west of the Hudson—Utica was a center of Methodist antislavery activity—but there were also many in western Pennsylvania and eastern Ohio. And even though Orange Scott believed that there were few abolitionists of his religion further west than Cleveland, they were active enough to control McKendree College in Illinois and form pockets of resistance to the ecclesiastically imposed silence on slavery. Scott reported in 1838 that 6 of the 16 Northern conferences had an antislavery majority, and he might also have added that 3 more conferences had large, active, and troublesome minorities. The Methodists probably had about 700 ministers out of over 3,000 who would be willing to preach and vote against slavery, and perhaps as many more lay or "local" preachers. In all, Scott claimed that there were 50,000 abolitionists in the entire church—probably as accurate an estimate as is possible.[39]

[39] The estimates are based upon statistics derived from the *Minutes of Annual Conferences*, II, 275, 679. See also *Liberator*, August 24, 1838, p. 135. *Zion's Watchman*, February 11, 1837, p. 22; June 10, 1837, p. 91; June 3, 1837, pp. 87–88; July 8, 1837, p. 108; September 9, 1837, p. 142; September 23, 1837; p. 150; November 18, 1837, p. 183; January 13, 1838, p. 2; February 3, 1838, p. 18; March 31, 1838, p. 50; April 28, 1838, p. 66. Fradenburgh, *History of the Erie Conference*, II, 400, 497, 499. Conable, *Genesee Conference*, pp. 427–429. Scott, *Appeal*, pp. 135–136. *Philanthropist*, July 8, 1838, p. 4. *Emancipator*, March 2, 1837, p. 174; September 21, 1837, p. 80; and Benjamin Kavanaugh to Willbur Fisk, July 26, 1838, Fisk Papers.

Obviously so large a body of converts led by so energetic a trio as Storrs, Scott, and Sunderland, were important to those most closely associated with the American Anti-Slavery Society and its auxiliaries. Theodore Dwight Weld very early warned James G. Birney against representing abolitionism as a Presbyterian enterprise since only about one-third of the antislavery converts belonged to that denomination and the Baptists and the Methodists were "beginning to come over" in large numbers.[40] William Lloyd Garrison thought the Methodists important also. His *Liberator* confidently followed Methodist abolition activity after 1833, encouraging the conventions, attacking the *Christian Advocate and Journal* in its support of ecclesiastical "oppression," and taking "pot-shots" at notable Methodist antiabolitionists.[41] The *Emancipator* did the same, condemning the Church for giving up its antislavery tradition. James G. Birney published an account of Orange Scott's activities and speeches at the General Conference of 1836 to show just how far the Church had in fact betrayed its heritage. Birney's successor as editor of the *Philanthropist,* Gamaliel Bailey, zealously reported Methodist antislavery exploits.[42]

William Goodell, editor of the New York Anti-Slavery society's *Friend of Man,* faithfully supported Methodist abolitionism in upper New York state and printed the articles of one of its most ardent leaders, Luther Lee. The *Herald of Freedom* at one time was almost a public diary for George Storrs and in 1836 was urging New Hampshire Baptists, Presbyterians, and Unitarians to speak as forcefully against slavery as had the orthodox Congregationalists and the Methodists.[43] Methodists were important to the antislavery revivals not only because they were members of the largest

[40] Theodore Dwight Weld to James G. Birney, September 26, 1835, in Dumond, *Letters of Birney,* I, 246.
[41] See for example *Liberator,* January 16, 1836, p. 11.
[42] See for example *Emancipator,* March 15, 1838, pp. 178–179.
[43] See for example, *Friend of Man,* October 3, 1838, p. 269; November 7, 1838, p. 392. *Herald of Freedom,* October 1, 1836, p. 122; October 8, 1836, p. 125.

Protestant sect in America but also because abolitionists wanted the churches, as America's institutionalized morality, to denounce the sin of slavery.

Many abolitionists were discouraged, however, for they were opposed by ecclesiastical leaders of all denominations. Consequently, they began to repudiate "organized religion." William Lloyd Garrison joined Stephen Symonds Foster to call for all true antislavery men to "come-out" from "hypocritical" churches that were tainted with the sin of slavery. Foster called the clergy a Brotherhood of Thieves and accused the Methodist Episcopal Church of containing less virtue than all of the brothels of New York City, an accusation which made Garrison blanch.[44] This distrust of the institutional church was a part of the Garrisonian abolitionists' emphasis upon a "perfectionism" that demanded disassociation from all evil whether slavery, or force, or more minor forms of selfishness. As a concomitant to his new-found ideas, Garrison began to support Henry C. Wright's "nonresistant" theories of "no human government" which emphasized that only God could rule mankind, and that therefore, only He should be trusted.

Amazed and dismayed, Orange Scott became one of the editor's most outspoken critics. "Trust in God and leave all to him?" he asked incredulously. "As well might you trust God to edit and print your paper, without any human agency." Trust in God and no human government? "What is it shields you from northern and southern vengeance

[44] See William Lloyd Garrison to his wife, November 27, 1842, Garrison papers. For a discussion of the "come-outers," see Parker Pillsbury, *The Acts of the Antislavery Apostles,* Concord, N.H., 1883. See also Stephen Symonds Foster, *The Brotherhood of Thieves,* Boston, 1844, p. 40. In a letter to Amos A. Phelps, October 20, 1837, Elizur Wright, editor of the *Emancipator,* condemned Garrison's perfectionism and his use of the *Liberator* to propagate his "sectarian" ideas. "If we follow the Liberator in its present track," he predicted, "the clergy will have us flat on our backs before another anniversary. . . . Those who swallow him hereafter must swallow his religious dogmas. . . ." Phelps Papers.

now?" Scott demanded, "Not the irresistible power of God as much as the fear of human laws." The way to destroy slavery was not to create chaos by repudiating human laws, Scott insisted, but to reform the existing government and abolish the laws that upheld racial servitude. To reform government, abolitionists would have to vote for men who would be most likely to work against slavery.[45]

Scott was following the elegant and persuasive Southern abolitionist, James G. Birney, who, together with the New York philanthropists, Lewis and Arthur Tappan, favored using political pressure to achieve abolition. Abolitionists should be asked to vote for men who would be most likely to support the cause of the slave, Birney believed; Garrison, however, repudiated such a request.[46] In the struggle that ensued, Scott, La Roy Sunderland, George Storrs, and their colleagues, Daniel Wise, Phineas Crandall, and Luther Lee, led the New England Methodists against Garrison's "folly." And in November 1838, the Methodist antislavery convention at Lowell, Massachusetts, urged abolitionists to exercise their political rights in fighting slavery. With this and other signs of Methodist disapproval of Garrison's course, Scott anticipated a successful subversion of the editor's influence within the Massachusetts Anti-Slavery Society.[47]

The signs, however, were wrong. The chief conspirators, against Garrison—Scott, Henry B. Stanton, and Amos A. Phelps—were disastrously unsuccessful in their attempts to dislodge Garrison from his powerful position. The harried editor himself was disheartened to find among his enemies the best known antislavery agents in the state, but he struck

[45] *Liberator,* October 26, 1838, pp. 171–172; November 16, 1838, p. 184.
[46] Barnes, *Anti-Slavery Impulse,* pp. 146–170. Birney, *Life of Birney,* pp. 295–313.
[47] *Zion's Watchman,* December 1, 1838, p. 190. *Liberator,* March 22, 1838, p. 43. Henry B. Stanton to Amos A. Phelps, June 1, 1839; La Roy Sunderland to Phelps, June 24, 1839; Phelps to William Lloyd Garrison, July 8, 1839, Phelps Papers.

back vigorously and won his fight at the convention in January of 1839. Stanton hoped to get Scott appointed general agent of the Massachusetts Anti-Slavery Society in order to have an anti-Garrisonian in that important job, but he failed. Stanton had also wanted the society to support a new abolitionist paper, but it would not. He tried to get the convention to require abolitionists to "vote for the slave," but it refused. As Scott had warned him, most of the delegates were *Liberator* abolitionists and they supported their leader with "clamor" and votes. One of the few good things that Stanton could recall after the disaster was that "a very large corps of Methodists were present, and went right and with their whole hearts, almost to a man."[48]

Scott threw himself wholeheartedly into the succeeding fight against Garrison. He charged that the editor's *"consummate nonsense"* of no human government could very easily subvert the abolitionist organization itself. He scolded the editor of the *Herald of Freedom* for not joining the fight to save abolitionism, urged Phelps to be more active in opposing Garrison's "foolery," and joined in forewarning fellow abolitionists of the danger of Garrisonianism if it should prevail at the national convention in May 1839. In order to institutionalize their opposition to both Garrison and slavery, the dissidents formed the Massachusetts Abolition Society which Scott supported vigorously. In his campaign to strengthen the new organization, Scott optimistically pledged *"nine tenths* of the Methodist influence in the state for a new state society."[49] He stumped local abolition meet-

[48] Henry B. Stanton to James G. Birney, January 26, 1839 in Dumond, *Letters of Birney,* I, 481–482. William Lloyd Garrison to George W. Benson, January 5, 1839, Garrison Papers. Henry B. Stanton to Amos A. Phelps, January 13, 1839; Orange Scott to Phelps, January 15, 1839, Phelps Papers. Stanton to Elizur Wright, January 26, 1839, Wright Papers.

[49] Orange Scott to James G. Birney, May 12, 1839, Weston Family Papers, Boston Public Library. Circular letter sent by Scott and Amos A. Phelps, April 16, 1839; Scott to Phelps, June 27, 1839, Phelps Papers. *Herald of Freedom,* April 6, 1839, p. 23; April

ings, talking so much about going to the polls for the slave that someone started a rumor that he would shortly run for Congress. Once he was heard "screaming at the top of his voice about Slavery's being a creature of law" and therefore capable of being destroyed only by law. And when a meeting at Lowell voted to hear both sides of the question concerning the obligation of abolitionists to vote, the canny evangelist spoke first and then, before his opponent could reply, had moved and carried a vote to adjourn. Such tactics made Theodore Dwight Weld deplore Scott's attitude as "the spirit of slaveholders undiluted."[50]

The Methodist opposition to Garrison was outspoken but futile. *Zion's Watchman* supported Scott's warfare, and accused the volatile editor of the *Liberator* of mistakenly supposing that he was actually the whole abolitionist movement. Wrote Sunderland: "We go for truth, for God, and the slave. But we put it to any candid man who has been familiar with the Liberator, for the last year, if he can say, before heaven, that he solemnly believes that paper has said as much against slavery, within six months, as it has against certain abolitionists in . . . Massachusetts. What religious or antislavery paper has been so much filled with bickering, and personal strife?" The Methodist editor worked behind the scenes as vigorously as did Scott upon the stage, but their energy had been expended futilely. The Massachusetts Abolition Society soon became powerless. The Garrisonians captured the American Anti-Slavery Society in 1840, whereupon the Methodist Leaders—Scott, Sutherland, and Storrs

---

13, 1839, p. 26; April 27, 1839, pp. 34–35. *Liberator*, April 5, 1839, p. 54; April 19, 1839, p. 64.

[50] Theodore D. Weld to Gerrit Smith, October 23, 1839 in Gilbert H. Barnes and Dwight L. Dumond, eds., *The Letters of Theodore Dwight Weld and Angelina Grimké Weld and Sarah Grimké, 1822–1844*, New York, 1934, II, 810. *Friend of Man*, October 30, 1839, p. 12. Lucia Weston to Deborah Weston, July 1839, and n.d., 1839; Maria Chapman to Mary Weston, n.d. [1839], Weston Family Papers.

—seceded with Birney and the New York abolitionists to help organize and administer the American and Foreign Anti-Slavery Society, or "new organization."[51]

Although there were some exceptions, most Methodist abolitionists were united in their support of Scott and Sunderland. They believed that the antislavery movement should continue to try to convert the government as well as the Church. What else they believed and how fervently they believed it is left to general speculation. Certainly they thought slaveholding a sin and accepted the definition of "immediate emancipation" which Orange Scott had outlined in 1835; they repudiated colonization, and apparently agreed with Luther Lee's explanation of moral responsibility; they thought that the Church should actively oppose slavery; and they resented the "gag" supported by the bishops because open discussion of slavery was one of their chief goals. Although they scored the inequalities that Negroes suffered in the North, they were so busy fighting church leaders that they never expended time or energy to remedy the situation. They pleaded for conversion as a precondition to action—and conversion was a long time coming. Guides to the antislavery faith were plentiful: in *Zion's Watchman,* in *Zion's Herald,* in Sunderland's *Antislavery Manual,* and in Scott's *Appeal to the Methodist Episcopal Church,* as well as in the myriad of official abolitionist papers. Early in the abolitionists' great push following the General Conference of 1836, Sunderland even printed a "CREED" which outlined the basic tenets of Methodist abolitionism.[52] The emphasis, as ever, was upon the decision to effect moral change by practical action whether discussing slavery in the Church and thereby wielding moral influence, or by voting and wielding democratic power.

It is also a speculative venture to ask who these 50,000

---

[51] *Anti-Slavery Reporter,* June, 1840, p. 3. *Zion's Watchman,* January 11, 1840, p. 6.
[52] *Zion's Watchman,* September 28, 1836, p. 155.

or so abolitionists were that repudiated Garrison and ecclesiastical authority "for the sake of the slave." They certainly were not a displaced elite angered by the new industrialism, for Methodists did not usually come from the former ruling classes. They certainly cannot be explained as ministers seeking to regain their moral control over a wayward people since their most ardent opponents were ministers. They cannot be dismissed simply as "fanatics" since their opposition differed little from them in dedication and vigor. Nor were they all younger men. Most of the Methodist abolition leaders such as Scott, Storrs, and Sunderland were born after 1800, but Seth Sprague of Duxbury, Massachusetts, was seventy-eight years of age when he presided over an antislavery convention in 1838. Father of the noted Massachusetts jurist, Peleg Sprague, Sprague was one of the most active abolitionists in Methodism and in the Bay State. His son, Seth, Jr., was also an abolitionist and both Spragues proudly proclaimed their antislavery ideas when they ran against each other for the Massachusetts legislature in 1839—the father as a Democrat and the son as a Whig.[53] Timothy Merritt was also an elderly man when he lost his position as assistant editor of the *Christian Advocate and Journal* because he was an abolitionist. Mild-mannered, considerate, learned, and exceedingly patient, Merritt was certainly not a "Young Turk" bent on exercising moral authority.[54] But Merritt and Sprague, Scott, Sunderland, and Storrs were merely representatives and leaders of the abolitionists; they were not the whole community of antislavery men. Perhaps the only generalization possible is that abolitionists were converts of a new, different kind of revival, but a revival nevertheless.

In preaching for a revival of antislavery enthusiasm, the

[53] *Liberator,* November 8, 1839, p. 179. *Friend of Man,* July 4, 1838, p. 213.
[54] *Zion's Herald,* December 21, 1836, p. 202; December 28, 1836, p. 206; January 18, 1837, p. 9; and thereafter sporadically for eight months.

abolitionists had by 1839 achieved some notable successes. To be sure, not all Methodist antislavery men were as ardent as Orange Scott, or La Roy Sunderland, or George Storrs, but for the moment they enthusiastically followed those three men in a course which was "proscribed" but not defeated by Methodist authorities. The ecclesiastical leaders—editors of the *Christian Advocate and Journal,* prominent men such as Fisk and Bangs, and the bishops—protested that their dedication to colonization was all the "antislavery" action that circumstances allowed. They feared that public controversy among Methodists would drive either the South or New England into secession. Consequently, they tried all of the tactics at their command to silence agitation on slavery: church trials, parliamentary maneuvers, journalistic propaganda, a "compromise" plan of peace, and appeals to ecclesiastical unity. None of the plans of the antiabolitionists succeeded in containing their opponents' ideas. Although abolitionists had neither gained what they wanted nor could expect to do so within the immediate future, they had grown in strength during their clash with Northern ecclesiastical antiabolitionism and had caused no little alarm.[55]

[55] For an opposite view see Charles Swaney, *Episcopal Methodism and Slavery,* Boston, 1926, pp. 79–89. Swaney emphasized the great difficulties which abolitionists faced rather than their growth. Instead of being "crushed" between 1838–1839, they were steadily gaining influence.

CHAPTER VII

CLASH OF ALTERNATIVES:
North and South
1836–1840

THE fears of Northern churchmen were well founded, for the successes of Methodist abolitionists frightened and disgusted Southern ministers. Pressed to theoretical extremes by their own emotions, lack of perspective, and intense concern for the place of the Church in Southern society, Southern conferences began to defend slavery. This flat refusal to follow the advice of the General Conference not to discuss the question of Negro servitude went unopposed by the bishops and their associates, but it nevertheless frightened them. Many believed that Southerners had not only betrayed their Northern friends, but the Methodist antislavery heritage as well. Dedicated to church unity as they were, Northern conservatives tried to avoid issues which might conceivably have split their denomination. But caution led them even further into a morass of moderation as they fought for the Church not only against abolitionists but also Southerners.

The first Southern reactions to the General Conference of 1836 revealed resentment of its failure to elect a man as bishop "simply because he owned slaves." Many Southern delegates—men who wielded considerable influence because of their position—resented what they believed was a "proscription" of slaveholders and, by implication, the South.[1]

---

[1] William Winans to William Dowsing, June 17, 1836; Winans to Ebenezer Hearn, June 30, 1836, Winans Collection. George Lane to Willbur Fisk, December 13, 1837, Fisk Papers.

In July 1836, William A. Smith, a colonizationist and the newly appointed editor of the *Virginia Conference Sentinel* printed a circular favoring a Southern General Conference should the derogation of slaveholders continue. In any case, he thought that Southern Methodists should print their own newspaper and incorporate their own book concern in order to give themselves a "position of independence." To add to the suspicious nature of his communication, Smith suggested that it be kept private, but it was soon widely discussed after *Zion's Herald* publicized its contents. The *Herald's* editor also printed parts of the *Discipline* which opposed slavery, and asked if Smith were the only Methodist who "bowed the knee to the image of Mammon."[2]

The editor of the *Pittsburgh Conference Journal* was no less shocked. It was the "height of presumption," he declared, for slaveholders to expect to be given an office which included presiding over people "conscientiously opposed both to their principle and practice." In reply, Smith shrieked: "There it is! and can anything be worse? more uncivil or more unrighteous, or more expressive of the degradation to which these men would reduce the whole southern portion of the church, by affixing upon it not only severe and unmerited censure, but also the odium of ecclesiastical disability."[3] This outburst startled and frightened many Northern leaders, but Stephen Olin, president of Randolph-Macon College in Virginia, wrote to one of them that many ministers thought Smith "isolated." Nevertheless, he cautioned, "There is every reason to believe that a perseverance in this course will lead to separation. Still our friends are not disposed to be hasty in the matter." Dissatisfaction was not easily abated, however; Nathan Bangs and some of his friends

[2] *Zion's Herald,* September 21, 1836, p. 150; October 26, 1836, p. 171.
[3] *Zion's Watchman,* October 12, 1836, p. 163. See also September 7, 1836, p. 142; October 5, 1836, p. 159; October 19, 1836, p. 167.

anxiously asked Willbur Fisk to visit Virginia and the Carolinas to help keep them within the Church.[4]

Unlike the Northern conservatives, abolitionists were almost pleased with Southern reactions to the General Conference because they revealed Southern Christianity's "apostasy." Smith's circular was interpreted and reported by La Roy Sunderland and other abolitionists as a self-condemning statement. The abolitionists pointed out that in order to be acceptable, Southern ministers had lowered the "standards" of the gospel to a "level with the prejudices and institutions of the country."[5] The abolitionists, however, were not surprised. Since their earliest public pronouncements, they had questioned not so much the kindliness as the devotion to Christian principles exhibited by Southern slaveholders and their apologists. And abolitionists understood the Southern Methodists' highest service to the Negro, the Mission to the Slaves, not as the great moral cause of Southern Christianity, but as a demonic and grotesque misuse of the gospel. The abolitionists could frequently admit that Southerners were sometimes charitable to the slaves, but never that they were just.[6] Such a dismissal of the efficacy of Southern Methodism would certainly call forth a reply.

The Smith circular was but the first of many Southern Methodist statements vindicating themselves to the North and assuring the South that they were not the antislavery "fanatics" their predecessors had been forty years earlier. In more forceful language than they had employed since the Denmark Vesey conspiracy, South Carolina Methodists followed much the same path as Smith, although without his threats of schism.[7] In 1837 they published a sermon

---

[4] Stephen Olin to George Coles, November 10, 1836, Coles Letters. See also George Lane to Willbur Fisk, December 13, 1837, Fisk Papers.

[5] *Zion's Watchman*, June 29, 1836, p. 101. See also the *Emancipator*, September 15, 1836, p. 77; November 2, 1836, p. 105.

[6] See *Philanthropist*, August 4, 1841, p. 2.

[7] See above, Chapter II. For an excellent interpretation of the pro-

by one Samuel Dunwody which they considered a true scriptural statement on slavery. Dunwody, whom an acquaintance called "a good man, but by no means a pleasant one," attempted to vindicate slavery on ground which was becoming quite familiar in the South. He pointed out that slavery was not a moral evil in some circumstances because God had allowed it in the days of Noah and Abraham. True, God had destroyed slavery by releasing Israel from Egyptian overlordship, but He had never released the children of Ham from the curse by which Noah had sent them into servitude in the first place.

In the New Testament, Dunwody found further proof that in some circumstances, that is under Roman rule, slavery had been accepted by church leaders. Finally Dunwody added a pietistic touch to his vindication of slavery by maintaining that good men could own slaves, presumably because as Christians, they would obey the Bible in treating slaves well and caring for their eternal salvation. The Southerner found it unfair for Northern Methodists to have allowed slaveholders to join the Church and afterwards to condemn slavery as a "moral evil." If Northerners really believed slavery so evil they would never have accepted slaveholders as Methodists. Dunwody closed his sermon by claiming that he was "no advocate for slavery," but rather for the doctrine "in which the principle of Slavery is justified in a variety of instances."[8] Gershom Cox repudiated Dun-

---

slavery argument and to whom it was addressed, see Ralph E. Morrow, "The Proslavery Argument Revisited," *Mississippi Valley Historical Review*, XLVIII (June, 1961), 79–94. See also William Sumner Jenkins, *Pro-Slavery Thought in the Old South*, Chapel Hill, 1935.

[8] Samuel Dunwody, *A Sermon upon the Subject of Slavery*, Columbia, S.C., 1837, pp. 12, 19, 27, 30, 31. The South Carolina Conference acclaimed the sermon as answering the "objections of those who contend that Slavery is always a Moral Evil." See South Carolina Conference Papers for 1837. Also William Winans, Diary, May 30, 1832, Winans Collection.

wody's arguments and cynically commented that he was happy to know that the South Carolinian was "no advocate for slavery." La Roy Sunderland despaired of a Methodist minister who could, with the approval of a Methodist conference, say that "a system which reduces thousands of American females to the condition of prostitutes, and which shuts up immortal minds in darkness and sin, and, as far as it may, fits the oppressor and the oppressed for eternal perdition, IS ACCORDING TO THE WILL OF GOD!!!" And in the same fashion, he continued for seven weeks.[9]

Southerners seemed intent upon providing copy for abolitionist newspapers and arousing antiabolitionist fears. In December 1837, Bishop Thomas Morris, former editor of the *Western Christian Advocate,* a colonizationist, and a self-styled opponent of slavery, presided over the Georgia Conference as its ministers "discussed" slavery and abolition—which was presumably contrary to the sense of the General Conference. With appropriate allusions to "spilling the last drop of blood that warmed their hearts before submitting to the doctrines of Northern fanatics," the Georgia preachers accused abolitionists of "perverting" the *Discipline's* statement on the "evil of slavery" to mean that slavery was a "moral evil." Thereupon, with bluster and not a little self-delusion, the ministers resolved: "It is the sense of the Georgia Annual Conference that slavery, as it exists in the United States, *is not a moral evil.*"[10]

A few weeks later, William Capers, chief promoter of the Methodist Mission to the Slaves, led a discussion by

[9] *Maine Wesleyan Journal,* July 22, 1837, p. 2. *Zion's Watchman,* July 22, 1837, p. 114; July 29, 1837, p. 118; August 5, 1837, p. 122; August 12, 1837, p. 126; August 19, 1837, p. 130; August 26, 1837, p. 134; September 2, 1837, p. 138; September 9, 1837, p. 142.
[10] *Southern Christian Advocate,* January 5, 1838, p. 114. George Round to Willbur Fisk, February 8, 1838, Fisk Papers. Round was an observer at the conference.

181

South Carolina ministers as they attempted to arrive at an official pronouncement upon slavery. He warned his colleagues that although all Southern ministers believed that slavery was not a moral evil, it would be best not to say so lest abolitionists make too much of such a statement. Therefore, he suggested a resolution that since slavery was not a proper subject "for the action of the church . . . this conference will not intermeddle with it farther than to express our regret that it has ever been introduced, in any form, into any one of the judicatures of the church." Just before the resolution passed unanimously, Capers observed that not only the North, but also the General Conference should understand that the South Carolina Conference meant to "convey the sentiment fully and unequivocally" that slavery was "not a moral evil," that is, a "sin." He continued, "If slavery were a moral evil, the church would be bound to take cognizance of it; but our affirmation is that it is not a matter for *her* jurisdiction, but is exclusively appropriate to the *civil government,* and of course not sinful."[11] The abolitionists were quick to seize upon such pronouncements as evidence of proslavery Methodism.

Even supposedly harmless decisions from the South were transformed into damaging testimony. It was almost ironic that the one conference in slaveholding territory which had tried to be consistent with the early Methodist antislavery tradition should be linked with the proslavery declarations of the Georgia and South Carolina clergy. The Baltimore Conference had instructed church committees dealing with infractions of the General Rule against buying and selling slaves that they should pay attention not to the facts but to the "qualifying circumstances." In other words, the judges were to consider the motives and problems involved in the cases before them. The radical antislavery men, however, accused the Baltimore Conference of justifying the slave

[11] *Ibid.,* January 26, 1838, p. 125; also February 2, 1838, p. 130.

182

trade "in some circumstances." Thus, the North was presented with three Methodist conferences that either appeared to condone the slave trade or openly defended slavery.[12]

Abolitionists were quick to compare the position of Southern Methodists with that of John Wesley. The *Emancipator* bewailed "Methodism under the influence of slavery," and with other papers printed extracts from the Canadian Methodists' *Christian Guardian* which apostrophied: "Sainted spirit of the venerable Wesley! Could shame and anger disturb thy deep and holy tranquility, this would call them into exercise!"[13] William Brown of *Zion's Herald* demanded to know if American slavery were not sinful, why did Wesley call it "the vilest which ever saw sun?" And La Roy Sunderland cynically asked if Southern conferences were really taking the advice of the General Conference to refrain from agitating the subject of slavery. "If slavery is neither a moral nor a political evil," he went on, "our Discipline might as well propose measures for the extirpation of the smallpox."[14]

Orange Scott was incensed. Convinced that the Methodist Episcopal Church was the proper foundation of abolitionism, he, Storrs, Sunderland, and two colleagues called for a great Methodist antislavery convention at Utica, New York, in the spring of 1838. Smith and the Southern conferences had gone unrebuked by church authorities, Scott pointed out, and he asked the abolitionist community: "Are you prepared to submit to such things *in Silence?* Will you not *remonstrate?* Will you not fly to the rescue?"[15] By way of reply,

[12] *Zion's Watchman,* April 29, 1837, p. 66. Elliott, *The Great Secession,* columns 172–173.

[13] *Emancipator,* January 18, 1838, p. 146; February 15, 1838, p. 163. Scott, *Appeal,* p. 16.

[14] *Zion's Watchman,* March 3, 1838, p. 34; also January 13, 1838, p. 6. *Zion's Herald,* March 21, 1838, p. 30.

[15] Orange Scott to W. Lindsey and William Taylor, March 29, 1838, New England Methodist Historical Society Papers. See also *Zion's Watchman,* February 24, 1838, p. 31. *Maine Wesleyan Journal,* February 24, 1838, p. 4.

200 delegates went to Utica in May. Jared Perkins, leader of New Hampshire Methodist abolitionism, joined Seth Sprague in presiding over the emissaries from 12 conferences, from Maine to Michigan. Orange Scott and Luther Lee addressed them on "the sin of slavery under all circumstances"; and a Negro local preacher described how his wife had been bought by a Methodist minister who had freed her only to sell her children. Thereupon, the offended delegates urged their Southern brethren to "hasten the glorious day of emancipation."[16] The reactions of the abolitionists to Southern statements were not, however, so important as those of their Northern antagonists.

Although the *Christian Advocate and Journal* did not refer to the Georgia resolutions, some of the men whom the paper represented were stunned by the outbreak of proslavery statements which William A. Smith's circular had presaged. Bishop Elijah Hedding was particularly upset and disgusted. He had devoted his prestige and power to the prevention of abolitionist agitation only to be betrayed by Southerners. To President Fisk he wrote, "I did hope we should get along better 'till I saw those wretched Resolutions from the Georgia Conference. I had no idea that any conference could pass such Resolutions; I see not how they can be justified." He then added, "If the southern conferences can be restrained and corrected, we may yet live, after (perhaps) losing a part of New-England."[17] Charles Elliott of the *Western Christian Advocate* wondered who "in his senses" could deny that slavery was a sin, and other

[16] The following conferences were represented: New England, New Hampshire, Maine, New York, Philadelphia, Troy, Oneida, Black River, Genesee, Erie, Michigan, Baltimore. Abolitionists from the following sent letters: New Jersey, Ohio, Illinois, Pittsburgh. See *Zion's Watchman*, May 12, 1838, p. 74. Also June 2, 1838, p. 85, May 19, 1838, p. 78; May 26, 1838, p. 81. Also Matlack, *Slavery and Methodism*, p. 179.

[17] Elijah Hedding to Willbur Fisk, March 19, 1838, Fisk Papers. See also *Christian Advocate and Journal*, January 12, 1838, p. 83.

moderates began to ask if they ought not to counter the action of the Southern conferences. Those in the Pittsburgh and Genesee conferences joined abolitionists to compensate for the Baltimore Conference decision by condemning the slave trade.[18] Responsible churchmen suggested that abolitionism might spread more easily now that the South had departed from the *Discipline,* and one Westerner wrote Fisk: "Have I been mistaken in supposing heretofore that every conference in the union maintained that the system of American Slavery was a moral evil and that this doctrine was distinctly recognized in Wesleyan & American Methodism, and must I now be taught forsoothe, my error in this respect by conference resolutions & by & by perhaps by the decision of the General Conference? And that instead of being a moral evil, Slavery is found to be only a Political, Civil, or domestic evil?" Gershom Cox wryly observed to the Connecticut educator that "the South will no longer *lean* on you for a defense of slavery."[19]

Other incidents continued to make Northern antiabolitionists wary of their Southern friends. President Fisk was much taken aback by William Capers' reaction to the pacification plan of Gershom Cox. Capers, editor of the new voice of Southeastern Methodism, the *Southern Christian Advocate,* repudiated pacification as a thoroughly abolitionist proposal. He maintained that the peace plan rested on fallacious reasoning and was offered for an objectionable purpose. He treated Cox's basic assumption that slavery was evil but not all masters equally guilty in a cavalier manner. Without the appreciation that Cox had shown for the complexities of social moral responsibility, Capers denied

[18] Elliott, *The Great Secession,* column 175. F. W. Conable, *History of the Genesee Annual Conference of the Methodist Episcopal Church,* New York, 1866, pp. 406–410. Elliott's remarks were conveyed to Willbur Fisk by Samuel Luckey in a letter of January 3, 1838, Fisk Papers.

[19] Gershom Cox to Willbur Fisk, March 21, 1838; John Clark to Fisk, March 19, 1838, Fisk Papers.

that "moral evil" was a proper evaluation of "systems," "relations," or situations of races. Moral evil, he said, related only to "the depravity or viciousness of man brought into palpable transgression of the law of God, for which the perpetrators are answerable each for himself." Sin was not a predicament or a condition for Capers, but merely a bad action by a bad man. Thus he was quite incapable of seeing the questionable nature of his own situation. Having bound themselves so closely to slavery as a system, Southerners could not stand off and evaluate it—nor for that matter could Northerners appreciate the problems involved in it. If sin were an evil act of willful men, as Capers said, slaveholding could not be a sin, nor slavery sinful since good Christian men held slaves. Those who attacked such good men were therefore suspect and one could not have fellowship with them. Quite simply, Capers thought the pacification proposal objectionable because it would make peace with men who warred on slavery and slaveholders—it did not throw the rascals out.[20] Capers' arguments aroused President Fisk to object strenuously to the Southerner's "misunderstanding," but Dr. Luckey of the *Christian Advocate and Journal* cautioned the educator to keep quiet lest he produce a "derangement of the present state of things."[21] Once again Southern words brought anxiety and frustration to Northern conservatives.

Through 1838 and on into 1840 Northern churchmen watched with apprehension as Southerners counteracted everything that Hedding, Fisk, Luckey, and Bangs had done for the sake of ecclesiastical unity. By the end of 1838 Capers was following one of William A. Smith's suggestions by urging Southern Methodists to establish a publishing house in Charleston. Nathan Bangs was profoundly distressed. "I have but little hope of preventing them from

---

[20] *Southern Christian Advocate*, August 3, 1838, p. 26; August 10, 1838, p. 30; August 17, 1838, p. 34.

[21] Willbur Fisk to Samuel Luckey, September 3, 1838; Luckey to Fisk, September 8, 1838, Fisk Papers.

pursuing their object," he wrote to Willbur Fisk, "as it seems to me that they are preparing for a separation in perhaps both Church and State. And though firmly opposed to Abolitionism I cannot so far yield to the South as to justify slavery even were it necessary to hold the church in union."[22] Fisk and Bangs nevertheless succeeded in dissuading Capers only to be faced with another schismatic move. Southerners insisted upon having their own subsidiary to the Methodist Book Concern. Thus, Bishop James O. Andrew urged the establishment of a "Southern Book Room" for the sake of the South's *"domestic institutions"* and the Church's "best interests." Finally in April of 1840 the institution opened.[23]

Most of the disagreement between Southerners and their Northern colleagues was prevented from erupting into open controversy. But a public debate did ensue over a proposed revision of the General Rule on liquor, an issue which once again separated Capers from Nathan Bangs. The latter supported a petition from the New York Conference that the General Conference make the regulation on "spiritous liquors" forbid not only their use but also their sale. Capers would not have any change in the General Rules. "What!" he cried, "shall we make arbitrary laws for the church of God and Lord it over the consciences of his people? Shall we put the General Conference in the place of the Lord Jesus Christ? Shall we dare to cast out souls from his fold, for the crooking of a pin, or rumpling a feather? God forbid!" But Capers was not worried about pins or feathers; rather, he knew that the New England Conference had prayed the General Conference for a change of the General Rule on slavery that would have excluded slaveholders from the Church. "What principle would be violated," he went on, "suppose you pass this law at General Conference, if you

---

[22] Nathan Bangs to Willbur Fisk, December 23, 1838, Fisk Papers.
[23] Nathan Bangs to Willbur Fisk, January 14, 1839; Fisk to Samuel Luckey, January 7, 1839, Fisk Papers. *Southern Christian Advocate,* March 27, 1839, Extra; January 24, 1840, p. 2; February 7, 1840, p. 3; April 17, 1840, p. 2.

should then go farther *and pass the one prayed for by the New England Conference?* . . . If you pass this law, you may shake to unloosing the hold of confidence which keeps us together."[24] The threat of disunion was never very far from Southern Methodist lips.

Behind these bold words about disunion was hatred and fear of abolitionism. Although pleased with the antiabolitionism of Fisk and Bangs, Southern Methodists had their own views of what the political writer and Methodist preacher, William G. Brownlow, called the "demon of Abolitionism."[25] Leading churchmen such as William Winans and Capers agreed with the layman who thought the abolitionists "a little cracked." The editor of the *Southern Christian Advocate* believed abolitionists to be subjects "of an infatuation of incalculable power both to fever the brain and chill the heart." Capers substantiated a charge that they were also heretics by analyzing one of La Roy Sunderland's theological ramblings. But the editor and his fellows did not denounce other heretics and enthusiasts because the latter were not troubling the South with "improper intermeddling with the subject of slavery"—because they were not trying to transform Northern conferences into "abolition machines."[26] The abolitionists were the enemy because, as William Winans said, they were "so lost to common sense as to contend for the emancipation of Slaves within our own country."[27]

---

[24] *Southern Christian Advocate,* November 1, 1839, p. 78. See also September 6, 1839, p. 47; October 4, 1839, p. 62; November 22, 1839, p. 90; February 21, 1840, p. 142. *Christian Advocate and Journal,* November 15, 1839, p. 49; December 13, 1839, p. 65.

[25] *Tennessee Whig,* June 13, 1839, p. 1. William Winans to Willbur Fisk, October 5, 1837; Gabriel P. Disosway to Fisk, June 11, 1838, Fisk Papers. Also *Southern Christian Advocate,* February 16, 1838, p. 139.

[26] *Southern Christian Advocate,* February 2, 1838, p. 131; April 6, 1838, p. 166. Also November 17, 1837, p. 86 and June 28, 1839, p. 6. William Winans to Matthias Winans, December 23, 1836, Winans Collection.

[27] William Winans to Matthias Winans, December 23, 1836, Winans Collection.

Southern Methodists, being as much Southern as Methodist, resented not only the antislavery revivalist demands to repent of an act they did not believe sinful, but also a sectional imperialism which had arisen first in 1819. The Missouri controversy of that year was the background against which Southerners cynically read abolitionist attacks upon the South and it was not surprising that Methodists informed their Northern brethren that Southerners were better judges of their situation than they.[28] A mild-mannered Maine editor, Moses Springer of the *Maine Wesleyan Journal,* thought that Southerners were deluding themselves. He wrote: "If the human mind operates in this as on other subjects, our situation is far better for forming a correct estimate of its moral qualities than that of our Southern brethren." Southerners' judgement was "biased by personal interest," he insisted, whereas Northerners were "uncorrupted by a bribe." If everyone practised the injunction not to "interfere with our practice," no one would be able to condemn sin at all, he went on, unless perhaps Southern nature were different from human nature.[29]

Since their nature was indeed quite human, Southerners did not take such statements lightly. "If the North has its fanaticism on the subject of abolition," wrote William Winans to President Fisk, "the South has its chivalric notions in regard to foreign interference in domestic concerns."[30] Even so calm and intelligent a man as William Capers shared those notions. Although he did not resort to chivalric threats, Capers did boast of Southern superiority and sneer at Northern meanness. An example of the latter he believed was an antislavery article by a minister who had had the audacity to report a sojourn in the South to the detriment of his hosts. And Capers roundly scolded the *Western*

[28] Sydnor, *Development of Southern Sectionalism,* p. 241. *Southern Christian Advocate,* January 24, 1840, p. 126.
[29] *Wesleyan Journal,* February 21, 1840, p. 2. The name of the paper was changed September 20, 1839.
[30] William Winans to Willbur Fisk, October 5, 1837, Fisk Papers. Winans to Matthias Winans, January 15, 1838, Winans Collection.

Christian Advocate for its "indignation" at the Congressional "gag" on antislavery petitions. Indeed, anything which appeared to justify abolitionists was anathema to him, and particularly embarrassing was the Section on Slavery in the Methodist *Discipline* which began "What shall be done for the extirpation of the evil of slavery?" The imperious editor discussed the question and its rather weak answer as a "dead letter" which was "foreign alike from the constitution and aim of the Methodists as applied to the South." He went on to assure Southerners that the General Rule against "the buying or selling of men, women, or children with an intention to enslave them" was merely historical. He reminded his readers that Southern conferences denied that slavery was a moral evil and printed, probably not without satisfaction, the statement of a non-Methodist that the Methodist Episcopal Church was "beyond suspicion on the subject of slavery."[31]

Men like Capers could remember only too well when Methodists had not been "beyond suspicion on the subject of slavery," and this memory was partially responsible for their earnestness in denying that slavery was a moral evil. Capers could remember when the antislavery enthusiasm of his youth had failed. He could remember that the General Conference of 1816 had admitted defeat before slavery. He could remember the General Conference of 1820 and the Missouri controversy, and the public suspicion of Methodists after the Denmark Vesey conspiracy, a suspicion which had induced Southern Methodists to declare publicly for the first time their acceptance of slavery. Capers, above all, could remember the difficulties he had met day by day, planter by planter, as he tried to establish a Mission to the Slaves. He was not alone in his memories although few were so

[31] *Southern Christian Advocate,* November 23, 1838, p. 90; December 28, 1838, p. 110; January 4, 1839, p. 114; April 19, 1839, p. 174; December 6, 1839, p. 98; See also William Winans to Matthias Winans, August 29, 1838, Winans Collection.

dedicated to the Mission as he. After antislavery preaching had failed, the Methodists believed that the Mission was the proper work of Southern Christianity. Their missionaries were trustworthy Southerners, they insisted. And Capers in a fit of frustration—but with much experience to legitimatize a statement which in a different context would seem ludicrous—wrote that slavery "TENDS TO THE SALVATION OF THE NEGROES."[32]

Most Methodists could accept this moral argument for having killed the antislavery tradition of their church, but it was primarily a rationalization. The Mission was never much more popular among average Southerners than abolitionist ideas were among average Northerners. Quite simply church leaders had found in 1785 that Methodists would not give up their slaves. This early discovery was reinforced time after time. And time after time the Church decided that converts were more important than conversion. Furthermore, the signs of salvation and evidences of Christian morality which were valued by Methodists were exhibited by slaveholder, slave, and nonslaveholder alike. Thus, the more learned preachers could imagine themselves in much the same situation as Paul the apostle in ancient Rome. The impossibility of ridding the Church of slavery became an explanation, then a vindication, and finally a justification of what had once been considered a sin—and this before anyone ever heard of William Lloyd Garrison. Clearly the early Methodist churchmen had been in a paradoxical situation, but their early compromises were remembered later for their virtue rather than for their ambiguity. Had Asbury's torment over slavery been passed on, perhaps the churchmen would not have denied that slavery was a moral evil and therein attempted to limit the realm of One Whom they claimed was Lord of the Universe.

This reaction of Southern Methodists could hardly be di-

---

[32] *Ibid.,* January 24, 1840, p. 126; Also December 28, 1838, p. 110. South Carolina Conference *Minutes* for 1839, pp. 30f.

vorced from the growing sectional antipathy of the time. Although the South controlled the federal government, it was becoming increasingly sensitive to what it considered Northern attacks upon Southern institutions. Southerners particularly resented the abolitionist petitions to Congress where the venerable and ingenious John Quincy Adams, delighted in "baiting" Southern congressmen. As the South also curtailed freedom of dissent, it is not surprising that Southern citizens who happened to be Methodists complied. Actually Methodist success guaranteed their oneness with the consensus of the community, for when they became more prestigious, more widely scattered, and more responsible members of society, they adopted the trappings and social ethics of what Ernst Troeltsch has called the *Church* as opposed to the *sect*. In his monumental *Social Teaching of the Christian Churches,* Troeltsch said, "The fully developed Church . . . utilizes the State and the ruling classes, and weaves these elements into her own life; she then becomes an integral part of the existing social order; from this standpoint, then, the Church both stabilizes and determines the social order; in so doing, however, she becomes dependent upon the upper classes, and upon their development."[33] The "upper classes" in the South were the slaveholders; whether rude or genteel they determined the character of society.

Thus, by 1840 there were three parties within the Methodist Episcopal Church. The Southerners were publicly unanimous in their dedication to preventing any action adverse to slavery and they threatened to secede from the Church in order to maintain their acceptable position in the South. The abolitionists were a troublesome minority in the North who demanded the Church return to the antislavery faith of the fathers. The conservatives (Northern antiabolitionists) hoped to keep the Church unified and had

[33] Ernst Troeltsch, *The Social Teaching of the Christian Churches* (Olive Wyon, translator), New York, 1931, I, 331.

tried to prevent abolitionist controversy by imposing a rule of silence on the subject of slavery. They failed in the North as well as in the South for the abolitionists were growing in friends and converts and the Southerners were passing resolutions that contradicted the *Discipline.* Assailed from all sides, the conservatives were understandably apprehensive of the General Conference of 1840 which they feared might dissolve into a clash between the three moral positions—a clash that would in turn dissolve the Church. What did finally occur at that conference reveals not only what was happening to the Methodist Episcopal Church, but also to the nation.

Abolitionists throughout the denomination looked upon the General Conference as the great test of Methodist antislavery principles; some joined the conservatives in anticipating that it would end in schism. La Roy Sunderland, harried by ecclesiastical trials and temporarily suspended from ministerial duties, was disheartened by the great power of slavery in the Church. Confident, nevertheless, of eventual victory, he repudiated abolitionist secessions in the West as "bad policy"[34] The major questions before the General Conference he knew would involve conference rights, temperance, the election of bishops, and the "Excision of the Abolitionists." To get rid of the radical antislavery men, the South, Sunderland predicted, would find some excuse to refuse Orange Scott his seat at the meeting, thereby forcing the New England Conference to walk out. Indeed, he expected the South to do almost anything to get the abolitionists to leave the Church. But Sunderland continued to hold out hope that in the end it would be the Southerners and not the abolitionists who would have to leave.[35]

While Sunderland gazed into his crystal ball, Orange Scott

---

[34] *Zion's Watchman,* September 14, 1839, p. 146; January 4, 1840, p. 2; February 29, 1840, p. 33; April 25, 1840, pp. 66–67. *Wesleyan Journal,* May 1, 1840, p. 2; May 8, 1840, p. 2.

[35] *Ibid.,* February 15, 1840, p. 26.

was optimistically trying to get the General Conference to take action that would guarantee a Southern exodus. Although Scott's purpose was not to split the Church, the success of his program could have had no other result. He supported the memorial from the New England and New Hampshire conferences which proposed to expel slaveholders, and encouraged the signing of petitions which urged the General Conference to act against slavery in some way: even a strong statement against it would be sufficient. Through the publication of a new paper, the *American Wesleyan Observer,* he also tried to boost abolitionist morale and to increase pressure against "the power of slavery" in the Church.[36] Consistent with this latter purpose, he and his colleague supported the election of abolitionist delegates to the conference, but the radical antislavery contingent was little larger than it had been in 1836. Many Northern conferences such as Maine, Genesee, Erie, and Oneida had been nudged into antislavery paths during the past four years, but they were not yet prepared to excommunicate slaveholders nor to disrupt Methodism with what they believed were "party" measures.[37]

The conservatives anticipated the General Conference with little joy. Southern proslavery pronouncements did nothing to encourage them; even the arch-conservative members of the Ohio conference had been repelled enough by the Georgia and South Carolina resolutions to announce that they "all considered slavery a great moral evil."[38] Bishop Hedding agreed, and explained to the New Hampshire Conference that he believed slavery "wicked . . . and the laws that sustained it abominable and cruel and ought not to

[36] *Zion's Herald,* November 13, 1839, p. 182.
[37] Mudge, *New England Conference,* p. 287. Stephen Allen and W. H. Pilsbury, *History of Methodism in Maine, 1793–1886,* Augusta, 1887, pp. 113–114. *Zion's Herald,* June 19, 1839, p. 98. *Journal of the General Conference of the Methodist Episcopal Church,* Baltimore, 1840, pp. 15–67.
[38] *Western Christian Advocate,* October 4, 1839, p. 94.

exist. Slaveholders ought to be ashamed of them."[39] Further-more, major public events were constant reminders of Southern demands that the North make slavery a national institution. The right of Americans to petition their elected representatives was being curtailed by the Southern imposed "gag" in Congress, and the Southern clamor for the annexa-tion of the new Republic of Texas revealed the voracious ap-petite of what abolitionists had condemned as the "slave power." Unwilling to fight for the rights and sanctity of slavery, the Methodist churchmen were constantly reminded that the South required more than they were willing to give.

For the sake of peace, however, they would still try to alleviate Southern apprehensions. Alarmed by slavery's ag-gressions and demands, conservatives were not yet prepared to make Negro servitude the primary issue in the contro-versies within the Church. Rather, they believed with Dr. Samuel Luckey of the *Christian Advocate and Journal* that the major question before the Church was its unity for politi-cal as well as for ecclesiastical reasons. Just before the con-ference met, Luckey wrote: "That the prevalence of pure religion exerts a conservative influence upon the state as well as the church, no one, it is presumed, will dispute." Methodism, he pointed out, had contributed toward creating a strong moral atmosphere, "but let this Church divide and break up into separate and disjointed fragments, how much will this binding influence be weakened, if not entirely de-stroyed!" The Church therefore should check the zeal of those who would destroy that unity "by the impetuosity of uncontrolled passions." It was obvious that Luckey al-luded to the abolitionists, but he and Bangs and Hedding also agreed that Southerners had gone too far. Willbur Fisk would have agreed, also, but he was dead.[40]

Thus, when the Methodist General Conference met in

---

[39] *Zion's Watchman*, August 3, 1839, p. 121.
[40] *Christian Advocate and Journal*, April 24, 1840, p. 141. Holdich, *Life of Fisk*, pp. 452–454.

Baltimore, Maryland, in May of 1840, the loyalties of its members were put to the test. Most Americans did not yet have to make the difficult decisions arising from the growth of sectional loyalty. True, the abolitionist revival of the 1830's was still active, but the problems of the economic depression weighed upon many, the hopes for the annexation of Texas enlivened others, and the great circus-revival of Jacksonian political life was then preparing to take advantage of American enthusiasm for Indian fighters and Old Heroes in the election of William Henry Harrison. But neither the depression nor Henry Clay's difficulties with his party were the chief concern of the Methodist General Conference—nor was theology or ritual. Almost 150 delegates, including more than half of the last General Conference and the antagonists, Orange Scott, Nathan Bangs, William Winans, and William Capers, discussed the issue which abolitionists had made central with their activities and preaching. From the first gavel to the last, the conference discussed the Church's responsibility to society in light of the existence of American Negro slavery.[41]

The bishops set the theme for the deliberations in their address to the conference on May 4. They accused abolitionists of contravening the "Christian and pastoral counsel" of the last General Conference by agitating in terms of "crimination and reproach"—agitation the bishops condemned as contrary to Methodism. The General Rule on Slavery testified to Methodist sentiments "on the principle of slavery, and the slave trade," they said; the Church had never demanded emancipation "in contravention of the civil authority," or wherever the slave could not "enjoy his freedom." Although Methodists had never suggested excom-

---

[41] Winans wrote to a friend about the presence of Scott at the General Conference: "No occasion has yet arisen to produce a collision between him and me. Should such an occasion occur, I do not intend to concede him the respect which I am always ready to allow to honorable antagonists." To Elijah Steele, May 9, 1840, Winans Collection.

munication for slaveholders, they had tried to regulate the exchange of slaves with "unhappy consequences both to masters and to servants." Methodists, said the bishops, had rejected direct antislavery action in favor of converting both masters and slaves in order that the duties of each might be discharged in a Christian manner. The Church would not interfere with "relations authorized and established by civil laws," but would insist upon the enforcement of the moral obligations of the gospel. "By a diligent devotion to this evangelical employment, with an humble and steadfast reliance upon the aid of divine influence, the number of 'believing masters' and servants may be constantly increased, the kindest sentiments and affections cultivated, domestic burdens lightened, mutual confidence cherished, and the peace and happiness of society promoted." To do this, the bishops suggested that the Church should be united in the understanding of its position on slavery, and to attain that end they asked the conference to define the meaning of the General Rule on Slavery.[42]

Abolitionists as well as the bishops wanted a new definition of the General Rule on Slavery; they introduced petitions day by day supporting some kind of antislavery statement. The English, too, added their own request to those of the American antislavery men. In their address to the conference they had written: "We are . . . strongly and unequivocally of the opinion that it is, at this time, the paramount Christian duty of the ministers of our most merciful Lord in your country to maintain the *principle* of opposition to slavery with earnest zeal, and unflinching firmness. May we not also be allowed, with the heartfelt solicitude of fraternal love, to entreat you that you will not omit or qualify the noble testimony which we have extracted, in a note to our address, from your book of Discipline,

---

[42] *Christian Advocate and Journal,* May 22, 1840, p. 157. The bishops did not include the Church's edict on slavery from the Christmas Conference of 1784.

but that you will continue to insert it there in its primitive and unimpaired integrity." The abolitionists must have been quite pleased, but the conference replied quite testily through William Capers' pen that Methodists under Thomas Coke, an Englishman, had tried once to emancipate all slaves under the jurisdiction of the Church and they had failed. Their duty was now to free men's souls and pay no attention to the "rights of Caesar."[43]

The Methodists did, however, "pay attention" to the "rights of Caesar"—considering them almost sacrosanct. When the Committee on Slavery reported the third week of the session, its chairman, Nathan Bangs, explained, "The General Conference, in its legislative capacity, has no authority to expound the General Rules of the Discipline." Furthermore, he insisted, Methodists could not now expediently express an opinion on slavery other than that which already existed in the *Discipline*. Nevertheless, in view of the *Discipline,* the committee regretted that annual conferences had in "some instances, expressed conflicting opinions on the item of slavery in the general rules, and on the subject generally." The committee, he continued, had concluded that the conferences "should closely adhere to the language of the Discipline as it now stands"—something the Southern conferences had failed to do. Orange Scott, a member of the committee, rose to object in a "dispassionate and conciliatory" manner to the Church's "quietude" on slavery. He pleaded for a "simple reaffirmation of a rule which had been once established . . . , some efficient interference on the part of the church." But the man most solicitous for the "rights of Caesar," William Capers, "drew tears from many eyes, by an earnest and affectionate appeal to those who professed so decided and inveterate a hostility to slavery, not to make a victim of the object of their sympathies, and immolate him through the success of their kind-

---

[43] *Ibid.,* September 30, 1840, p. 26. Wightman, *Life of Capers,* p. 376.

ness."[44] The General Conference then accepted the report of the Committee on Slavery, rejecting their 10,000 abolitionist petitioners.

The "rights of Caesar" were protected through many more abolitionist reversals. The "conference rights" controversy ended in the assembly's approval of the actions of the bishops in restraining the abolitionists in the war of resolutions. The delegates also overturned a censure against Daniel Dorchester which had been voted by the New England Conference after he had abruptly adjourned an abolitionist quarterly conference.[45] Then the assembly worked out a procedure to allow the New York Conference to try La Roy Sunderland as it saw fit without appeal to the conference of which he was a member.[46] As if to indicate that antiabolitionists anticipated an effective campaign against the editor, Nathan Bangs' Committee on Slavery triumphantly reported numerous "irregularities" and forgeries in the abolitionist petition from New York—much to Orange Scott's embarrassment. Possibly the most symbolic repudiation of abolitionism, however, was the conference's recommendation of the

[44] *Ibid.*, May 29, 1840, pp. 162–163; June 15, 1840, p. 169. *Journal of the General Conference*, 1840, pp. 48, 69. The *Southern Christian Advocate* opposed naming a committee on slavery because it was a "practical abandonment of the principle of noninterference which gave so much satisfaction to the southern portion of the church, and was hailed as a harbinger of peace." May 22, 1840, p. 194.

[45] *Ibid.*, May 22, 1840, p. 158. *Journal of the General Conference*, 1840, pp. 48, 99.

[46] The New York conference was accustomed to charging La Roy Sunderland with immorality and un-Christian conduct for his tempestuous activities as an abolitionist only to have his home conference of New England clergy acquit him. The procedure was necessary because Sunderland was a superannuated minister of the New England Conference residing within the bounds of the New York Conference. The new *Discipline* allowed a minister in the above circumstances to be "held responsible to the annual conference within whose bounds he may reside, who [should] have power to try, acquit, suspend, locate or expel him, in the same manner as if he were a member of said conference." *Discipline*, 1842, p. 66.

199

organization most abused by the radical antislavery men, the American Colonization Society.[47] The abolitionists, it seemed, were being crushed on every hand.

They might have expected much of their bad fortune, but no one anticipated acceding to the "rights of Caesar" in quite the manner resulting from the case of Silas Comfort. A delegate to the 1836 General Conference from the Oneida Conference of New York, Comfort had moved to Missouri with some hope of investing in western lands. He had, however, accepted a church in St. Louis where he became involved in a trial of rather broad social implications. One of Comfort's parishioners was determined upon a clandestine rendezvous with one Mrs. Mary Jane Bolgiana and sent her a note by a Negro messenger. Mrs. Bolgiana replied "You are a Villain and if you knew me you would not send such notes to me. I am a Divorced lady and have had trouble enough with a man never to wish to see one as long as I live." She told Comfort of the incident and he brought the "Villain" to trial before a church board that found him guilty of "ungentlemanly and unchristian conduct" upon the testimony of the Negro who had carried his note. Thus condemned, the "gentleman" appealed to the quarterly conference of the church on grounds that he had been convicted in a church court on testimony inadmissible in a civil court of law.[48]

The Missouri Conference called Comfort to account for his actions. The minister explained that trial for moral conduct was "not a civil transaction" but strictly ecclesiastical; that Negroes might possibly be morally superior to those whom society had awarded superior "civil" rank. Comfort

[47] *Christian Advocate and Journal,* May 22, 1840, p. 158; June 5, 1840, p. 166. *Journal of the General Conference,* 1840, pp. 59–60, 70.

[48] Mrs. Mary Jane Bolgiana to A. M. Rucker, May 1, 1839 in a note from the recipient to the sender of the same date. See also Silas Comfort to John Comfort, October 24, 1836, Silas Comfort Papers, Syracuse University.

insisted that the state did not prescribe how the Church should act on New Testament principles. Since the state had said nothing on Negro church membership, Comfort insisted, the Church could do as it wished in dealing with its members. The beleaguered preacher concluded that if slavery were the civil institution everyone said it was, the civil authorities had no business delimiting what the Church should do within its jurisdiction. The annual conference, however, accused Comfort of an "error of judgment," whereupon he appealed to the General Conference.[49]

Comfort's ground for appeal was that the testimony of 88,000 Methodists would be automatically voided if the decision of the Missouri Conference were allowed to stand. Andrew Munroe of Missouri answered that Comfort's actions were questionable because of the "delicate relations between the races in St. Louis" and because of abolitionist excitement. But George Peck, a colonizationist and an antiabolitionist from New York's Oneida Conference, observed that state enactments did not prescribe ecclesiastical procedures. Stephen G. Roszel, who had long demonstrated his dislike of slavery in the Baltimore Conference, disagreed because ecclesiastical laws in conflict with civil authority would endanger the Church. Thereupon he offered a resolution that the General Conference support the action of the Missouri Conference, but after some debate the resolution was lost.[50]

Wary of the effect of the assembly's refusal to affirm the action of the Missouri Conference, Ignatius A. Few, a distinguished preacher from Savannah, Georgia, and pro-

[49] Silas Comfort, Remarks on the Admission of the Testimony of colored persons in Ecclesiastical Investigations, Missouri Conference, 1839. A. M. Rucker to Silas Comfort, May 3, 1839; Rucker to Messers. Richard B. Dallam, John Goodfellow and James E. Blount, May 4, 1839, Comfort Papers. See also *Christian Advocate and Journal*, May 29, 1840, p. 161.

[50] *Journal of the General Conference*, 1840, p. 57. *Christian Advocate and Journal*, May 29, 1840, p. 161.

spective president of Emory College, submitted a resolution: "That it is inexpedient and unjustifiable for any preachers to permit colored persons to give testimony against white persons, in any state where they are denied that privilege in trials of law." The consequent discussion revolved around the problem of the proper relationship between the Church and the law. Jotham Horton, New England abolitionist, held that the laws of men were not above the laws of God. Roszel of Baltimore did not wish to vindicate the laws excluding Negro testimony, but he thought that Methodists must observe them for the sake of ecclesiastical "prosperity" and the "success of the Gospel." He undoubtedly had recalled the troubles that the Baltimore Conference had encountered twenty years earlier when some of its ministers had got involved in law suits for preaching against slavery. Nathan Bangs had no such memory and he was disturbed by the implications of the Few resolution. In a flight of oratory that swept him past his intended remarks, he proclaimed that he preferred martyrdom to yielding to civil laws that defiled conscience! The applause from the abolitionists unnerved him; the South, however, persisted. Few appealed to the conference not to endanger work with the Negroes and thus divest Southern Methodists of their "ministerial robes." William A. Smith of Virginia tried to inject a discussion on the morality of slavery into the proceedings, turning upon Bangs as if the antiabolitionist were a traitor. Finally, the reliance of the Church upon the suffrance of society carried the balance of victory for the Few resolution 74 to 46.[51] It was a victory for the South, but the abolitionists had found much support.

Disturbed over the implications of the General Conference's action, Daniel Ostrander of New York nine days later introduced a resolution to reenact history. He and Nathan Bangs proposed and the assembly passed a statement

[51] *Ibid.*, p. 60. *Christian Advocate and Journal,* May 29, 1840, pp. 161–162.

that the General Conference would not entertain the appeal of Silas Comfort although it already had. Then George Peck asked reconsideration of the Few resolution, and its author rose to his feet. The refusal of the conference to support the Missouri decision had already been publicized throughout the South, Few said, "and it would be madness to withhold the antidote." He turned upon Bangs and the moderates. "Are you [so] afraid of bringing down upon you the wrath of abolitionists, of foolish and unreasonable men, that you wish to rescind this resolution? And are you entirely careless of the indignation of the South, and, to secure their favor, are willing to do an act which shall encourage the slave to plant his knife into the heart of his master, with the hope of having his name blazoned on the page of history with that of Brutus. I am tired of these sickly sympathies with agitators. If you push this thing, let us go; it is not our fault . . . . This is the Rubicon, sir. I announce it seriously and sorrowfully, this is the Rubicon; pass it not." Bishop Hedding calmly and patiently explained that some of those present had merely thought it "inexpedient to express any opinion on this delicate subject," and hoped to "place ourselves just where we were before." After much heated debate, which now took place not between abolitionists and their antagonists, but between North and South, William A. Smith offered a resolution to compromise the moderates. He suggested that annual conferences be allowed to determine when to make exceptions to the Few resolution. The North and East voted against the South and West, and the border conferences divided their votes so that the final tally was 69 to 69. The deadlock could not be broken; the Few resolution remained in force.[52]

Still dissatisfied with the predicament created by the Comfort case and the Few resolution, Bishop Joshua Soule on

[52] *Christian Advocate and Journal,* June 5, 1840, p. 166. *Journal of the General Conference,* 1840, pp. 62, 88. Clark, *Life of Hedding,* p. 558.

the day before adjournment offered resolutions which attempted to vindicate the Church to the South, antislavery men, the Negroes, and anyone else who might be interested. The conference in passing them stated that the decision of the Comfort case was not to be understood as necessarily approving Negro testimony against white men, the Few resolution was not to prohibit Negro testimony where it could be peaceably admitted, and the General Conference was not to be interpreted as questioning the piety or integrity of colored Methodists.[53] Nevertheless, William Winans was thoroughly satisfied. He wrote a friend that on the Few resolution, "the views of the South finally and *fully* prevailed, and by a respectable majority."[54]

The "rights of Caesar" were vindicated not only by the Few resolution but also by the Judiciary Committee of the General Conference in its report on the Westmoreland case. The Baltimore Conference had withheld ordination from men of the Westmoreland Circuit in Virginia because they were slaveholders. Thus aggrieved, they had complained to the General Conference that Virginia law did not allow liberated slaves to remain free after residing in Virginia a period of time; they pointed out that the *Discipline* "allowed" men to be ordained in such cases. Although the committee admitted that the *Discipline* did not direct the ordination of a man if he were a slaveholder, and although they pointed out that the conference had a right to choose its own members, they found that the owning of slaves "constituted no legal barrier to the election or ordination of ministers."[55] It appeared that slavery and the "rights of Caesar" had indeed conquered the General Conference of the Methodist Episcopal Church.

[53] *Ibid.*, June 12, 1840, p. 171. *Journal of the General Conference,* 1840, p. 109.

[54] William Winans to Alexander Talley, July 20, 1840, Winans Collection.

[55] *Christian Advocate and Journal,* June 12, 1840, p. 171. *Journal of the General Conference,* 1840, p. 129.

There were, however, indications that Northern conservatives were preparing to resist Southern demands that the Church accept and condone slavery. These conservatives or antiabolitionists had implied that Southern conferences had broken the spirit of the *Discipline* in their discussions of slavery; led by that slightly pompous but devoted churchman, Nathan Bangs, they had begun to swing their support away from Southern proposals. The votes on issues which could have been interpreted as dividing strictly between "antislavery" and "proslavery" gave the former 35 per cent of the tally, almost a threefold increase over 1836. Furthermore, the conservatives angered many Southerners by "dodging" the issue which had led William A. Smith to threaten Southern secession after the last General Conference. They refused to elect a bishop and therein avoided the question of whether or not a slaveholder could hold that office. William Winans reported, "A feeling of keener resentment among the Southern preachers I have never witnessed."[56] There was also great resentment at the refusal of the conservatives to censure the New England Conference for its abolitionism. Bishop Hedding pointed out that much of the abolitionist excitement had been caused by the Georgia resolutions and that since the General Conference had declined an opinion on the Georgia Conference it should refrain also from commenting on New England. In spite of William A. Smith's exaggerated absurdities about the truth of the Georgia resolutions, the conference backed Hedding.[57] The moderates had conceded much to the South, but their suspicions and a sense of betrayal were slowly alienating them from the men who had trampled upon the Methodist antislavery tradition even more violently than they.

The Pastoral Address of the General Conference to Amer-

[56] William Winans to Obadiah Winans, June 8, 1840, Winans Collection.

[57] *Christian Advocate and Journal,* June 12, 1840, p. 170. *Journal of the General Conference,* 1840, p. 107.

ican Methodists reflected the resignation of the delegates to the moral diversity in the United States and in the Methodist Episcopal Church. It also revealed a sense of lost innocence. Unlike that of the last General Conference, the Address did not condemn "agitation" because there was "far less occasion to fear from the causes of dissension than there was at the last meeting of [the] conference." Nevertheless, the delegates pleaded with Methodists to understand the delicate nature of the political and ecclesiastical problems of the country. So diverse were the customs and institutions of the nation that it was "not to be supposed an easy task to suit all the incidental circumstances of our economy to the views and feelings" of everyone. The delegates prayed, therefore, that those who disagreed with their actions should "at least give [them] the credit of having acted in good faith, and of not having regarded private ends or party interests, but the best good of the whole family of American Methodists."[58] Thereupon the Church's leaders urged greater effort in teaching morality and saintliness of life.

In their difficulties with slavery and abolitionism, Methodist churchmen were little different from their counterparts in other denominations. Quakers, whose numbers were few in the South and who did not have a large national constituency, for the most part continued their antislavery quietism. Quaker abolitionists might be tempted to form special societies, as had their Methodist brethren, but the Friends' position was not complicated by a conception of the Church and society which hampered other Christians.[59] The Methodists, Baptists, and Presbyterians, in spite of their moral austerity, did not pose themselves against the world; rather they assumed that Christian morality was irrelevant to social structures. The Synod of South Carolina and Georgia denied that the General Assembly of the Presby-

[58] *Ibid.*, July 3, 1840, p. 181.
[59] Drake, *Quakers and Slavery*, pp. 133–151.

206

terian Church had any right to speak on the civil institution of slavery, and maintained slavery had never been a sin. The Baptist *Southern Watchman* spoke of Southern Baptists as a "distinct and separate people" who had "their domestic institutions to protect and vindicate in conformity with the word of God."[60] And John England, Roman Catholic Bishop of Charleston, said that the "existence of slavery as a social institution, accepted both by scriptural authority and by the tradition of the Church was compatible with the exercise of true religion."[61]

There was less unanimity of opinion further north. For a while the Methodist Protestants avoided the issue of slavery by "gagging" their official paper and leaving action on slavery to the discretion of the annual conferences. Elsewhere, antislavery Baptists were disturbing the peace of their loosely knit denomination by forming a Foreign Provisional Missionary Committee in 1840, an institutional repudiation of slaveholding Christianity. And Presbyterians were also afflicted with their own antislavery evangelists, wrestling with both the "New School" heresy and the abolitionist social heresy in their schism of 1837. The division of the Presbyterians into New and Old Schools was not, however, a proslavery-antislavery division. Many of the Old School Presbyterians in Ohio followed the Lane Seminary antislavery revivalists, and the New School General Assembly of 1840 refused to reaffirm the condemnation of slavery which Presbyterians had pronounced in 1818. The division of 1837 actually put conservatives in power in both branches of Presbyterianism so that although the denomination had split with the help of the abolitionist issue, the resultant parts were not strictly sectional. A myth of national unity could still be maintained.[62]

[60] *Southern Christian Advocate*, December 1, 1837, pp. 94–95.
[61] Rice, *American Catholic Opinion in the Slavery Controversy*, p. 66.
[62] Drinkhouse, *History of Methodist Reform*, II, 307–310. Putnam,

That the moral unity of the churches and the nation, however, was quite tenuous is clearly demonstrated by the Methodists. Abolitionists in that denomination and throughout the North, were awakening their fellow Americans to the evil of a system generally and complacently accepted. The controversies they engendered in the Church facilitated the dissemination of their gospel. They were often immoderate, but moderation was not a virtue for them; in the face of evil it was a sin. Orange Scott explained in righteous indignation: "Our statesmen and doctors of divinity can fold their hands and calmly say, 'Keep still. . . .' It is nothing to them that two and a half millions of American citizens are groaning in chains! 'They are not their brother's keeper.' Opposition to SIN is a dreadful *thing;* but *sin itself* is a small matter, compared with agitation! What a paradox we are to surrounding nations—and what a stench in the nostrils of the Almighty! I blush for our institutions; I blush for our religion."[63]

In short, the abolitionists wanted the Church to make no excuses for slavery, to vindicate no slaveholder. They could have passed mild and general antislavery resolutions disapproving slavery, but they wished to be more specific. Slavery was evil not only in principle but also in the United States. The Methodist *Discipline* asked "What shall be done for the extirpation of slavery?" And the abolitionists on firm Methodist historical and moral ground wanted that question answered definitely and energetically. By raising the questions involved with slavery, abolitionists had revealed how

---

Baptists and Slavery, pp. 19ff. Victor B. Howard, "The Anti-Slavery Movement in the Presbyterian Church, 1835–1861," unpublished Ph.D. thesis, Ohio State University, 1961, pp. 55–88, 89ff, 144–154. One study has placed too much emphasis upon the abolitionist-antiabolitionist dichotomy in the Presbyterian division. See C. Bruce Staiger, "Abolitionism and the Presbyterian Schism of 1837–1838," *Mississippi Valley Historical Review,* XXXVI (December, 1949), 391–414.

[63] Scott, *An Appeal,* p. 128.

Christian morality was intertwined with social mores. Although they may have been unrealistic to have expected the South and the Church to repent under their preaching, and although their lack of complicity with slavery made them unable to comprehend the difficulties of emancipation, at least they did not sanctify those difficulties nor shy away from the fact that slavery must be destroyed. Uncompromised by responsibility to institutions, abolitionists believed themselves to be chiefly responsible to principles. Consequently, they were free to denounce ecclesiastical "tyranny," Southern "oppression," and the "sin" of slaveholding. The abolitionists were the conscience of the Church and the nation; as a self-righteous conscience, however, they were never very pleasant.

Southern Methodists thought abolitionists particularly unpleasant. Because Methodists had been attacked as antislavery fanatics a generation earlier, it is not surprising that they assured the Southern public that they were "sound on the slavery question" and demonstrated it by their three demands of the North: no proscription of slaveholders in the election of bishops, no opposition to Southern law, and no agitation. The main question facing the Southern churchmen was the place of the Church in a society which accepted slavery as a normal, amoral "fact of life." Thus, in replying to their nemeses, Southern Methodists addressed not so much the abolitionists as their own compatriots who linked antislavery agitation with sectional aggression and hypocrisy.[64] The South answered Methodist abolitionism with three arguments. The first was to deny that the Church had the right to comment on such a "civil" institution as slavery. Second, since the Church denied itself authority over slavery, slaveholding could not be considered a sin, a conclusion which irrevocably linked the Southern portion of Methodism to sectional institutions and a tenuous social system. The third complaint which the South reiterated over

[64] Sydnor, *Development of Southern Sectionalism*, p. 241.

and over again was that the agitation on slavery endangered the Mission to the Slaves.

In defending the Church's place in the South, however, the Methodists were actually defending slavery "as it existed in the United States." Although Southern Methodists disagreed amongst themselves as to the extent to which they would carry their case, they presented to the world unanimity on the subject of slavery. When Georgia and South Carolina ministers spoke out in no uncertain terms in order to keep the Church respectable in a slave society, the rest of the South in their silence accepted the lead of their more vocal brethren and united with them in the General Conference to create a solid Southern voting bloc. The members of this bloc undoubtedly spread their discontent among the ministers and people whom they represented. To add to the growing self-consciousness of Southern Methodism, denominational journals such as the *Southern Christian Advocate* and *Richmond Christian Advocate* further sharpened Southern sentiment in the midst of a society becoming increasingly self-conscious. Many Southern churchmen probably regretted the existence of slavery, but they would not—and on their own premises could not—move against it.

Institutional conservatives wrestled with the problem of keeping the differing parties within the Church without giving each everything it wanted. In 1836 the conservatives had stood with the South against the abolitionists and had later suffered repeated attacks for refusing to allow antislavery revivalists to express their opinions on their own terms. Contrary to abolitionist charges, the issue was not so much over the right of free speech as the integrity of the Church, since both abolitionists and conservatives claimed to speak for the good of Methodism.[65] In a way, both of them did:

[65] Charles Swaney, *Episcopal Methodism and Slavery*, pp. 76, 89, also believed that the issue was merely one of free speech and refused to try to understand the problems with which the conservatives were confronted.

the abolitionists as the conscience of Methodism and the conservatives as its center of responsibility. But the conservatives soon found that their fight with the abolitionists was being sabotaged by Southern pronouncements on slavery; they had to bear the brunt of abuse hurled at them by Southerners who wished to censure New England abolitionism.

The conservatives were a *via media* in a conflict over the source of responsibility. Abolitionists were responsible to the principles of human freedom. Southerners were responsible to their congregations as good Protestants, to the good order of society as decent citizens, and to the Mission to the Slaves as ministers of the Gospel. Conservatives were responsible to a decent, well-ordered society and the institutional, historical, and moral integrity of the Church. Such integrity forbade social and rhetorical recklessness in both the North and the South. Although increasingly estranged from Southern proslavery apologists, the conservatives still managed to be true to their primary concern—Methodist unity. In their desire to maintain a national institution, however, they had failed to keep the Church free of implication with the slavery they professed to abhor. The dissatisfaction demonstrated in the General Conference of 1840 revealed that the dilemma of unity and slavery would have to be resolved soon—perhaps within the next four years. The delicate and symbolic issue of the election of a slaveholding bishop could not be postponed forever.

CHAPTER VIII

REALIGNMENT OF ALTERNATIVES:
The Conservatives Discover Antislavery
without Abolitionism
1840–1844

REFLECTING upon the implications of the Few resolution and the power of growing antislavery sentiment, Northern Methodist conservatives began to cut their moral ties with the South. This psychological schism did not mean that Methodist officials would now repudiate colonization and expel slaveholders, thus purifying the Church from contamination as radical antislavery men demanded. The ecclesiastical leaders merely wanted to hold their church and their consciences in suspended animation. But their opponents complained that to be against slavery and not slaveholding—as the conservatives tried to be—was to be unaware of the nature of moral responsibility. The antislavery revivalists had fought the antiabolitionists too long to be very much impressed with the antislavery ideals that they professed to hold. Consequently convinced of the impossibility of converting Methodist officialdom to abolitionism, and discouraged by the obsequity to the "rights of Caesar" revealed in the General Conference, the most radical abolitionists followed George Storrs, La Roy Sunderland, and Orange Scott out of the Methodist Episcopal Church. Fearful of ecclesiastical disintegration in the North, and finally convinced that they should openly defend their antislavery heritage, Northern conservatives explained to abolitionists that the Church was their proper home—a distinct departure from the General Conference of 1836. Thus, by

1844 most Northern Methodist leaders were agreed that their church should not again accede to slavery. This determination was increased in the face of Southern demands for the election of a slaveholding bishop. And when it was learned that a Southern bishop had already acquired slaves, the Church's unity was tested in the surcharged atmosphere of suspicion, recrimination, and revivalistic emotionalism.

The Few resolution became the "scarlet letter" that signified the shame of the Methodist Episcopal Church. Ministers would probably continue to accept or refuse Negro testimony in church trials at their own discretion, but the General Conference, in passing a resolution to follow civil procedure in such matters, had indicated what abolitionists had constantly contended: Negroes could not be accepted on the basis of Christian equality in a church that had sacrificed its independence of civil pressures. In the Old Northwest and Iowa as well as in the South, Methodists would theoretically be unable to accept Negroes into the full life of the Church because of popular feeling.[1] This dependence upon ordinary morality was probably more damaging to the self-respect of Northern conservatives than the actual disqualification of the Negroes' rights to full church membership. The depth of the embarrassment felt by the Northern Methodists is easily understood when the requirements of the Few resolution are contrasted with the reaction of the President to an incident that occurred during the 1840 political campaign. Upon the testimony of two Negroes, a court-martial had condemned an officer of the United States Navy. The defendant appealed the verdict, but President Martin Van Buren let it stand despite the condemnation of his action by Southern Whigs. Comparing the decision of the court-martial with that of the Methodist General Conference, the editor of the *Anti-Slavery Reporter*

[1] For a discussion of the testimony of Negroes against white men in Northern courts, see Leon F. Litwack, *North of Slavery*, Chicago, 1961, pp. 93–97.

commented: "And how should such conduct tinge the cheek of every Christian. An [sic] United States' Court Martial acting on higher moral principle than the Methodist Episcopal Church of the United States."[2]

Abolitionists everywhere joined in shaming the Methodists for their inability or lack of desire to stand against "the world" in passing the Few resolution. Said the *Colored American:* "It reflects upon the piety of the Church, because she regards [Negroes] as sufficiently worthy to be members of the Church, and yet [to] have not piety enough to be believed even on oath." The *Pennsylvania Freeman* and the *Friend of Man* agreed with those sentiments and the *Herald of Freedom* pointed out that even though the scriptures said that God was "no respecter of persons," the Methodist Episcopal Church was! In much the same manner, the *Philanthropist* suggested, "The Conference has shown greater respect for a wicked civil regulation, than for the rights of man, the claims of their poor brethren, or the authority of God."[3] La Roy Sunderland reported that Baltimore Negroes had petitioned the General Conference to rescind the Few resolution, but to no avail. Addressing the frustrated memorialists, Sunderland said, "You cannot tell of wrongs against you. THE CHURCH WILL NOT HEAR YOU."[4]

Methodists in the North joined the outspoken editor of

---

[2] *Anti-Slavery Reporter* [organ of the American and Foreign Anti-Slavery Society or New Organization], January, 1841, p. 117. Also *Raleigh Register and North Carolina Gazette,* June 26, 1840, p. 3; July 7, 1840, p. 3; July 10, 1840, p. 3. William Winans to Edmund Smith et al., September 2, 1840 referred to one of the many "outrages" of the Democratic administration, "that most alarming innovation in the customs of the South—admitting the testimony of colored persons against a white man, in a trial within the limits of a Southern territory." Winans Collection.

[3] *Colored American,* June 20, 1840, p. 2. *Friend of Man,* June 17, 1840, p. 140; also July 1, 1840, p. 150 and July 15, 1840, p. 160. *Herald of Freedom,* June 13, 1840, p. 63. *Philanthropist,* June 23, 1840, pp. 2–3.

[4] *Zion's Watchman,* June 20, 1840, pp. 95, 98.

Zion's Watchman in his repudiation of the Few resolution. In Maine, distraught ministers were moved to prepare counter-resolutions for presentation at the next General Conference, and in western New York, moderates and abolitionists of the Genesee Conference denounced the voiding of Negro testimony as an action which would "operate as a strong inducement to the depraved propensities of human nature."[5] Other annual conferences and various local congregations agreed. Even the bishops began to relent in their opposition to "antislavery principles." Although Bishop Joshua Soule prevented the New England Conference from disagreeing with the Few resolution in 1840, Bishops Thomas Morris and Robert Roberts allowed the New Hampshire Conference to do so before joining them at an antislavery meeting.[6] The New York Conference, as thoroughly antiabolitionist as it was, eventually voted to request the General Conference to rescind the resolution, indicating just how far alienation from the South had gone. In fact, one disgruntled churchman, probably Nathan Bangs, told confidants at the Methodist Book Concern that the North would make no more "concessions" to the South.[7] Northern Methodists of all persuasions were finally officially cognizant of the situation that abolitionists had been talking about for almost eight years; slavery had been interwoven into the ethical fabric of Southern Christianity.

Northern sensitivity to Southerners' affirmation of their pe-

---

[5] *Christian Advocate and Journal,* September 30, 1840, p. 26. Allen and Pilsbury, *Maine Methodism,* pp. 118–120.

[6] *Zion's Herald,* August 19, 1840, p. 134; October 21, 1840, p. 170; November 11, 1840, p. 181; September 21, 1842, p. 52. *Christian Advocate and Journal,* September 30, 1840, p. 26. *Wesleyan Journal,* August 21, 1840, p. 2. Matlack, *Slavery and Methodism,* p. 63.

[7] William Winans was furious with this change. To rescind the Few resolution would be to create public opinion favorable to "dislocation" of the South from the rest of the Church. See William Winans to James Sewell, October 27, 1843; also a draft of a letter Winans sent to Daniel DeVinne, an abolitionist and a former friend, August 31, 1841, Winans Collection.

culiar social structure did not mean that antislavery revivalists were about to convert their coreligionists to an abolitionist program. On the contrary, the actions of the General Conference of 1840 seemed to indicate that official Methodism would never use its moral power to oppose slavery as it had when Francis Asbury called for antislavery petitions in 1800. In spite of the many Methodist converts to abolitionism, the ruling elders of the Church had been unwilling to satisfy abolitionists; rather, they had satisfied Southerners. As the abolitionists understood their situation, a little gain in antislavery power in the General Conference could not compensate for the humiliation of "forged" petitions, the embarrassment of the Few resolution, and the pious irrelevance of supporting colonization. Nevertheless, Methodist antislavery men such as Orange Scott hoped to arouse their fellows for yet another assault upon the Church's hierarchy by forming a Methodist antislavery society that would consolidate Wesleyan abolitionism, prevent secessions by demonstrating that good Methodists could be good abolitionists, and perhaps intimidate the next General Conference with ineluctible moral power.[8]

Scott called abolitionists to New York City in October of 1840 to institutionalize American Methodist abolitionism and to speak out against the "savage, barbarous, murderous" Few resolution. Not only did Scott and his colaborers intend to create what became the American Wesleyan Anti-Slavery Society, but they also hoped to explore the possibility of forming a new missionary organization which, like that of the antislavery Baptists, would use no funds collected from slaveholders. Denying that such a plan would be schismatic, Scott emphasized that he had no intention of leaving the Church, for abolitionists had more claims to it than slaveholders. And since Scott and his colleagues were not anxious to secede, they wished to demonstrate that they, as responsible churchmen, were concerned not only for the Church's

[8] *Zion's Watchman,* September 12, 1840, p. 146.

purity, but also for its institutional responsibilities such as the mission to preach the gospel.

Although the abolitionists found it impossible to create a new missionary organization, they did form their antislavery society under the presidency of Cyrus Prindle of Middlebury, Vermont. In the course of the meeting the delegates asked the *Christian Advocate and Journal* to open its columns to a discussion of slavery and abolition—but without success.[9] The executive committee of the new antislavery society therefore concluded that the "slavery power" still controlled the Church. Were the editors of the *Christian Advocate and Journal,* the bishops, and the antiabolitionists in general, therefore, bad men? The abolitionists thought not; they pointed out: *"The strength of the slave power consists in the countenance extended to the system by professedly good men.* A practice prevalent only among *wicked* men, especially one so abominally wicked as that of enslaving human beings, could not be tolerated in civil society. Hence, it can only exist by seducing professedly good people to believe that 'circumstances' render it necessary for them to adopt it, or justify the practice of those with whom they are connected." Since the Methodist Episcopal Church was connected with slavery, its officials could not be expected to condemn it, the abolitionists continued. "But this *connection* with slavery, this dominion which the slavery PRINCIPLE has obtained in the church, is the grand reason for our associate action in the same church against it."[10] The abolitionists revealed to the disinterested observer that they were more sophisticated moralists than their opponents

[9] *Zion's Herald,* November 4, 1840, p. 177; November 11, 1840, p. 181. *Wesleyan Journal,* November 3, 1840, p. 2.

[10] *Zion's Watchman,* October 31, 1840, p. 174. The official paper of the American and Foreign Anti-Slavery Society, the *Anti-Slavery Reporter,* was pleased with the new antislavery society, and in apocalyptic language, intoned that Methodists must either "set themselves in defense of slavery or cease to obstruct the peaceful measures which their Christian brethren are putting forth for its overthrow." November, 1840, pp. 69–70.

had supposed. But it remained to be seen whether they would be at all successful in convincing Methodists to assert more pressure against the Church.

The invitation to form new antislavery societies was answered positively in a few places, but there was no mass conversion. Abolitionists were most active in the hitherto unorganized West. During the autumn of 1840 in Wayne County, Indiana, Methodists formed a Wesleyan Anti-Slavery Society and seven months later they organized a state society.[11] In Cincinnati and Cortsville, Ohio, and in the Genesee Conference of New York, Methodists met to establish new societies, repudiate the Few resolution, and to protest slavery's control of the Church.[12] In New England, Luther Lee began to edit a new Methodist abolitionist journal, the *New England Christian Advocate,* and in May abolitionists formed the American Wesleyan Anti-Slavery Missionary Society on the principles that Orange Scott had outlined at the New York meeting the past October.[13] Methodists also joined other abolitionists in their regular requests to Congress to grant the right of petition to all Americans, prohibit the coastwise slave trade, abolish slavery in Florida and the District of Columbia, and make constitutional and statutory adjustments that the federal government might not sanction slavery.[14] By the first anniversary celebration of the American Wesleyan Anti-Slavery Society in 1841, however, the endeavor to consolidate Methodist abolitionism was not a notable success. The economic depression had precluded an adequate treasury and the antislavery revival had somehow lost its momentum, for only

---

[11] *Philanthropist,* September 23, 1840, p. 1; also April 23, 1840, p. 1.

[12] *Zion's Watchman,* June 5, 1841, p. 89. *Philanthropist,* December 9, 1840, p. 3; April 28, 1841, p. 1.

[13] *Zion's Herald and Wesleyan Journal* [merger of the *Herald* with the *Wesleyan Journal*], March 24, 1841, p. 47. *Zion's Watchman,* June 12, 1841, p. 94.

[14] See *Anti-Slavery Reporter,* September, 1841, p. 28.

16 societies reported themselves auxiliary to the national organization. Nevertheless, Methodist abolitionists had great hopes for the West—there were 5 auxiliaries in Ohio, 2 in Michigan, and 1 in Indiana.[15]

In order to help increase the strength of Western abolitionism, Ohio Methodists called a convention at Cincinnati in October of 1841. The meeting was under the presidency of Samuel Lewis, a prominent lawyer, sometime Superintendent of Ohio Common Schools, a president of the Ohio State Anti-Slavery Society and a Methodist local preacher. Under his distinguished guidance, the assembly heard speakers promise victory for antislavery principles. They were also read a letter from the ailing Orange Scott in which the evangelist had enthusiastically written, "Mobs are retreating to the very borders of slavery—and slaveholders are beginning to be looked upon as other impenitent sinners." Scott asked if slaveholders should not be refused fellowship with true Christians, and some of the delegates answered in the affirmative.[16] But the assembly repudiated the schismatic implications of their attitude by passing resolutions against secession from the Methodist Episcopal Church. As for following the directives of the General Conference, the delegates would practice loyal disobedience: they condemned the Few resolution and promised not to carry it into effect even though it applied to Ohio as much as to South Carolina. Although conservative churchmen might look upon such conventions as schismatic (by implication perhaps they were) Methodist abolitionists wanted very much to remain true to Methodism as well as abolitionism.[17]

The convention's acts revealed not only the pressures in the dilemma of secession or reformation, but also the influence of political abolitionism. In spite of objections, the assembly recommended that Methodists use their elective

---

[15] *Zion's Watchman,* October 16, 1841, p. 166.
[16] *Philanthropist,* November 10, 1841, p. 4.
[17] *Ibid.,* October 7, 1841, pp. 2–3.

franchise to effect legislative action against slavery. Such action was quite consistent with the beliefs of the chief Methodist abolitionists. One of the major issues which had separated Garrisonians from the followers of James G. Birney, the obligation to vote for abolition principles had been warmly supported by Orange Scott and his New England colleagues. A few Methodists supported the Liberty Party when it nominated Birney for the presidency in 1840, and continued to do so as it survived the avalanche of votes for William Henry Harrison and Martin Van Buren.[18] In the rapidly growing West, Guy Beckley, a Methodist minister, and former agent of the American Anti-Slavery Society, edited the *Signal of Liberty* which became a small but insistent voice for the Liberty Party, Methodist abolitionism and the Michigan Anti-Slavery Society.[19] Samuel Lewis of Ohio spoke for the Liberty Party at Methodist conventions over which he presided and in 1843 announced for Congress on the Liberty ticket. He attempted to gather all antislavery men into the party regardless of the strictness of their abolitionism because, as he pointed out, the South made no distinctions between the different shades of antislavery opinions.[20]

The paths of political activism were also traveled by Methodists in the East. James C. DeLong, one of the most energetic of the Methodist laymen in the New York State Anti-Slavery Society, ran on the Freeman's ticket for New York state senator from Oneida County in 1840. And Jared

[18] For a discussion of political abolitionism, see Filler, *Crusade Against Slavery,* Chapter 7.

[19] See *Signal of Liberty,* January 5, 1842, p. 2; January 19, 1842, pp. 2, 3. Beckley was president of the Michigan Wesleyan Anti-Slavery Society and followed Orange Scott's leadership as best he could especially in supporting the antislavery missionary society and the petitions to annual conferences against the power of slavery in the Church.

[20] *Philanthropist,* October 22, 1842, pp. 2, 3. See also January 18, 1843; p. 2; July 5, 1843, p. 3; September 30, 1843, p. 3. *Emancipator and Free American,* November 10, 1842, p. 111.

Perkins of the New Hampshire Conference and Phineas Crandall of the New England Conference ran for Congress under Liberty Party auspices in 1842.[21] It apparently was not too difficult to adapt Christian evangelism to the political "revivalism" of the Jacksonian era.

A few candidates and conventions did not mean, however, that Methodist abolitionists were entirely satisfied. They could never really free themselves from the pessimism which had been induced by the General Conference of 1840: it clouded all their efforts and seemed to turn all hope into despair. La Roy Sunderland was particularly depressed. The energetic little evangelist had become a symbol of contentious Methodist abolitionism, and a Methodist abolitionist's orthodoxy could be tested by whether or not he approved of *Zion's Watchman*. Gradually, Sunderland came to realize the great improbability that abolitionists would take the Church by storm. He mused over the antiabolitionists' power in the annual conferences and confessed that they had forced him to give up his parchments as a "traveling preacher" and settle for the status of a lay minister. Discouraged with the powerlessness of abolitionism, he turned his fertile and imaginative mind to discussing those fascinating subjects dealing with the nature and power of the mind and its relation to electrical energy—"Electricity, Galvanism, and Electromagnetism."[22] As its editor flagged, so did the *Watchman:* Sunderland was forced to offer books as special premiums to get subscriptions, and finally the publishers sold the paper.[23]

During the eighteen months from January 1841 to June

---

[21] *Emancipator and Free American,* October 20, 1842, p. 94; December 29, 1842, p. 138. *Friend of Man,* August 12, 1840, p. 174.

[22] *Zion's Watchman,* August 15, 1840, pp. 130–131. For Sunderland's articles on "electro-magnetism" see September 11, 1841 to November 13, 1841.

[23] *Ibid.,* May 29, 1841, p. 86. *Zion's Herald and Wesleyan Journal,* November 9, 1842, p. 176.

1842 Sunderland summarized his views on the power of slavery in the Church. Over and over again he tried to explain the essential Methodist ground of abolitionism and the "false love of denomination" which guided the Church's leaders. Perhaps the defense of slavery came from sensitivity to criticism, he mused, and from a want of self-denial for any principle save that of institutional stability. Like the New York antislavery convention of 1840, Sunderland saw as the basic problem the fact that the bishops who defended the South and slaveholders were "good men." Many slave-holders, too, were "unquestionably actuated by as pure motives as those which have carried our bishops into such strong measures to put down abolition." No ordinary class of men—only holy men—could have crushed abolitionism. And now that the first burst of revivalistic enthusiasm had been exhausted, the General Conference had constantly rejected abolition principles; in fact, Sunderland thought that slavery would never be expelled from the Church by official action. He wanted to urge his readers to fight on, to redouble their efforts, but his heart was not in it. Redouble efforts to be embarrassed, scorned, humiliated, and almost excommunicated? In June of 1842 the disheartened editor was finally facing the possibility of secession—a decision which he had fought against since 1833 and as late as the Ohio convention the autumn of 1841. He concluded that if the abolitionists could not reform Episcopal Methodism, they would have to withdraw from it.[24]

Orange Scott was also despondent over the future of anti-slavery action within the Church. Forced to rest because of ill health, Scott pondered the fortunes of abolitionism after the General Conference of 1840. Oppressed in body, he became depressed in spirit; he desperately wanted peace

[24] See a selection taken from the *New York* [*Zion's*] *Watchman* in the *Liberator*, June 10, 1842, p. 89. See also *Zion's Watchman*, January 23, 1841, p. 14; February 27, 1841, p. 34; March 20, 1841, p. 46; April 3, 1841, p. 54; April 10, 1841, p. 58; April 24, 1841, p. 66; May 15, 1841, p. 78.

and silence after so much "sound and fury." But there was conscience—perhaps he should leave the Church in one last protest against slavery, for he joined Sunderland in despairing of reformation. First, however, he tried to atone for some of the animosity which his violence had wrought. He wrote letters of apology to the bishops, who, he had already admitted in the *American Wesleyan Observer,* were not so guilty of usurpation as he had once thought. And in June of 1842 he wrote to *Zion's Herald* what must have been for him a difficult letter. In it he compared his impetuosity to that of Saint Peter's in Gethsemane—he had been right but he had been unwise. "I now regret," he confessed, "that the debate on both sides assumed, at so early a period, so hostile a character . . . and that I contributed my full quota to such a result." He went on to question the usefulness of antislavery conventions and even denominational antislavery societies, suggesting that political action was the best solution to the problem of slavery.[25] Surely, Scott and Sunderland had shed much of the vibrant, revivalistic optimism which had thrust them into the vanguard of the antislavery movement.

The despair these two Methodists felt at the prospect of converting their church to abolition principles was quite probably intensified by both James G. Birney's pamphlet, *The American Churches the Bulwarks of American Slavery,* and the Garrisonian attacks on "denominational abolitionism." Birney, whom Scott and Sunderland had acknowledged as their leader in the schism of the American Anti-Slavery Society in 1840, exposed "proslavery" churches with appropriate allusions to the Few resolution and the General Conference debates of 1840.[26] Garrisonians not only attacked the antiabolitionist ecclesiastics but also the ministers who

---

[25] *Zion's Herald and Wesleyan Journal,* June 15, 1842, p. 96. Matlack, *Life of Scott,* pp. 185, 193, 195–203.

[26] James G. Birney, *The American Churches the Bulwarks of American Slavery,* Boston, 1843 [published first in 1840], pp. 14ff.

tried to serve both the Church and abolitionism. With sarcasm and personal abuse, Garrisonians attacked all "so-called" Christians who would not "come-out" of those churches which refused to condemn slavery. Lydia Maria Child, editor of the official journal of the purged American Anti-Slavery Society scornfully accused Scott and Sunderland of having "treacherously betrayed the slave into the hands of proslavery influence" because they still adhered to the Methodist Episcopal Church.[27] New England Methodist abolitionists were not only harangued from afar, but also in their own churches, for "come-outers" did not disdain to interrupt Christian worship by heckling and impromptu sermons.[28]

Garrison himself constantly berated those who loved the Church more than the slave, for he believed that by separating from institutions implicated with sin, the pure would somehow help the Negroes. Garrison believed that associating with what Henry C. Wright called a "Brotherhood of Manstealers" or Stephen S. Foster called a "Brotherhood of Thieves" was to prostitute ones antislavery principles. An antislavery man would be suspected of adhering to heterodox abolitionist ideas by associating with "sinners." As for the denominational antislavery societies he had once praised, the editor of the *Liberator* charged that they were *"framed not to aid the progress of abolition principles, but to prevent their going too far—to serve the church, not to serve humanity."*[29] The charge indicated a false dichotomy; knowing this and deeply stung by attacks upon

---

[27] *National Anti-Slavery Standard,* November 19, 1840, p. 94.

[28] Parker Pillsbury, *Acts of the Anti-Slavery Apostles,* pp. 182, 307.

[29] *Liberator,* October 21, 1842, p. 166; also August 13, 1841, p. 130. Also Stephen Symonds Foster, *Brotherhood of Thieves, passim.* Also *National Anti-Slavery Standard,* February 4, 1841, p. 139 which claimed that ministers opposed reform because it "disturbed" their power.

the clergy, Scott attempted to fight the "come-outers" and to defend ministers as proper abolitionists. After one of his bouts with the purists, the once friendly *Herald of Freedom* reported that Scott had "groaned out his naked opinion with all the impudence of Yankee sect, and all the importance of the Episcopal high church which characterizes the order of our priesthood."[30] The harangues, attacks, sneers, and scorn continued as Garrison taunted his clerical abolitionist enemies for having betrayed the true faith. Where was Orange Scott, the *Liberator* demanded. Where was Orange Scott "who once shook the Methodist hierarchy to its foundation with his antislavery thunder? Morally defunct."[31]

The pressure exerted against Scott and the Methodist abolitionists came not only from their erstwhile colleagues in the antislavery revival, but also from conservative churchmen. The tone of the conservatives' arguments had changed, however; whereas they had once encouraged abolitionism by forcefully opposing it on every issue, they now followed a more diplomatic course which was less easily countered. They adopted the theme to which they had privately adhered but up to now had not expressed publicly for fear of unnecessarily antagonizing the South: Methodists are opposed to slavery but do not wish to expel slaveholders because of the great complexity surrounding the question of slavery.

The man who most represented the new stance was Thomas E. Bond, Sr., a veteran lay preacher from Baltimore, a physician, a colonizationist, and a former pamphleteer against the Methodist Protestants or Radicals who had twelve years earlier seceded from the Church because of its hierarchical structure. A forceful and sometimes witty writer, Bond assumed the editorial direction of the influential and official *Christian Advocate and Journal* in 1840 after

[30] Quoted in Pillsbury, *Acts of the Anti-Slavery Apostles,* p. 231.
[31] *Liberator,* August 12, 1842, p. 127.

Samuel Luckey had only too happily resigned.[32] Although Bond claimed that he wished to avoid discussing abolitionism, he could not eschew criticizing the New York Convention which Orange Scott had called to organize the American Wesleyan Anti-Slavery Society. Bond believed that such meetings were too similar to the activities which had led to the Methodist Protestant schism in 1828. Indeed, Bond called Scott's followers "radico-abolitionists" to associate them with the "radicals" who had left the Church over a decade earlier and to disassociate them from abolitionists who would balk at secession from the Methodist Episcopal Church now.

Bond cynically asked why Methodists would even want to join Wesleyan antislavery societies. If they wished to exclude all who "irrespective of circumstances," were affiliated with slavery they would be "unrighteous and cruel" and in violation of the injunction to love ones neighbor. Methodists could join political antislavery societies, Bond believed, but they could not in good conscience form organizations for the purpose of expelling people from the Church because they were involved through no fault of their own in social and moral evil. The sinfulness of slaveholding could be determined only by searching men's motives, the editor explained, and that could be done only by God. To make slaveholding a sin, he went on, "the participation must be voluntary, and with a knowledge of the evil; but a man may participate in a moral evil, without knowing it to be such; or, knowing it to be such, the participation may be of necessity, and therefore involuntary." Each person must judge for himself, wrote Bond, how he would fulfill the command to love his neighbor, but "No rule of the Church [could] prescribe the amount of his obligation." The editor concluded that Methodist antislavery societies could not

---

[32] Ira A. Easter to R. R. Gurley, January 10, 1839, American Colonization Society Papers. James Floy to John McClintock, February 2, 1840, McClintock Papers.

rightfully prescribe "absolute" laws of conduct. Bond would admit that slavery was a moral evil, but not that slaveholders *per se* were any more flagrant sinners than other men. The only thing Methodist antislavery societies would accomplish, he insisted, was un-Christian dissention and schism.[33]

Bond was no more enamored with Southern slavery apologists than he was with "radico-abolitionists"; unlike his predecessor as editor he did not try to soothe the South with silence. When a slaveholders' convention in Annapolis, Maryland, put pressure on the legislature to remove all free Negroes from the state, Bond excoriated the proposed law as unjust, inhumane, and "mad." He was pleased that his son and other prominent Maryland Methodists and ministers had memorialized the legislature in opposition to the proposal and warmly congratulated the Maryland Senate when it rejected the bill after it had passed the House. "The righteous shall be had in everlasting remembrance," he wrote. Although a few abolitionists were pleased with Bond's "war upon slavery," their enthusiasm was not shared by Methodists in South Carolina who attacked the editor for "discussing slavery." Bond was repelled. "Ought so flagrant an ultraism to have been tolerated and acquiesced in," he demanded, "because it occurred south of Mason and Dixon's line?"[34]

Bond's strictures against "radico-abolitionism" were repeated in both New England and Ohio. In Boston, *Zion's Herald* acquired a new editor the autumn of 1840 in the person of Abel Stevens, one of the signers of the counter-appeal of 1835. His assumption of an office usually held by friends of abolition did not portend an end to abolitionist articles in the *Herald,* but it did mean that the journal

[33] *Christian Advocate and Journal,* September 23, 1840, p. 22; November 18, 1840, p. 54; November 25, 1840, p. 58; January 13, 1841, p. 86.

[34] *Ibid.,* March 9, 1842, p. 119; March 16, 1842, p. 121; March 23, 1842, p. 127; April 13, 1842, p. 138. *Signal of Liberty,* April 25, 1842, p. 2.

would be neither "a vehicle for radical sentiments" nor an "organ of personal attack and defense."[35] Despite some abolitionists' complaints against Stevens' moderation, the editor devoted a regular section of the paper to articles opposing slavery; he reported Southern attempts to crush John Quincy Adams in Congress, and tried on the whole to follow an antislavery but "non-radical" editorial policy. Stevens refused to be drawn into controversies over whether or not he had suppressed the rights of free speech of the abolitionists because, as he explained it, "Abolitionism is too good a cause to be marred with such discussions, and the distractions which must follow." Furthermore, he emphasized that Methodist abolition papers such as the *New England Christian Advocate* were of little further use because of the prevalence of abolition ideas.[36]

In the West, Charles Elliott, a colonizationist, assumed the direction of the *Western Christian Advocate,* and accepted Dr. Bond's distinction between the system of slavery and the people who held slaves. By virtue of their religious profession, Methodists were opposed to slavery, Elliott wrote, and those who were implicated with it would have to answer to God. As for abolitionists—they could be Methodists but they should not disrupt the Church.[37] Clearly antislavery ideas and the men who held them were more respectable in 1841 than they had been in 1836. Furthermore, the new tack of Methodist publicists was soothing many abolitionists, for ministerial meetings throughout New England reported that antislavery societies were more active than ever before, but that "radicalism" was dead![38]

[35] *Zion's Herald and Wesleyan Journal,* December 9, 1840, p. 198; also October 7, 1840 reprint of Bond's attack on "radico-abolitionists."

[36] *Ibid.,* June 9, 1841, p. 90; December 15, 1841, p. 198; January 5, 1842 and following issues, especially February 16, 1842, p. 26.

[37] *Western Christian Advocate,* September 25, 1840, p. 90; November 20, 1840, p. 122; April 23, 1841, p. 3.

[38] *Zion's Herald and Wesleyan Journal,* December 23, 1840, p.

The kind of antislavery sentiment expressed by official Methodist publications was not, however, altogether convincing to a reflective, dedicated abolitionist. It was too easily satisfied with being "opposed" to slavery without trying to use moral suasion, or political power, or disciplinary action to change men's minds. Such antislavery opinion was too content to rest on the virtue of its righteous convictions without trying to free the Negroes. The desire to be opposed to slavery and not to slaveholders revealed a willingness to accept an evil for which no one was responsible, a willingness to place oneself at the disposal of circumstances or the forces of history without taking seriously the nature of moral responsiveness, moral accountability, and moral action. In order to be moral, men must not only think, but also act. And the abolitionists were really demanding that slaveholders be more moral than even the prophets who preached at them—by taking charge of historical circumstances and freeing the slaves. The Church could have helped immensely, the radical abolitionists believed, by exerting moral pressure. But it remained passive when asked to act against slavery. In June 1842 Orange Scott wrote: "I have now no expectation that the M.E. Church will ever take action against slavery, so long as it exists in the country—or that a majority of the general conference, or of the church, will ever be abolitionized 'till slavery ceases in the land."[39]

Although Scott knew that he could minister in a thoroughly "abolitionized" sect only if he left the Methodist Episcopal Church, he put off his secession as long as possible. He confessed that he was "waiting in sullen silence for others to produce some change, or submit to things

---

208; June 16, 1841, p. 94; June 30, 1841, p. 102; August 18, 1841, p. 131; September 1, 1841, p. 138; November 17, 1841, p. 184.

[39] *Ibid.*, June 15, 1842, p. 96.

as they are."[40] Thomas Bond encouraged him to be "restored to the Church," but there were more powerful pressures upon him to leave it. The scorn of the "come-outers" and the realization that Birney had been at least partially correct in calling the churches the "bulwark" of slavery helped to make more sensible the secessions from Methodism which had been taking place since 1837. From Ohio, Michigan, New York, and Pennsylvania had come reports of withdrawals and soon the Wesleyan Methodists, as many called themselves, were becoming a denomination.[41]

In the summer of 1841 Utica seceders had discussed organizing a presbyterian Methodist church with a hierarchy neither of power nor of color, and in June 1842 the demand was even greater for a "Methodist Convention to be called immediately on the principle of *opposition to Episcopacy and to Slavery*."[42] George Storrs had left the Methodist Episcopal Church after the General Conference of 1840, complaining of "spiritual tyranny" and professing "no creed but the Bible."[43] Shipley Willson, who had helped to write the appeal of 1835, became a Unitarian, but La Roy Sunderland and Orange Scott still remained within the Church. Nevertheless, the latter was on the brink of secession the summer of 1841 when his former congregation at Lowell, Massachusetts, asked him to be their pastor contrary to the bishop's orders.[44] The many pressures from abolitionists,

[40] Orange Scott to Cyrus Prindle, April 25, 1842, in Matlack, *Life of Scott,* p. 193.

[41] *Zion's Watchman,* June 10, 1837, p. 91. *Friend of Man,* July 25, 1838, p. 224. *Signal of Libery,* October 31, 1842, p. 1; November 7, 1842, p. 2. Matlack, *Slavery and Methodism,* pp. 301–327. *Emancipator and Free American,* June 2, 1842, p. 18.

[42] *Friend of Man,* June 8, 1841, p. 127, July 6, 1841, p. 142. *Signal of Liberty,* June 27, 1843, p. 2.

[43] *Herald of Freedom,* October 2, 1840, p. 125. George Storrs to Gerrit Smith, December 16, 1841, Gerrit Smith Papers, Syracuse University.

[44] *Christian Register,* July 30, 1842, p. 122. *Christian Advocate and Journal,* August 25, 1841, p. 6; September 1, 1841, p. 9. Matlack, *Life of Scott,* pp. 198–199.

as well as from secessions and frustrations, could hardly encourage Scott to remain within the Church. Finally he shook off his "sullen silence" and the indecision which was so uncharacteristic of him and with Sunderland and their mutual associate, Jotham Horton, he seceded from the Methodist Episcopal Church—its slaveholders and its bishops—on November 8, 1842.[45]

The Scottite secession soon became formalized as the Wesleyan Methodist Church. Under the guidance of Scott's new paper, the *True Wesleyan,* Methodist radical abolitionists left the Church at an increasing rate and awaited the organizing convention of their new denomination which was scheduled for Utica, New York, in May 1843. Called into being ostensibly because the episcopal hierarchy had protected slaveholders, the Wesleyans created a presbyterian polity and purified their church from any association with slavery. The purity of the denomination would be guaranteed not only by the Wesleyans' refusal to accept the fellowship of slaveholders, but also by their emphasis on Christian "perfection." This doctrine which John Wesley had once made the peculiar belief of Methodists was being revived among American Methodists as well as Calvinists during the 1830's and 1840's. Although Scott and Sunderland had never preached it as a necessary adjunct to abolitionism and although some antiabolitionists were perfectionists, the new church would adopt Christian perfection as their peculiar doctrine in order to be true to Wesley's heritage. The pastoral address of the organizing conference at Utica explained: "It is holiness of heart and life that will arm you against every assault, that will give you moral power to oppose the evils and corruption in the world, against which we have lifted up a standard."[46]

---

[45] See Orange Scott, *The Ground of Secession from the M.E. Church,* New York, 1848, pp. 6, 14.

[46] Matlack, *Slavery and Methodism,* pp. 343–344. Also *Liberator,* January 13, 1843, p. 8. *Signal of Liberty,* February 6, 1843, p.

Those who had met to lift the standard represented 6,000 Methodist laymen and 80 ministers—a membership which more than doubled within a year. Scott declined the presidency of the new denomination in order to continue his role of prophet and preacher in the *True Wesleyan;* he was optimistic for the future once again. He promised the Utica convention that by seceding, the Wesleyans would exert a "greater amount of influence in the world, and even on other religious denominations," than had they remained within the Methodist Episcopal Church.[47] Events were to prove him quite correct.

Although some Garrisonians did not think that the Wesleyan secession was quite pure enough, the more thoughtful abolitionists agreed with Scott. Garrison thought that the Methodist seceders were not true "come-outers" since they had left the Church to escape only slavery rather than all of its sins. When the Utica convention had finished its work, the *Liberator* reported that since the new denomination could make rules for its membership, it would still place men in "shackles." Alas, the Wesleyans were more interested in being Methodists than Christians, for they would be governed by regulations rather than by principles. "When Methodists call themselves *Christians,*" the *Liberator* concluded, "they [are] greatly mistake[n]."[48] The primary reason for Garrisonian disregard of the Wesleyans was not their Methodism so much as their adherence to the America and Foreign Anti-Slavery Society which had repudiated the

---

2. Also see the following for a discussion of perfectionism and its relation to "social reform:" Timothy Smith, *Revivalism and Social Reform;* John Peters, *Christian Perfection and American Methodism,* Nashville, 1956.

[47] Matlack, *Life of Scott,* p. 213. Matlack, *Slavery and Methodism,* pp. 322, 328ff. Of the original churches in secession more than 55 were from New York, 14 from Massachusetts, 4 each from Pennsylvania, Vermont, and Connecticut, and 2 each from Michigan and Ohio, and 1 each from New Hampshire and Rhode Island.

[48] *Liberator,* June 23, 1842, p. 97; December 22, 1843, p. 202.

leadership and principles of the intrepid Boston editor.[49] To Gamaliel Bailey of the *Philanthropist,* however, the dispute between Garrisonians and Wesleyans was of less interest than the effect of the Scottite secession upon authority in general and the Methodist Episcopal Church in particular. Noting the past, rather ill-advised reaction of the Church to abolitionism, Bailey explained: *"Authority* must *bend* or be *broken."*[50]

Northern Methodist officials were convinced that they would have to bend. The increasing antislavery sentiment could neither be ignored nor allowed to become fuel for the secessionist fire which Orange Scott and his colleagues had kindled. Abel Stevens became the editorial statesman of ecclesiastical abolitionism in New England where the danger of a large schism was the greatest. In *Zion's Herald* he berated the defeatist attitude that made Methodists leave their church because it was connected with slavery; the logical extension of such sentiment into political terms would induce men to renounce their citizenship because some Americans held slaves. Involved though the Church was in the "inequity of slavery," it was also more involved in "abolition sentiment" than any other Christian sect, Stevens pointed out. "Some of the strongest men now fighting this great battle of freedom, are in our communion, and in our pulpits," he went on. "Whole conferences which once rejected antislavery resolutions now sustain them with scarce a dissent, and it cannot be doubted that soon, very soon, all our northern conferences will be of one mind on the subject."[51] Thomas Bond, too, tried to convince abolitionists

[49] See the report of Wesleyan opposition to the "Old Organization" or Garrison-controlled American Anti-Slavery Society in Abby Kelly's letter to Maria Weston Chapman, October 10, 1843 in the Weston Family Papers.

[50] *Philanthropist,* January 18, 1843, p. 2.

[51] *Zion's Herald and Wesleyan Journal,* December 7, 1842, p. 190. The *Northern Christian Advocate* from Auburn, New York thought that the separation would be small, and Bond in the *Christian*

that Methodists opposed slavery if not slaveholders. He spoke at antislavery meetings and printed a long discussion upon the slavery question between himself and an Ohio abolitionist. At last the *Christian Advocate and Journal* was opened to antislavery men even if only slightly. And even the strongly antiabolitionist Ohio Conference was moved by the evidence of growing antislavery feeling to protest that the Methodist Episcopal Church was opposed to Negro servitude.[52]

Anti-secessionist abolitionists in New England called conventions and printed pamphlets and articles to emphasize what Bond intimated and Stevens had boldly stated: Methodists could be abolitionists. A meeting in Boston denounced slavery as a sin, encouraged Methodists to act against slavery, and almost encouraged a separation from the South to "satisfy the consciences of honest and faithful abolitionists." A second meeting at Hallowell, Maine, passed resolutions almost as disruptive, but which emphasized that secession from sin was no way for moral men to combat it—that men must remain within the Church to fight its involvement with slavery. Stevens hurried to explain the surprising contentiousness of the resolutions as the work of "radicals" who had not yet left the Church. Nevertheless, further secessions purged Methodist abolitionism of its more "violent members," and rid it of its more extreme forms of anti-ecclesiasticism.[53]

Thus, encouraged, Stevens continued his editorial policy with the help of the many preachers who agreed with

---

Advocate and Journal observed that Scott, Sunderland and Horton had "abandoned us to our fate"; but he was worried about keeping New England: November 30, 1842, p. 62. *Northern Christian Advocate,* November 24, 1842, p. 134.

[52] *Christian Advocate and Journal,* July 12, 1843, p. 190; June 14, 1843 and following issues. October 25, 1843 for report of the Ohio Conference.

[53] *Zion's Herald and Wesleyan Journal,* January 25, 1843, p. 11. See the following issues to June 7, 1843.

pamphleteer Charles Adams of the New England Conference that the Methodist Episcopal Church was the legitimate home for true Wesleyan abolitionists. But neither Adams nor Stevens could prevent the New Hampshire Conference from proposing a division of Methodism along a line separating slaveholding and free territory.[54] New England Methodist leaders, knowing the strength of antislavery beliefs among their laymen, and firmly convinced that Methodism was by its very nature opposed to slavery, walked a tortuous path. Indices of antislavery sentiment in the North which encouraged abolitionists portended grave difficulties for the Church should slavery continue to be the subject of controversy in the General Conference.[55]

The new editor of the *Southern Christian Advocate,* William Wightman, had no sympathy for the difficulties of his Northern coreligionists. He might have refrained from discussing the New England conventions and thereby helped to becalm a small part of the antagonism which was being increased by sectional political controversy, but he did not. Although President Stephen Olin of Connecticut's Wesleyan University had assured him that the latest antislavery conventions were only attempts to keep the Church unified, Wightman could not be dissuaded from an irrational attack upon his "New England enemies." Both he and John McFerrin of the *Southwestern Christian Advocate* in Nashville suggested that the latest developments in New England made the fellowship of Methodists so "flimsy" as to be incapable of surviving the next General Conference. For Wightman and McFerrin there was no sorrow in the rent fabric of Methodism, but rather an opportunity to threaten even more destruction.[56]

[54] *Ibid.,* June 7, 1843, p. 90; August 23, 1843, p. 133 and throughout the next two years. See also Charles Adams, *An Address to Abolitionists of the Methodist Episcopal Church,* Boston, 1843, *passim.*

[55] See *Anti-Slavery Reporter,* March, 1843, p. 144.

[56] *Southern Christian Advocate,* March 10, 1843, p. 152; April

The publicists of Southern Methodism were in fact, doing their best to tear the South from the North. Although editors of church papers could not create public opinion, they certainly could focus against Northerners and abolitionists the antagonism which had been growing since the first days of the antislavery revival. Furthermore, the nation's political affairs were once again complicated by a discussion of slavery. The division of North and South was further facilitated by the influence of sectarian journals which lent their piety to political and economic as well as moral differences. Suspicion and doubt seemed burned into Southerners' souls when they thought of the North: Northern Methodists could simply not be trusted to protect the rights of their Southern brethren. They had listened too much to antislavery revivalists to be trusted; they had yielded too much to abolitionist principles.

Southerners believed that there was something definitely unsettling about the North where men dreamed of making over the universe, readjusting social relations, and converting the depraved South. Southern Methodists complained that when Yankee Methodists came South they were not content to notice the beauty of Charleston, but seemed compelled to mention the slave trade—a very unkind thing to do.[57] The editors of the *Southern Christian Advocate, Southwestern Christian Advocate,* and the *Richmond Christian Advocate* contrasted the Christian South with the heathen North. Southern Methodism was as "calm and placid as the surface of a mountain lake" whereas the North was

---

14, 1843, p. 172; August 25, 1843, p. 42. *Southwestern Christian Advocate,* February 10, 1843, p. 58. Stephen Olin to William Wightman, March 8, 1843, Eugene R. Hendrix Letters, Duke University.

[57] See for example *Christian Advocate and Journal,* February 14, 1844, p. 105; also January 3, 1844, p. 83; December 27, 1843, p. 79. *Southern Christian Advocate,* December 9, 1842, p. 100; November 13, 1840, p. 86; January 8, 1841, p. 118; April 7, 1843, p. 144.

"like an ocean in the uproar and rage of the storm." The South preached the gospel; the North, "extraneous" subjects. Northerners were pictured as acting in such ways as to perpetuate Negro servitude, whereas Southerners were portrayed as selflessly "penetrating swamps, visiting the Negro's cabin, breasting and braving the pestilent malaria" to take care of the slaves.[58]

Missionaries to the slaves were theoretically supposed to fulfill the moral obligation which Southern Methodists admittedly had to the Negroes. Thus fortified with their moral tribunes, they were particularly incensed with the abolitionists' assumption that slavery was a moral evil and slaveholders sinners. They reiterated the old excuses for slavery: it was the means of preaching to the Negroes, it was necessary to keep good order in society, it was none of the Church's business.[59] And if Methodists were not yet able to adopt a "positive good" theory for slavery, they were at least prepared to deny that slavery was either a moral evil or sinful. That is, slaveholders were not only guiltless because society gave them no choice but to be slaveholders, they were also guiltless because a master-slave relationship was simply not immoral. Thus, when Thomas E. Bond began to define slavery as a moral evil, Southern Methodists were incensed. Local congregations in the deep South accused him of abolitionism and demanded his removal from office. It was bad enough to have discussed slavery, they said, but it was even worse to have called it a moral evil.[60]

Put upon by conservatives as well as by abolitionists,

[58] *Southern Christian Advocate,* March 8, 1844, p. 154. *Southwestern Christian Advocate,* May 10, 1844, p. 102.

[59] *Ibid.,* October 27, 1843, p. 78. William Winans to Daniel DeVinne, September, 1843, Winans Collection. *Southwestern Christian Advocate,* February 20, 1841, pp. 62–63.

[60] *Ibid.,* July 14, 1843, p. 199; also August 18, 1843, p. 39. Bond replied, "Should the Church of which we are an unworthy member ever cease to testify against slavery as a moral evil, as we have defined that term, we shall seek a more pure communion." *Christian Advocate and Journal,* August 30, 1843, p. 10.

Southern Methodists looked to their spokesmen to vindicate their position in a slaveholding society. The statements of Southern conferences before 1840 and the votes of Southern delegates to the General Conference since 1832 had already indicated that Southern Methodists joined with the members of other churches in denying themselves jurisdiction over slavery. It remained for William Wightman, however, to develop a theory of relations between Church and state. Methodists had not hitherto scrupulously adhered to a strict theory of separation between the secular and the spiritual worlds. They preached to state legislatures, became chaplains to Congress, petitioned that body concerning its superintendence of the Indian trade, and perennially memorialized state assemblies for temperance legislation.[61] Methodists were supposed to believe that the Church should help to effect good laws for a better society. Furthermore, those laws which allowed men to do less than their duty, or to be less than God willed were not excuses for un-Christian conduct. For example, the Georgia Conference in 1843 warned Methodists that although laws might allow latitude in a declaration of bankruptcy, they could not "cancel moral obligation." The ministers cautioned, "Remember that civil law is not the measure of moral right—that an obligation once assumed is perpetually binding, whether expressed in the technicalities of the law or otherwise."[62]

Slavery, however, was in a different category. William Capers had explained in 1838 that slavery, "where it may exist as an element of the constitution of the country, an institution guaranteed by the laws—is not a moral evil."[63] William Wightman went on from Capers' position to demon-

[61] Christian Advocate and Journal, November 25, 1826, p. 1. December 16, 1826, p. 1. Southern Christian Advocate, August 19, 1837, p. 34; June 7, 1839, p. 202; September 27, 1839, p. 58. William Warren Sweet, Circuit-Rider Days in. Indiana, p. 197. Western Christian Advocate, November 15, 1839, p. 117.
[62] Southern Christian Advocate, March 3, 1843, p. 148.
[63] Ibid., March 9, 1838, p. 150.

strate how Christians were obligated to support constitutional law. Quoting Edmund Burke that "Religion is the basis of civil society," Wightman wrote that Christianity established in its followers an inner motivation to obey the law for the sake of "social order, public peace, security, and happiness." From their establishment in America, Methodists had recognized this fact, Wightman pointed out, for they had exempted from the antislavery rules those states where laws had prescribed slavery as virtually perpetual. Simply put, "canon law" bowed "submissively as it ought to do, to civil law."[64] Slavery was so interwoven into society that the Church could do nothing more than to make the master-slave relationship palatable. To depart from this religious approach to social relationships and to adopt the heresies of "Fanny Wrightism, Agrarianism—Mormonism—Radico-Abolitionism, or any other of these fooleries" would be to invite chaos. Countering Dr. Bond, Wightman denied that Methodism was opposed to slavery in any way. If it were, it would consequently be opposed to the state and therefore in a revolutionary position impossible for Christians. Wightman went on to warn that Southern ministers who valued their missions to the slaves would leave the Church should the General Conference ever depart from his doctrine of noninterference with the "rights of Caesar."[65] Although Wightman spoke as one man, subsequent developments were to show that he was not alone in the construction of his ideas.

The arguments in Southern and Northern church journals were not merely academic. They guided and reflected the thinking of those men who would make the decisions for the Church at the next General Conference. By the middle of 1843, ministers most concerned with Methodist unity and

[64] *Ibid.*, January 8, 1841, p. 118; also November 20, 1840, pp. 90–91; November 27, 1840, p. 94; December 4, 1840, p. 98.
[65] *Ibid.*, April 28, 1843, p. 180; also March 21, 1843, p. 176; September 8, 1843, p. 50.

the slavery question were anticipating the great quadrennial assembly with much anxiety. Decisions would be made which might possibly affect the entire structure of Episcopal Methodism. Abolitionists who followed Scott out of the Church had by their action made conservative churchmen appreciate the power of antislavery sentiment in the North. And the conservatives' reaction had alienated the South, just as the Southerners by their proslavery apology had formerly alienated the Northern conservatives. The test of the power of antislavery attitudes and the alienation of the parties within the Church would come at the General Conference in May of 1844. Thus, for over a year preceding that meeting, Methodists reflected and passed resolutions upon what should be done there.

Almost every Northern annual conference petitioned the General Conference to take more decisive action against slavery. The New York Conference, which had a reputation for antiabolitionism, circulated a resolution to alter the wording of the General Rule pertaining to slavery in order to make it more clearly relevant to every slaveholder. The rule had previously forbade the "buying and selling" of Negroes. Southern Methodists had come to interpret this provision as being opposed not to the buying of one slave or the selling of another, but to the slave trade: "buying *and* selling." The New Yorkers suggested that the rule read "buying *or* selling." It was an inconsequential suggestion when compared with the abolitionist galaxy of moral demands, but it was symbolic of the conservatives' desire to do "something," even if almost nothing, against slavery. And that "something," by altering the status quo would certainly mean to some Southerners that they could no longer trust even the antiabolitionists of New York to support them. Conference after conference in the North concurred with the New Yorkers' suggestion. And those beyond Ohio made their first public declarations against the "moral evil" of slavery, demonstrating that the South would have fewer allies than

240

it had had when the General Conference passed the Few resolution.[66]

Conferences where the antislavery revival had been intense were more outspoken than to suggest a minor change in the General Rules. The Genesee and Black River conferences in western and central New York were quite overwrought by abolitionist secessions as well as slavery's influence in the Church and supported resolutions to enlarge the General Rules to exclude slaveholders wherever and whenever the laws should allow emancipation. Although the proposal was little different from the all but neglected Section on Slavery in the *Discipline*, it would have had the effect of reaffirming the right of the Church to legislate on such matters. It would aslo have affected slaveholders in the border states and the District of Columbia.[67]

Elsewhere the Pittsburgh Conference of western Pennsylvania and Virginia was so zealous to appear opposed to slavery that it sent to the General Conference a delegate whom it had censured the previous year for abolitionist activities. And both the Pittsburgh and the neighboring Erie Conferences petitioned the General Conference to apply itself more rigorously in the fight against slavery and to rescind the Few resolution.[68] New England Methodists were even more aroused on the "slavery question." They raised an impassioned outcry when they heard a rumor that Bishop Beverly Waugh had had the temerity to ordain a slaveholder.

[66] "Journals of the Genesee Conference," III, 122. Fradenburgh, *History of the Erie Conference*, II, 507. Sweet, *Circuit-Rider Days in Indiana*, p. 324. "Minutes of the Illinois Annual Conference of the Methodist Episcopal Church," typescript copy in Duke University Library, p. 293 (1843). *Southern Christian Advocate*, February 2, 1844, p. 135. *Western Christian Advocate*, September 29, 1843, pp. 94–95. *Signal of Liberty*, September 4, 1843, p. 2.

[67] *Liberator*, August 25, 1843, p. 133. *Zion's Herald and Wesleyan Journal*, July 26, 1843, p. 120. "Journals of the Genesee Conference," III, 96.

[68] *Pittsburgh Christian Advocate*, August 17, 1843, p. 118; February 14, 1844, p. 15.

Bishop Elijah Hedding thought the reaction a "striking instance of the impetuosity of the times," but *Zion's Herald* did little to calm its hypersensitive readers so long as they did not propose to leave the Church.[69] In this atmosphere the abolitionists who had not yet seceded were encouraged to petition the General Conference to guard the Methodist antislavery tradition. The Maine, New Hampshire and New England conferences asked the governing body of Methodism to rescind the Few resolution and to prevent slaveholders from being elected to high office in the Church.[70]

The question of slaveholders in high ecclesiastical positions was of no little significance. James O. Andrew had been elected to the episcopacy in 1832 because the most obvious candidate, William Capers, was a slaveholder. Four years later, William A. Smith of Virginia had shaken Northern conservatives by demanding a Southern General Conference if the "proscription" of slaveholders continued in the election of bishops. The issue, which had been avoided in 1840 was sure to arise once again in 1844 because of the need for more bishops. Knowing the necessity of an election, Methodists braced themselves for a fight.

While Northeastern church members were demanding that no slaveholder be made bishop, William Wightman was leading a chorus of Southerners in requesting just the opposite. He suggested that the next General Conference elect a slaveholding bishop to "place the South in her proper position and attitude as an integral part of the M.E. Church. The dodging or refusing such an election, endorses on the part

---

[69] *Zion's Herald and Wesleyan Journal,* April 19, 1843, p. 63; June 28, 1843, p. 102; July 26, 1843, p. 120; January 3, 1844, p. 4; January 10, 1844, p. 6 and every issue thereafter through March 6, 1844, p. 40. See also *Christian Advocate and Journal,* January 17, 1844, p. 90.

[70] Minutes of the Maine Annual Conference of the Methodist Episcopal Church, 1841–1845, July, 1843, p. 13, in New England Methodist Historical Society papers. *Zion's Herald and Wesleyan Journal,* July 19, 1843, p. 116; August 9, 1843, p. 126.

of the General Conference the calumnies of the abolitionists . . . . The Southern Conference can have no duty
more solemn and imperative," he went on, "than to press,
at this crisis, their positive, undeniable claim to be placed
on the *same footing* with other divisions of the connection
in all appointments to office."[71] The editors of the church
papers at Richmond and Nashville agreed with Wightman.[72]

William Capers, however, tried to calm his colleagues
by pointing out that ability, not "previous residence," should
bear upon the election of a bishop. God has given us no
"right" to a slaveholding bishop, said Capers; and he added,
"I must confess I should doubt the heart of the Southern
man who would be willing to go to the North in the office
of Bishop, he owning slaves."[73] The superintendent of the
Negro missions was wary of the extreme sectionalism in
the Church and hoped to prevent demands which might
lead to schism. Nevertheless, Capers could not keep Southern
Methodists from being dissatisfied. A delegate to the General
Conference from Mississippi pointed out that some of the
South's finest men, including Capers, had not been made
bishop because of their owning slaves.[74]

Long opposed to what Wightman proposed, Northerners
found solace only in Capers' words. The *Northern Christian
Advocate* of western New York called the demand for a
slaveholding bishop a "rapid stride towards ultraism and
revolution."[75] Capers' observations, however, were welcomed
by Abel Stevens who explained that Methodists could not
lend the Church's support to Negro servitude by electing
a slaveholding bishop. One of Stevens' correspondents observed that such action would be "ecclesiastical suicide.
A greater insult to Christianity or to Methodism could not

[71] *Southern Christian Advocate,* May 3, 1843, p. 184.
[72] *Ibid.,* July 7, 1843, p. 13; October 13, 1843, p. 70. See also
Southwestern Christian Advocate, June 9, 1843, p. 110.
[73] *Ibid.,* October 13, 1843, pp. 70–71.
[74] *Southwestern Christian Advocate,* December 1, 1843, p. 22.
[75] *Southern Christian Advocate,* October 13, 1843, p. 70.

be offered. Even if it were morally proper it would certainly be inexpedient."[76] Dr. Bond in the *Christian Advocate and Journal* disregarded the morality of the question in an attempt to reconcile the two parties which were developing. To Northerners he complained of a New England movement for a convention to counter the Southerners' demands. As he explained it, the South hoped only to preclude sectional questions in episcopal elections. To Southerners, Bond said that slaveholding was not necessarily a moral disqualification for the episcopacy; he pointed out, however, that, as Saint Paul had said, all things lawful were not therefore expedient. Slaveholding bishops could not be accepted by Methodists in all parts of the nation and therefore could not exert all the good influence they otherwise might. The "prejudices" of Northerners might be unreasonable, he explained, but they nevertheless existed and should be taken into account.[77]

Bond's stand was very much like that of the Baltimore Conference in its objection to a slaveholding ministry. Since that Conference covered areas of Pennsylvania, Maryland, and Virginia, it had always attempted to prevent its clergy from being connected with slavery. Stressing its "central position" between North and South, the conference held that a slaveholder could not have the same beneficial influence among nonslaveholders as a minister who was unencumbered with "servants." The Baltimore preachers "deemed of Vital importance to the interest of *Methodism,* that this conference firmly maintain the Integrity of its character for Constancy, and Consistency unimpaired; retaining, and preserving that fair Model of primitive Methodism transmitted to us by our Fathers to serve as a Beacon light, elevated far above the stormy elements of contention."[78] Since a bishop traveled and presided in both slave and free territory, Bond maintained that a bishop must be acceptable

---

[76] *Zion's Herald and Wesleyan Journal,* October 25, 1843, p. 170; November 15, 1843, p. 181.

[77] *Christian Advocate and Journal,* December 20, 1843, p. 74.

[78] Report of the Committee on Slavery, 1844, Baltimore Conference Papers.

to the whole Church for the same reason that a minister of the Baltimore Conference had to be acceptable in Pennsylvania as in Virginia. The situation in 1844, however, was such that some Methodists in the far South thought that the Baltimore Conference was tinged with abolitionism and that a slaveholding bishop was a necessity. Obversely, some Northern Methodists believed that the Baltimore Conference was proslavery and that any acceptance whatsoever of slaveholding was sinful.

Thus, in a state of tension, Methodists awaited May 1 when their General Conference would meet. Although Northern churchmen protested that all was well, they must have known that such was not the case.[79] Abolitionists were demanding that slaveholders be excluded from high church offices, and the schism of Orange Scott effectively punctuated their demands. The conservatives were arming themselves against further abolitionist secession to the point of exhibiting more antislavery sentiment than ever before. Southerners were being schooled by men such as William Wightman to resist Northern proscription of their section's morality. The issue which abolitionists, conservatives, and Southerners had all agreed would determine the ultimate position of the Church on slavery was whether or not to elect a slaveholder to the prestigious and powerful office of bishop. And then the question became moot—or at least some Southerners thought so—for it was discovered that Bishop James O. Andrew had become a slaveholder. The news spread throughout Methodism from Texas to New England. Speculation and sectional moral conflict were now focused on one Georgia preacher who had no desire to be a bishop in the first place.[80]

[79] *Zion's Herald and Wesleyan Journal,* May 1, 1844, p. 70. *Christian Advocate and Journal,* May 1, 1844, p. 150.

[80] William Winans to Charles K. Marshall, October 30, 1843; Winans to Henry Slicer, February 29, 1844, Winans Collection. John McClintock to his wife, March 31, 1844; McClintock to Robert Emory, April 4, 1844, McClintock Papers. B. M. Hall, *The Life of Rev. John Clarke,* New York, 1856, p. 226.

CHAPTER IX

CHOICE AND DISJUNCTION:
The General Conference of 1844

AMERICANS were thoroughly aroused about the nature and future of their Republic in the spring of 1844. The six-year depression was over and state governors were promising a new era of prosperity and economic integrity. Although the prospect of economic improvement was generally welcomed, other changes were not. Many people doubted if the Protestant character of the nation should be changed by an infusion of Irish Roman Catholic blood. Others doubted if the nature of the Republic should be altered by adding to it a great territory that would more firmly establish the power of slavery and therefore of the South. These doubts and misgivings about the future were increased by sectional and moral differences which were being magnified by the politics of the ensuing presidential election. If the Whig campaign of 1840 were any indication, the electioneering would raise passions to a revivalistic pitch.

The primary issue of 1844 was Texas and slavery. In September of 1843 political abolitionists met in the National Liberty Convention to renominate James G. Birney for president and to repudiate the power of the constitution to require immoral acts—such as the return of fugitive slaves. Abolitionists also continued their warning to the North that the power of slavery should not be increased by annexing the slaveholding Republic of Texas to the United States. Radical antislavery men found some unintended support in the other political parties. Before the major party conventions met in May of 1844, the front-running candidates for the Whig and Democratic nominations, Henry Clay and

Martin Van Buren, both disavowed any intention to annex the Lone Star Republic since to do so would involve the United States in war with Mexico. Not surprisingly, the temperatures of Southerners and annexationists rose several degrees; Southern leaders of the "Democracy" intrigued to deprive Van Buren of the nomination. In the spring of 1844, therefore, Americans could read *Niles' National Register* and either enjoy or suffer the travail of the Democratic party as well as speculate upon Martin Van Buren's political survival in the face of disapproval by the South and Andrew Jackson. They could reflect on how the issues devolving from slavery were beginning to weaken the political unity of the nation. And if they were interested in how much slavery had affected the churches as well as the politicians, those same readers could find on the last page of the *Register* references to the difficulties of the Methodist Episcopal Church.[1]

The difficulties of the church were not the result of transient issues any more than were those of the nation at large. The problem of slavery was entangled in the roots of American Wesleyanism just as in those of the Republic. And in 1844 the Methodist Episcopal Church acted out a drama which foreshadowed, although it did not predict, what would happen to the Union in 1861. The stage was the floor of the large, barn-like Green Street Chapel in New York, and the time was May 1844, a month of violence and intrigue. In Philadelphia some native-born Americans were rioting against Irish-born Roman Catholics; in New York City a great Whig meeting in "the Park" erupted into a riot due to the heat as well as politics. Political conventions met in Baltimore to nominate Whig and Democratic candidates for the presidency of the United States, and other conventions met in New York City to support

---

[1] See *Niles National Register,* March 30, 1844, p. 80; May 18, 1844, p. 192. Also September 16, 1843, p. 47; January 20, 1844, p. 324; May 4, 1844, pp. 46ff.; June 1, 1844, pp. 209ff. James C. N. Paul, *Rift in the Democracy,* Philadelphia, 1951, pp. 114f.

abolitionism, peace, Christian missions, education, temperance, and the Bible. Amidst all of this activity and tension, the delegates to the Methodist General Conference bowed their heads in a convocation prayer before they energetically attacked each other over the question of slavery.[2]

The conference which met on May 2 was a much different one from the assembly of four years earlier. The membership was about the same, except that Orange Scott now followed the proceedings from the visitors' gallery rather than from a delegate's seat. The change was in the delegates' minds. The Northern conservatives were fed up with concessions to the South, and the abolitionists were ready to follow the lead of their erstwhile nemeses in the fight against slavery's influence on Methodism.[3] Although the Southern delegates had not changed their goals, they were far more aggressive than at Baltimore a quadrennium earlier. Apparently encouraged by the demands of their politicians for extension of slavery and the admission of Texas, Southern Methodists were ready to fight against the proposed repeal of the Few resolution, the exclusion of slaveholders from high office, or any attempt to censure Bishop James O. Andrew for becoming a master. In fact, Southern delegates were prepared to resist any General Conference action which would in any way make the Methodist Episcopal Church appear to be even slightly concerned over the existence of slavery.

Yet when the meeting began, no delegate could have shut slavery out of his thoughts as he heard Bishop Joshua Soule slowly read the Episcopal address to the General Conference.

---

[2] See the *New York Herald,* May 3, 1844, p. 2; May 7, 1844, p. 1; May 8, 1844, p. 1; May 10, 1844, p. 1; May 11, 1844, Supplement, p. 1. Robert D. Clark, *The Life of Matthew Simpson,* New York, 1956, p. 118.

[3] James Porter, "General Conference of 1844," *Methodist Quarterly Review,* 53 (April, 1871), 242. Porter was one of the abolitionist leaders in the General Conference of 1844.

To a casual visitor the speech must have seemed exceedingly dry and perhaps a little too long. Undoubtedly even some of the delegates may have wondered why the meticulously careful Soule emphasized the power of the General Conference—but the bishops were concerned that the conference realize that the Church relied upon it for continued ecclesiastical unity and peace. Thus, in a "tremulous" voice, Soule read: "According to our ecclesiastical organization you are, under God, the constitutional body in which the conservative elements of the peace and unity of the Church repose; and consequently . . . all your acts should be the result of calm deliberation, and calm analysis, guided by enlarged and enlightened views, and accompanied with much prayer." Soule then explained that the office of bishop was executive; and that bishops were "amenable" to the General Conference for their conduct, doctrine, and administration. This point implied that the General Conference could call bishops to account for their conduct—but no one objected.

Soule droned on explaining that Methodist bishops belonged to the whole Church and therefore of necessity traveled throughout the United States. The itineracy was supposedly one of the peculiarities of Methodism which guarded against being seduced by local mores whether one was a bishop or an elder. But the bishops were led to complain of "localism" in habit and custom. Although Soule did not discuss the environmental effects of slavery upon the ministry, he and his fellows did deplore the existence of Negro servitude, adding that the Church had "no control" over it. Since Methodists could not leave Negroes helpless in their plight anymore than whites, the bishops proposed expanding the missions to the slaves. Lest the suggestion be misunderstood or misused by partisans for their various ends, the bishops cautioned no one to think that "a state of servitude is more favorable to the success of the Gospel . . . than a state of Freedom. Facts will clearly show that this is not the case."[4] With these cautious words of admonition, the bishops released the floor for the business of the conference.

That business was designed to be done in committees concerned with education, missions, temperance, and publications. But organization and careful planning could not prevent the Church's most urgent concern from coming to the floor; the conference managers had surprisingly not prepared for this. On the second day of the meeting the delegates heard a memorial from the Providence (Rhode Island) Conference denouncing the Few resolution and slavery. Nathan Bangs moved that the memorial be referred to a committee on slavery. Amidst much excitement William Capers opposed receiving such documents because they im-

---

[4] *Christian Advocate and Journal,* May 8, 1844, p. 154. The story told in this chapter is somewhat different from that sanctioned by official Methodist historiography, a thesis recently outlined in Emory Stevens Bucke, ed., *The History of American Methodism,* 3 vols., New York, 1964, I, 47–85, especially 83–85. The theory is that an old discussion about the nature of the episcopacy had divided the North and South and that at the General Conference of 1844 the South defended "the coordinate relationship between the General Conference and the general superintendency." That is, the South believed that the bishops and General Conference were equal in power and the former not officers of the latter. When Southerners lost constitutional arguments necessitated by Northern votes on Bishop Andrew's case, they had to leave the Church. The emphasis has been on the question of constitutionality rather than the problem of slavery. Although Southerners did not object to the sentiments expressed in the opening address to the General Conference of 1844, the latest Methodist history emphasizes Southern sensitivity to such constitutional issues as would have been raised when the bishops claimed to be "amenable" to the General Conference. It should be pointed out that prior to the General Conference of 1844 there were no widespread debates over episcopal powers; but there were heated discussions about a slaveholding bishop. And only after the question of Bishop Andrew's slaves came up did anyone raise the constitutional question of who could do what to whom and how. Slavery and slaveholders were much more important to Southerners than "constitutionality." The denial that slavery divided the Church is simply unsupported by evidence.

plied that Methodists were willing accomplices in evil. Furthermore, he believed that a committee on slavery would unnecessarily disrupt the deliberations of the conference. In the back of his mind, Capers was probably thinking of Bishop Andrew's new status of slaveholder which caused the North so much alarm. His efforts were useless, however, for he was defeated in his attempt to keep a discussion of slavery out of the deliberations.[5] Petitions against slavery and slaveholding officials poured in to be referred to the committee on slavery, a display of "antisouthern" feeling which antagonized the stout, excitable William A. Smith of Virginia. Having made Northerners nervous with threats of secession in 1836, he was not now hesitant in objecting to Northern attacks on slaveholding Christians.[6]

Smith's greatest effort, however, was in conducting the appeal to the General Conference of one Francis A. Harding. Harding was a minister of the Baltimore Conference which had a well-deserved reputation for preventing its preachers from being associated with slavery. Since the earliest Methodist antislavery rules had been written, the Baltimore Conference had consistently maintained its peculiar position between the North and South despite objections from pro-slavery men. In 1843, for example, the conference had withheld ordination from candidates who had some connection with slavery. The next year five men again were investigated and notified that their ordination would be deferred because the Baltimore Conference would "not countenance the connection of any of its members with slavery directly or indirectly." The statement was no surprise, but rather the expression of an accepted principle; all of the men obeyed the direction to divest themselves of their slaves without selling them or giving them away. A sixth man, however, would not yield. Having become "connected with slavery"

[5] *Ibid.* Also *New York Herald,* May 4, 1844, p. 2.
[6] *Ibid.* Also *Zion's Herald and Wesleyan Journal,* June 12, 1844, p. 98.

through marriage, Francis A. Harding was "deprived of ministerial character" until he agreed to emancipate his slaves. Harding then appealed to the General Conference.[7]

Smith's efforts on Harding's behalf were a mixture of casuistry, sophistry, and self-righteous indignation. He explained that the slaves which the Baltimore Conference had told Harding to emancipate were not his but his wife's. Smith maintained, however, that even if Harding could emancipate the Negroes, to do so would work a hardship upon them because they could not by law remain in Maryland. They would be torn from their families! He added innocently that Harding had promised the Baltimore Conference that he would send the Negroes to Liberia if he received their consent and his wife's permission, but the eager Virginian did not explain that that consent was never given. Smith then accused the Baltimore Conference of breaking the Methodist *Discipline.* The Section on Slavery required ministers to emancipate their slaves only when practicable and where the liberated persons could "enjoy their freedom." Furthermore, the General Conference of 1840 in the decision upon the Westmoreland case had found that slaveholding was no legal barrier to ordination. In opposing the Westmoreland decision and the *Discipline,* the Baltimore Conference was as bad as the abolitionists, Smith claimed. And then, after denying that Southern Methodists thought slavery a social good, he wandered through the heights and depths of what amounted to an apology for Negro servitude until he concluded by saying that ministers should not "meddle in politics."[8]

The next day, May 8, tough little John Collins of the Baltimore Conference took the floor to answer Smith. After dismissing the Virginian's remarks on slavery as uninformed

[7] Baltimore Conference Journals, III, 264, 266, 267, 273, 290 (1843). Baltimore Conference Papers for 1843 and 1844.

[8] *Christian Advocate and Journal,* May 15, 1844, pp. 157–159; also July 31, 1844, p. 203.

and not to the point, Collins emphasized that the issue was whether Harding or the Baltimore Conference would yield. The conference had found that Harding had refused to do anything that the law allowed him to do in manumitting the slaves in question. Furthermore, it made little difference whether the slaves were Harding's or his wife's—he was still their master. And after all, Collins pointed out, no pious woman would keep her slaves if by so doing she jeopardized her husband's ministry. Harding knew the historic position of the Baltimore Conference, and he knew that he would make himself ineligible for the traveling ministry if he married a slaveholder. The Baltimore Conference, Collins insisted, believed that the Church was more important than personal feelings: "No Methodist minister has the right to do just as he pleases." Admit one slaveholder to the ministry, Collins went on, and the Baltimore Conference could no longer assume the independent position which it had held for so long. He added that to allow Harding to continue his ministry as a slaveholder would strengthen the "localism" which the bishops had deplored in their address. Therefore, Collins promised that he and his colleagues would never retract their decision. "We cannot," he concluded, "sacrifice our ground to accommodate Mr. Harding or any other man who may choose to become a slaveholder."[9]

The discussion upon the Harding case greatly disturbed Southern Methodists almost to the point of threatening to disrupt the Church. For three days the delegates exchanged

---

[9] *Ibid.* Another more accessible report of the General Conference Debates is Robert Athow West's *Report of Debates in the General Conference of the Methodist Episcopal Church, Held in the City of New York, 1844,* New York, 1844. The present author, however, first went over the debates in the *Christian Advocate and Journal* which gives the scholar a sense of time and process as well as the editorial reactions to what was going on in the Conference. The *Advocate's* reports with those of the New York daily papers were the first to be read and from them Methodists throughout the country could partially relive the tragedy of their church.

verbal blows until finally on May 11, the General Conference voted 117 to 56 against reversing the decision of the Baltimore Conference. For the first time in the history of the Methodist Episcopal Church, Southerners had lost an important vote.[10]

William A. Smith was livid with rage as he took the floor to excoriate the conference amidst calls of "order, order!" Smith demanded that the delegates' decision be referred to the bishops but with such language that the presiding officer, Joshua Soule, reprimanded him for his "disrespectful" manner. Tempers were cooled, however, as Peter Cartwright of Illinois used his effective but slightly indecorous humor to make the delegates laugh at themselves. Soule then ended the meeting but not the hostility which had erupted during it. Reviewing the conference the following day, the reporter for the *New York Herald* cynically wrote: "This pious and exemplary body of sectarian preachers of 'peace and good will towards men' had a very exciting and edifying debate on yesterday," which, he concluded, would widen the breach between the North and the South.[11] Southern delegates agreed, for they believed themselves terribly abused. The *Richmond Christian Advocate* called the decision on the Harding appeal the first act of disunion and the *Southern Christian Advocate* described it as "disingenuous and injurious to the Southern church; and . . . in direct opposition to the laws of the land and

---

[10] *Ibid.* Also *Journal of the General Conference of the Methodist Episcopal Church,* New York, 1844, pp. 33–34. All of the Baltimore Conference voted with the North to uphold their own decision. The delegate from Texas and one delegate from Missouri voted with the North. The rest of the South voted in a bloc. Nine delegates from conferences half in the North and half in the South voted with the latter.

[11] *New York Herald,* May 12, 1844, p. 2. The *New York Tribune, New York Express,* and *Christian Register* of Boston also followed the proceedings. See *Christian Register,* June 1, 1844, p. 87; *Southern Christian Advocate,* May 24, 1844, p. 198. Also *Niles' Register,* May 18, 1844, p. 192.

the laws of the church—John A. Collins and the whole clique of Abolitionists to the contrary notwithstanding."[12]

So great was the convulsion resulting from the Harding case that William Capers feared for Methodist unity. He knew that the North would soon bring up the question of Bishop James O. Andrew's slaves and he wanted to forestall the division which such action would surely bring. Therefore, on Tuesday, May 14, the apostle to the slaves asked the General Conference to appoint a committee to pacify the Church. For several moments a pall of silence lay upon the conference, and then, amidst calls for unity from all sides, a committee was organized with three Southerners, two conservatives, and one abolitionist.[13] One of the most influential of the Southern delegates, Lovick Pierce of Georgia, explained to John Early, one of the members of the committee, what he considered to be acceptable to the South. The Section on Slavery in the *Discipline* should be changed as much as possible so that the Church could legislate only on the slave trade, the separation of families, and the treatment of slaves. Pierce warned Early against allowing the *Discipline* to continue to express hopes for the "extirpation of slavery." Such an expression would be dangerous, for "the abolitionists [would then be] engaged in the appropriate work of the Methodists. And we of the South must

[12] *Southern Christian Advocate,* May 31, 1844, pp. 202–203. *Christian Advocate and Journal,* May 29, 1844, p. 167 for reference to the *Richmond Christian Advocate.* Also Franklin N. Parker, ed., *A Diary-Letter Written from the Methodist General Conference of 1844 by the Rev. William Justice Parks,* Emory University Publications, Sources and Reprints, Series ii, p. 19. Thomas Stringfield to his wife, May 13, 1844 in Thomas Stringfield Papers, University of North Carolina.

[13] *Christian Advocate and Journal,* May 22, 1844, p. 161. The Southerners were William Capers, William Winans, and John Early. The conservatives were L. L. Hamline of Ohio, a colonizationist; Stephen Olin, President of Wesleyan University and a former member of the South Carolina Conference. The abolitionist was Phineas Crandall of the New England Conference. See also the *New York Herald,* May 15, 1844, p. 6.

recede. For in this work we cannot and do not participate."[14] During the discussions of the committee, however, the Southern delegates were primarily concerned with the predicament involving Bishop Andrew. They suggested limiting his jurisdiction to those places where his status as master would be acceptable, but such a proposal was clearly contrary to the ideal of the itinerant episcopacy. All the other problems separating the South and North seemed as insoluble as that concerning Andrew; the committee reported on May 18 that it could agree on no plan to reconcile the two parties.[15]

After the conference adjourned for the day, the Northern and Southern delegates met in separate caucuses in order to determine their strategy during the inevitable debate concerning Bishop Andrew. The issue had not yet been raised on the floor of the conference, but its introduction there was only a matter of time. Furthermore, with the Harding appeal having gone so badly for the South, there was little expectation that Bishop Andrew would fare any better. In principle the Harding and Andrew cases were similar. The bishop, however, was the perfect example of a man caught in a situation over which he had no control. It was quite true that he had become a slaveholder contrary to episcopal custom as well as the wishes of Northern Methodists, but he had had little choice in the matter. He had been bequeathed a young Negro girl whom he could have freed and sent either to Liberia or a free state. But the law forbade manumission within the state of Georgia where Andrew lived, and the girl preferred to remain with him. Sometime later, he received a Negro boy in the same manner as the girl although he expected to send the youth to the North

---

[14] Lovick Pierce to John Early, May 14, 1844, John Early Papers, Randolph-Macon College.

[15] *Christian Advocate and Journal*, May 22, 1844, p. 161; June 12, 1844, p. 173.

when he was old enough to go. Thus Andrew was a slave-holder twice over when he married his second wife. Because Mrs. Andrew owned slaves and because the bishop did not want to be their master, he secured them to her by a deed of trust.[16] But neither Andrew's reticence nor his legal arrangements could satisfy the abolitionists. William Lloyd Garrison called him a "man-thief" and New England Methodists demanded the episcopacy be purged of slavery.[17]

Andrew was both troubled and annoyed. Although he was a bishop and therefore belonged more to the Church than he did to himself, he considered the objections to his status as master "an inpertinent interference with [his] domestic arrangements." Thinking that much of the opposition to his owning slaves was self-righteous hypocrisy, he was nevertheless personally prepared to relieve the Church of its predicament by resigning.[18] Thomas E. Bond had reminded him that a slaveholding bishop would "tie the friends and defenders of the Church hand and foot, and put them into the hands of their bitterest enemies"—the abolitionists. Bond had therefore suggested that Andrew resign without any reference to slavery since it was generally known that he wanted to retire anyway.[19]

The more Andrew thought about his part in the whole affair, the more he was convinced that he should in fact resign; thus at the Southern caucus he announced that he

[16] *Ibid.,* May 29, 1844, p. 168.

[17] *Liberator,* June 14, 1844, p. 94. *Western Christian Advocate,* October 11, 1844, p. 101. Even moderates like John McClintock of Dickinson College desired the episcopacy to be purged, see his letter to Robert Emory, May 16, 1844, McClintock Papers. Also James Porter, "General Conference of 1844," *Methodist Quarterly Review,* LIII (April, 1871), 242.

[18] James O. Andrew to his daughter, May 14, 1844; Andrew to his wife, May 16, 1844 in Smith, *Life of Andrew,* pp. 355, 357.

[19] *Western Christian Advocate,* October 11, 1844, p. 101. *Christian Advocate and Journal,* June 19, 1844, p. 178. Smith, *Life of Andrew,* p. 343.

wanted to do so. The Southerners refused to allow it! They believed themselves "most rabidly pressed" by the Northerners and feared that Andrew's resignation would be a "fatal concession" to their importunate enemies. The Northerners were equally adamant in their determination to purge slavery from the office which represented the whole Church.[20] Andrew's personal feelings were irrelevant once the two sides had chosen to make him the symbol of the Church's relation to slavery. Long-suppressed emotions were about to be released with all the bitterness and recrimination that good men could express.

The battle over Bishop Andrew and slavery began with a few skirmishes on May 21. The conference asked the committee on episcopacy to ascertain the nature of Andrew's relation to slavery and the bishop thereupon wrote a letter explaining his situation. The North and South then called separate meetings, but before the conference could adjourn into its two parts, there was a sharp exchange resulting from Southern charges that the North intended to make the South secede. Thus forewarned of the impending conflict, on the following day Alfred Griffith of the Baltimore Conference launched the initial attack with a resolution requiring the Reverend James O. Andrew "to resign his office as one of the bishops of the Methodist Episcopal Church." The grounds were that having become a slaveholder contrary to the Church's policy, Andrew had placed himself in a position embarrassing in nonslaveholding sections of the nation. Furthermore, Andrew had been nominated as a nonslaveholding Southerner in 1832, and his "innovation" could not have come at a less propitious time considering the present agitation over slavery.[21]

With his resolution, Griffith had crossed the psychological barrier between convert and overt opposition. Nevertheless,

<hr/>

[20] Parker, ed., *Diary-Letter Written by William Justice Park,* pp. 15ff. Thomas Stringfield to his wife, May 22, 1844, Stringfield Papers.
[21] *New York Herald,* May 22, 1844, p. 1.

the Baltimore delegate tried to soften his blow by delimiting the discussion to the question of whether or not the General Conference could regulate its officers in their administration of ecclesiastical business as the episcopal address had implied. Griffith concluded that the conference could require a bishop to resign if he could no longer do his duty. Although Andrew's moral conduct was above reproach, he simply could not exercise his episcopal office in all parts of the Church. Therefore, as an administrative expedient the General Conference must ask him to resign.[22]

William Winans of Mississippi arose to answer Griffith and to take full advantage of the decision to allow unlimited debate. Furiously attacking Griffith's argument, Winans' harsh voice rose almost to a scream as he questioned the facts and lacerated the argument of the Baltimore delegate.[23] Although the Mississippian had long opposed the "proscription" of slaveholders in episcopal elections, he vehemently denied that it had been Methodist "usage" not to elect a slaveholder as bishop. The Methodists would have had such a superintendent in 1832 but for the "management and trickery" of the Baltimore Conference, he declared. He then went on to discount Griffith's explanation of the inexpediency of having a slaveholding bishop preside in the North for fear of driving that section from the Church. Winans promised that if the conference passed the proposed resolution, the South would be cut off. It seemed that the General Conference would have to choose between the morality of two expedients.[24]

The debate then developed into a long-winded wrangling between conservatives and Southerners about "expediency" and abolitionism. Of course, not all the speakers could be held to the points at issue because of the emotional tension

---

[22] *Christian Advocate and Journal,* May 29, 1844, p. 165. *Journal of the General Conference,* 1844, p. 64.
[23] *Zion's Herald and Wesleyan Journal,* May 29, 1844, p. 87.
[24] *Christian Advocate and Journal,* May 29, 1844, p. 166.

of the proceedings. But Southern arguments tended to take the "high moral ground" of depreciating the expediency urged upon the conference by the conservatives. Such expediency, Southerners agreed, was merely a cover for abolitionist principles. Those principles, foreshadowed as they were by early "intermeddling of the Methodist Church with the question of slavery," had hurt true religion by turning men's minds from salvation to questions of no more concern to the Church than the tariff. Southerners admitted that the antiabolitionists had fought abolitionism, but not out of sympathy for the slave or the South. Rather, the antiabolitionists, it was claimed, had acted entirely for the sake of the North, and proved their sectional prejudices by demanding Andrew's resignation. The Southerners quite inaccurately insisted that the question of a man's relation to slavery had never been raised before in the election of bishops. The conservatives on the other hand maintained that slaveholding had been a traditional disqualification for the episcopacy because the Methodist Episcopal Church had always opposed slavery and always would. The Northerners then stepped back from the implication that Andrew's status was therefore immoral and called it merely an unfortunate impediment. To try the impossible task of mending the breach between North and South and yet keep antislavery men within the Church, James B. Finley of Ohio offered a substitute resolution that Andrew "desist" from his duties so long as the "impediment" of his slaveholding remained. The fact that Andrew was not asked to resign did not, however, affect Southern arguments.[25]

Although the *New York Herald* observed that the General Conference had deliberated long enough for men whose "chief concern" was with heaven, the meeting had begun to enthrall the public. Throngs of strangers poured into the visitors' gallery to witness rather than read about an actual

[25] *Ibid.*, p. 167.

debate over slavery between Northerners and Southerners.[26] The discussion rambled over history and ethics with no apparent order, but as it continued, the positions hardened. The discussants, however, attempted to avoid the appearance of extremism. The Southern Methodists refrained from defending slavery as a positive good and the Northern conservatives constantly followed President Stephen Olin's lead in evaluating slaveholding. The head of Wesleyan University explained that to own a slave was not necessarily wrong in itself, it was simply unacceptable to Northerners. After such statements as this, the abolitionists would dissent on grounds of conscience, but usually they abstained from the debates as if by prearrangement.[27] Like the abolitionists, the Southerners seemed to be pushing the conservatives to come right out and say that Andrew was a bad man who had done a sinful thing. But the Northerners insisted that Andrew was indeed a justly admired, honorable, Christian gentleman caught in unfortunate circumstances which left the Church no choice but to ask him to do a painful but necessary thing. No one liked the predicament, the conservatives insisted, but Andrew was the only man who could do something about it.

The debate took on a fascination of its own, the South constantly talking of innocence, the North steadfastly refusing to speak of guilt. Southerners emphasized Andrew's purity and William A. Smith of Virginia even went so far as to deny that Andrew was a slaveholder in any "offensive" or "actual" sense because he had never intended to be one. He then accused the General Conference once again of being under abolitionist influence. If the Finley substitute passed, he went on, Southern Methodists would be "in a direct con-

[26] *New York Herald,* May 24, 1844, p. 2; May 25, 1844, p. 1.

[27] James Porter, an abolitionist leader, claimed that the conservatives had agreed to prosecute the case against the bishop if the abolitionists would only remain quiet. See Porter, "General Conference of 1844," *Methodist Quarterly Review,* LIII (April, 1871), 242.

nection with an abolition Church." The result would be to jeopardize work with the slaves and to cut Methodism off from the South. He concluded by implying that a cynical North was opposed to a virtuous South. George Pierce of Georgia, a close friend of Andrew's, agreed. The North was suspect not only for its emphasis upon expediency, but also for its disrespect for the law. As evidence, he alluded to the decision in the Harding case which had been based upon the "preposterous doctrine" of the Baltimore Conference that the "purposes and usages [of Methodism were] paramount to the law of the land." Finally John A. Collins of Baltimore could hold back no longer. "The Methodist Episcopal Church," he said emphatically, "never compromised her opinion on slavery—she was always opposed to it." Winans of Mississippi thereupon called the Baltimore Conference a Brutus to the South amidst much excitement and cries of objection.[28]

The debate reached such a state of intensity that it was almost impossible to conduct it at all—"a half dozen [men] rising and addressing the President at the same moment." The Southerners would yield neither to Northern pleas of expediency nor to appeals to the Methodist antislavery heritage. Because Andrew's case involved "the southern ministry at large," Southerners would not suffer any action on slavery which would suggest even the slightest influence of abolitionism.[29]

The abolitionists themselves usually remained aloof from the debates, a fact which conservatives hoped would make the Finley substitute more acceptable. Knowing the South's sensitivity to antislavery pressure, Northerners had tried to emphasize the practical aspects of the Andrew case rather than its moral character. Consequently they spoke of the power of the General Conference to control its officers and

[28] *New York Herald,* May 30, 1844, p. 1. *Christian Advocate and Journal,* June 19, 1844, p. 180.
[29] Thomas Stringfield to his wife, June 1, 1844, Stringfield Papers.

directed the debate into an exposition of differing conceptions of the Methodist constitution. Although the radical antislavery men had little interest in this aspect of the discussion, they nevertheless wielded a significant amount of power. They quite firmly believed that the primary issue of the Andrew case was whether or not the Methodist Episcopal Church would identify itself with the acceptance of disapproval of slavery. The abolitionists believed that if Andrew remained an effective bishop while he was a slaveholder, the Church would demonstrate that it no longer followed its *Discipline* in opposing slavery. Andrew therefore had to be removed from power. With this in mind the abolitionists willingly kept quiet except when the "expediency" arguments of the conservatives were excessively revolting to them.

The role of the radical antislavery minority was that of a conscience and of a potential threat to those who strayed from a minimal antislavery position. Abolitionists had shocked the North into a discussion over slavery, preaching their revival against discouraging odds. And although Northern conservatives had been alienated from Southerners because of the latters' proslavery statements, abolitionists were quite active in keeping that alienation alive. The Scottite secession had frightened churchmen who knew that New England was not yet completely satisfied with protestations that the Methodism was by its very nature opposed to slavery. The abolitionsts exercised power in the General Conference not in their words, which were few, but in their moral influence and their ability to disrupt the Church. Perhaps the abolitionists supplied the courage for the conservatives' innermost convictions, for the latter thought themselves more opposed than disposed to slavery.

The abolitionists' role was best exemplified in the circumstances surrounding the eleventh hour attempt of the bishops to conciliate North and South. On May 31, Bishops Waugh, Morris, Hedding, and Soule suggested that the conference

263

postpone a decision on Bishop Andrew's case until 1848 since during the next quadrennium the issues might be resolved without splitting the Church. Many Southerners seemed willing to follow their superintendents' suggestion, but New England would not postpone the inevitable. The abolitionists conferred with Bishop Hedding to tell him what their spokesman, James Porter, told the conference the following day—New England could not remain within the Church unless Finley's resolution were passed. On June 1, therefore, Hedding informed the conference that he receded from the hitherto unanimous declaration of the bishops, Nathan Bangs thereupon moved that it be tabled, and the assembly did so by the close vote of 95 to 83. The abolitionists' importunity and Hedding's influence probably provided the element of victory.[30]

The last hope for conciliation gone and the speakers exhausted, John A. Collins moved that the conference vote on Finley's substitute resolution. Immediately the delegates decided 110 to 69 that it was "the sense" of the General Conference that Bishop James O. Andrew "desist from the exercise of his office" so long as he remained "connected with slavery."[31] Although the wording was equivocal, the intent and result of the resolution were quite clear.

The South then began to find a way to secede from the Methodist Episcopal Church. William Capers hoped that a complete split would be avoided; he had been ordained

[30] Elliott, *The Great Secession*, columns 310–313. John Nelson Norwood, *The Schism in the Methodist Episcopal Church, 1844,* Alfred, New York, 1923, pp. 77–79.

[31] *Journal of the General Conference,* 1844, p. 84. The South voted as a bloc against the resolution with the one exception of John Clarke of Texas who had recently come to that conference from the North. Northerners joined their Southern brethren in some instances: 5 from Illinois; 3 from the Philadelphia conference (Pennsylvania, Delaware and Maryland); 2 from the New Jersey conference, and 1 each from the New York, Ohio, and Michigan conferences. The Baltimore Conference split its vote 5-5.

by Francis Asbury and deplored the idea of destroying what the venerable bishop had created. On June 3, therefore, he offered a series of six resolutions for the purpose of setting up two coequal general conferences with jurisdictions defined primarily by the extension of slavery. Capers suggested, however, that the Church be not completely divided. The Methodist Book Concern and the missionary enterprise should be under the joint control of North and South thus perpetuating a bond of unity between the two sections. The suggestions were referred to a committee under Capers' chairmanship, but his hopes for a thread of union were crushed. L. L. Hamline of Ohio argued effectively against the practicality of Capers' proposal and the committee finally reported to the conference on June 5 that it could not agree on the resolutions.[32]

Determined that disagreements should not dissuade them, the Southern delegates then announced that they intended to leave the Methodist Episcopal Church in any case. The witty and well-known Democratic politician, writer, and Methodist preacher, Augustus Baldwin Longstreet of Georgia, read the unanimous declaration of the Southern members of the conference that: "The continued agitation on the subject of slavery and abolition in a portion of the Church; the frequent action on that subject in the General Conference; and especially the extrajudicial proceedings against Bishop Andrew, which resulted, on Saturday last, in the virtual suspension of him from his office as superintendent, must produce a state of things in the south which renders a continuance of the jurisdiction of this General Conference over these conferences inconsistent with the success of the ministry in the slaveholding states." The conference referred the statement to a committee of nine men who were also ordered to attempt an amicable adjustment

[32] *Ibid.,* pp. 86–87, 103, Robert Paine to Nathan Bangs, January 31, 1846, Nathan Bangs Papers, Drew University.

of the difficulties over slavery. Should the attempt fail, and no one doubted that it would, the committee was to devise a "mutual and friendly division of the church."[33]

Before the committee reported, the South presented an apology for the path it would be forced to take. Henry Bidleman Bascom of Kentucky read a "long, elaborate, and argumentative" protest against the action of the General Conference in the case of Bishop Andrew.[34] Bascom, primary author of the document, called the acceptance of the Finley substitute "a violation of the fundamental law, usually known as the compromise law of the Church on the subject of slavery." The Kentuckian claimed that the slaveholding and nonslaveholding sections of the nation had always constituted two parties within the Church, but that in 1816 they had compromised their differences. Describing the compromise as if it were a treaty of confederation, Bascom said that the South had conceded the right to resist Northern interference. The North on the other hand had conceded that while the Church moved against slavery it would never exclude slaveholders from either the membership or the ministry wherever emancipation was illegal or impracticable or the emancipated slaves could not "enjoy their freedom." The North by condemning Andrew for being a slaveholder had broken the compact.[35]

Bacom's reference to a so-called "compromise law on slavery" was exactly what Northerners in all Christian charity said that it was—"as unfounded on fact as it [was] ingenious in its legal casuistry."[36] The early antislavery preachers in the Methodist Episcopal Church had been Southerners, and the decision to excommunicate slaveholders no longer and to do obeisance to the law was not a compromise between two constituent parties within the Church,

[33] *Ibid.*, pp. 109–111.
[34] *New York Herald,* June 8, 1844, p. 1.
[35] *Journal of the General Conference,* 1844, pp. 186–190.
[36] *Ibid.*, p. 203.

but between the Church and the "world." Nevertheless, Bascom went on to argue from the premise of his imaginary treaty. He also denied that expediency had any relation to the Andrew case; it was a matter of law alone. And the Methodist law said that a man could not be deprived of his orders if he could not manumit his slaves. Therefore, the General Conference action was an extrajudicial if not an illegal trial. Because bishops were not officers of the General Conference and did not have to answer to it, that body had exceeded its powers! Finally, Bascom accused the Church of assuming an improper role by attacking so essential "an element of society" as Negro slavery, an institution which had become a "household reality in the Methodist Episcopal Church in the United States."[37]

In reply to the protest of the minority, Northerners maintained that they were merely defending the Church's integrity against dangerous innovation. They pointed out that the so-called "compromise law" had never existed, a fact demonstrated by a study of history and the application of common sense. The issue between North and South was not over consistency with a nonexistent article of confederation, the conservatives claimed, but over whether or not the Church could legitimately allow Andrew to keep both his slaves and his office. The *Discipline* had always opposed slavery, the Northerners pointed out, although it had never specifically mentioned bishop's holding slaves because no one had ever dreamed that they would do so. Nevertheless, superintendents of the whole Church could hardly be allowed to contradict the spirit of the *Discipline* by binding themselves to the social morality of the South. By defending Andrew's innovation, Southerners had localized the episcopacy and compromised the essential character of Methodism. The General Conference could not allow it! Therefore, consistent with statements in the episcopal address of May 2, the highest judicatory in Methodism had

[37] *Ibid.*, pp. 191–197.

brought Andrew to account. The Northerners concluded that the responsibility for the then inevitable division of the Church lay with the South for trying to change Methodism and then seceding when it could not have its way.[38]

Emotionally torn and on the verge of disintegration, the General Conference limped to a close discussing slavery and separation. The committee on slavery, apparently deriving courage from the debate on the Andrew and Harding cases, asked the General Conference to rescind the Few resolution on Negro testimony and the assembly complied by a vote of 115 to 40. The conference also elected two Northerners to the episcopacy and attended to such matters as affected Bishop Andrew's status. The delegates decided to keep his name on official church publications, to continue his salary, and to allow him to decide what work he should do, if any. Finally, the committee of nine under the chairmanship of Robert Paine of Alabama reported a plan for the separation of the Methodist Episcopal Church into two parts. The committee suggested that all of the societies and conferences whose majorities wished to join the South might do so without fear of retaliation and that once the size of the two jurisdictions was determined, church property would be divided equitably between them. The plan also outlined several procedural matters which would take effect when three-fourths of the members of the annual conferences concurred in supporting the division of property. After the delegates adopted the proposal by an overwhelming vote on June 10, they adjourned. The North and South would not meet in general conference again for almost a century.[39]

Although the rent in the fabric of American Methodism was yet to be institutionalized, the damage to national unity was irreparable; the separation of the North and the South, inevitable. And although the parties involved in the recent

[38] *Ibid.*, pp. 199–210.
[39] *New York Herald*, June 8, 1844, p. 1. *Journal of the General Conference,* 1844, pp. 117–118, 135–137.

discussions reacted differently to their handiwork once they returned home, the essential differences revealed in the debates of the conference remained. When reflecting on the proceedings of the assembly, non-Methodists would be less interested in the ecclesiastical results than in the political and social implications, for the latter could escape no one. The Methodist Episcopal Church had divided over the question whether or not slavery could be accepted as an American rather than merely a Southern "household reality," as Bascom of Kentucky had called it. A vast majority of both abolitionists and Southerners agreed that the schism was preferable to continued association with sin (as the abolitionists saw it) or "unbridled fanaticism" (as Southerners understood it). Although many Northern ministers were less convinced of the virtue of the plan of separation then had been their representatives at the General Conference, they nevertheless approved the decision concerning Bishop Andrew and its implications. Northerners resented the attempt on the part of Southern Methodists to make Methodism accept slavery as a Methodist institution just as Southerners resented what they inferred was a hypocritical condemnation of their morality and way of life. But the abolitionists, as could be expected, were generally pleased with the action of the General Conference of 1844.

That is, abolitionists believed that the action of the Methodist General Conference was a step in the right direction. Orange Scott, the antislavery evangelist responsible for the rise of Methodist abolitionism, was not wildly enthusiastic about the conservatives' morality because they had acted for expedient rather than ethical reasons. To have been consistent in their conduct towards Andrew, he charged, the conference "should have made a law expressly against slavery." He wondered if Bishop Andrew had actually done "a hundredth part as much to sustain [Slavery] as Bishop Hedding? Nay, verily!" But Scott did not bewail the division; he rejoiced in it. "A division of the ME Church

269

will hasten the abolition of slavery in our country, it cannot be otherwise," he wrote. "Withdraw all Northern support from the abominable system of man stealing, and the traffic in human souls will soon wind up." Scott believed that the Methodist division presaged that of other churches and perhaps even of the nation. He went so far as to praise the day "when the ungodly national compact [should] be broken up! Slavery never could have flourished in this land . . . but for the connivance and support of the North."[40]

Other abolitionists shared Scott's outlook. They believed that although the Northerners had not been altogether honest in resting their case against Andrew on pragmatic ground, they had in their actions revealed the power of abolitonism. Northern antiabolitionists were obviously attending to the words and yielding to the influence of those whom they had previously mobbed—and it was rather satisfying to the abolitionists to watch the discomfort of their erstwhile antagonists. Wrote the *National Anti-Slavery Standard:* "We may rejoice, then, with great gladness that this Church is shaken to her very foundations . . . because like her giant sisters, whose shadows cover the land, and shut out the sunlight of Truth, she has been faithless to the great principles taught by him whom she declares her 'cornerstone.' " Other abolitionists were more kind, but none more pleased than the Garrisonian *Standard*.[41]

Methodist abolitionists also welcomed the decisions of the General Conference. The annual conferences which had been most influenced by the antislavery revival, especially the four in New England, supported by large majorities both the judgment concerning Bishop Andrew and the adop-

---

[40] *True Wesleyan*, June 15, 1844, p. 94; August 3, 1844, p. 123.
[41] *National Anti-Slavery Standard*, June 20, 1844, p. 10. *True Wesleyan*, June 29, 1844, p. 102. *Emancipator and Weekly Chronicle*, June 5, 1844, p. 23. *Cincinnati Weekly Herald and Philanthropist*, July 3, 1844, p. 1. *Philanthropist*, June 5, 1844, p. 1. *Liberator*, August 9, 1844, p. 126; August 30, 1844, p. 138.

tion of the plan of separation.[42] Rare as it had been for eight years, abolitionist satisfaction with the actions of the General Conference was comforting to such a churchman as L. L. Hamline, a newly elected bishop, a colonizationist, and a leading proponent of dividing the Church. He wrote to James B. Finley, author of the resolution suspending Andrew: "Where all was Strife and bitterness and 'war to the knife' but a little while ago, not a leaf stirs. Abolitionists are as calm and loving to their brethren as can be conceived, & say that if the Ch[urch] maintains its ground, they have done with [agitation] forever." Hamline added with equal pleasure that western New York as well as New England seemed to be saved from the "Scottite" secession.[43] Although the Methodist Episcopal Church still included slaveholders in the southernmost portions of its communion, the probability of internecine strife among Northern Methodists had diminished because the General Conference had taken what could have been interpreted as an antislavery position.

Although the Church had not been converted to abolitionist ideals, it most certainly had been rudely shocked into viewing more honestly what the radical antislavery men had said was the character of Southern Methodism. Alienation and disruption clarified positions and made opposition simple: the South was now the enemy because it had decided to repudiate the Methodist heritage. The result was that whereas conferences which had been most greatly influenced by abolitionism willingly adopted the plan of separation to get rid of slaveholding Methodism, former antiaboli-

---

[42] *Minutes of the New Hampshire Annual Conference of the Methodist Episcopal Church for the year 1844–45,* Claremont, N. H., 1845, pp. 11, 13. *Minutes of the Providence Annual Conference of the Methodist Episcopal Church, June 4, 1845,* Providence, 1845, p. 15. *Zion's Herald and Wesleyan Journal,* September 4, 1844, pp. 141, 142.
[43] L. L. Hamline to James B. Finley, September 14, 1844, James B. Finley Papers, Ohio Wesleyan University.

tionist conferences refused. They applauded the vote on Bishop Andrew's predicament, but they were less enthusiastic about dividing the Church—in fact, they refused to sanction it.

With the Ohio Conference many Westerners voted against voluntary division in the hope that Methodist union would be maintained. But this gesture was not necessarily one of brotherly love. If the South refused to remain with a church whose heritage was opposed to slavery, let it secede, but Westerners would not be a party to it! They and other Methodists called the plan of separation unconstitutional, and as they discussed whether or not the General Conference could arrange for a division, their antagonism against the South increased. When the final vote on separation was tabulated, 2,135 ministers favored division and 1,070 opposed it. Obviously the three-fourths majority necessary for constitutional separation was lacking. Almost all of the opposition, or 1,067 votes, came from Northerners of whom only 1,164 favored a peaceful schism. The Northern General Conference of 1848 thereafter repudiated the plan of separation, forcing the South to go to the civil courts in order to receive its equitable share of Methodist property.[44]

The bad feeling between the North and the South was intensified by Thomas E. Bond, the editor of the influential *Christian Advocate and Journal.* Although Nathan Bangs attempted to soothe injured feelings and effect as friendly a division as was possible, Bond used his pen as a "spear" in what he considered a just war against the South and Bishop Andrew.[45] Bond admitted the South's contention that compromise had characterized the history of the Church

[44] *Christian Advocate and Journal,* August 7, 1844, p. 207. *Western Christian Advocate,* August 16, 1844, p. 70; September 6, 1844, p. 83; September 20, 1844, p. 90; October 4, 1844, p. 99; November 1, 1844, p. 115. Norwood, *Schism in the Methodist Church,* pp. 103–104, 117–125, 141ff.

[45] Robert Paine to Nathan Bangs, January 31, 1846, Bangs Papers. *Western Christian Advocate,* October 11, 1844, p. 101.

and slavery, but he emphasized that the compromise had been between the Church and stern necessity rather than two ecclesiastical parties. True Methodists had always been opposed to slavery, the editor insisted, and the Southerners had departed from their heritage. Furthermore, they had been aided in their heresy, Bond charged, by Bishop Andrew who should have resigned rather than engulf Methodism in controversy.[46] For this and more personal attacks upon the Southern martyr, Bond was bitterly assailed by William Wightman of the *Southern Christian Advocate*. The Southerner accused the Northern editor of pushing the fight against the South for political as well as for ecclesiastical reasons, and added: "Dr. Bond is the most glorious example on record, or in the memory of living man, of enormous, immovable, happy self-conceit."[47]

Although other Methodist leaders knew that Bond's attitude was not calculated to quiet the South, they also knew that they could not do the one thing would have pacified the secessionists: repudiate the Methodist antislavery heritage. Even Charles Elliott of the *Western Christian Advocate* emphasized the essential antislavery character of Methodist Christianity as he attemped to keep Kentucky and Missouri Methodists within the fold. He pointed out that the conferences in those two states had always opposed a slaveholding ministry in strict adherence to highest Methodist principle. The Irish publicist of Western Methodism constantly emphasized that Methodists were simply unable to condone slavery due to their ethics and history.[48]

[46] *Christian Advocate and Journal,* June 19, 1844, p. 178; June 26, 1844, p. 182. *Western Christian Advocate,* October 11, 1844, p. 101.

[47] *Southern Christian Advocate,* June 28, 1844, p. 10; July 12, 1844, p. 18; July 19, 1844, p. 22; August 9, 1844, p. 34; August 23, 1844, p. 42.

[48] *Western Christian Advocate,* July 12, 1844, p. 51; September 6, 1844, pp. 82–83; September 13, 1844, p. 86; October 4, 1844, p. 98; October 11, 1844, p. 102; November 22, 1844, p. 126.

In this tack Elliott was joined by George Peck, a New York colonizationist who printed a widely circulated pamphlet defending the Northern position at the late General Conference. The conservatives were shedding the appeal to expediency which had shrouded their arguments in the New York assembly. Time, distance, and the decision to divide the Church freed them to rest their case upon principle: slavery was wrong. Wrote Peck: "The civilized world has signed and sealed the doom of slavery. It is a remnant of barbarism which cannot bear the light of the nineteenth century. And is this any time for the ME Church to give it her sanction?" Peck thought not; he thought that to have allowed a slaveholding bishop would have fixed the "odium" of slavery upon the Church. "We might endure any amount of persecution 'for righteousness sake,'" he pointed out, "but to be buffeted for our faults is not so comfortable."[49]

Southern Methodists denied that there was anything righteous about "intermeddling" in the relationship between master and slave. Consequently they resented the decision of the General Conference on Bishop Andrew and were generally agreed on the necessity to separate the slaveholding from the nonslaveholding sections of the Church. Southerners were not yet prepared to contradict Northern protestations of the essential antislavery character of Methodism by saying that slavery was a blessing, but they did emphasize that the Church did not discuss Negro servitude. William Capers, distraught as he was with the division and the increasing animosity between North and South, explained to conservatives that since they had acted in concert with abolitionists to suspend Andrew, they had in fact become an abolitionist Church. Southern Methodists could allow no derogation of slavery or slaveholding whatsoever.[50]

Capers' position was developed further by Augustus

[49] George Peck, *Slavery and the Episcopacy*, New York, 1845, p. 111.
[50] *Christian Advocate and Journal*, July 10, 1844, p. 190.

274

Baldwin Longstreet who wrote a pamphlet defending the relation of master and slave as too "sacred" to be interfered with—Saint Paul had implied as much in his epistle to Philemon. And Henry Bidleman Bascom in his brilliant if erratic *Methodism and Slavery* assured Southerners that Methodists could never be opposed to civil authority in any way.[51] In fact, most Southern Methodist assertions on slaveholding continued to be couched, as they had been since the Denmark Vesey conspiracy, in the form of assurances. Churchmen assured Southern politicians that Methodists accepted slavery; they assured Methodist masters that the laws allowed them no choice but to be slaveholders; they assured each other that the missions to the slaves were the proper "reform" of the Church in a slave society; they assured the nonslaveholder that slavery was a fact of life which no one could or should do anything about. The primary assurance of Methodist social orthodoxy, Southern churchmen could explain, was the separation from the North; it was an act, said one South Carolina minister, which proved that Methodists were as "entitled to the public confidence as the ministers of any other church."[52]

There were a handful of Southerners who were not quite so pleased with separation. The Baltimore Conference urged the calling of a special General Conference in 1846 to settle the differences between the North and South, but the last General Conference should have revealed the futility of calling another. The Holston, Missouri, and Kentucky conferences did not join their Baltimore brethren, but they did urge that conciliation rather than division should be the goal of Southern Methodists. In the event of schism, the Kentucky Conference and the Holston ministers of the Southern Appalachian highlands appealed to the South to

[51] Henry B. Bascom, *Methodism and Slavery*, pp. 6ff., 66ff., 75, 123. Augustus Baldwin Longstreet, *Letters on the Epistle of Paul to Philemon*, Charleston, 1845, *passim*.
[52] Whitefoord Smith, Manuscript Speech, Whitefoord Smith Manuscripts.

make no changes in the *Discipline* concerning slavery.[53] Nevertheless, the three conferences supported Bishop Andrew and disavowed the action of the General Conference, for even those ministers who were least pressed to take what could be called a proslavery position could not refuse to defend the piety of a slaveholding Christian. Such an attitude did not prevent some dissenters in Kentucky, Tennessee, and Maryland from talking of a compromise in which the South would agree to preclude slaveholders from the episcopacy if the North guaranteed to do the same with abolitionists.[54] But the hope for a compromise was futile because the proponents of conciliation were too few.

Most Southern Methodists were ready to leave a church ruled by Northern and "abolitionist" principles. Immediately after the General Conference of 1844, the Southern delegates had called upon their annual conferences to send representatives to Louisville, Kentucky, in May 1845 to contemplate appropriate action. Except for the three conciliatory conferences, all Southern ministers demanded separation because of the "dangerous precedent" set in the "illegal" decisions of the Andrew and Harding cases. In the balloting upon the plan of separation, only three preachers in the entire South registered any opposition, and the opinion of laymen was apparently almost as solid.[55]

[53] Resolutions of the Baltimore Conference of 1845, Baltimore Conference Papers for 1845. Resolution of the Holston Conference supporting the Action taken on Separation, Aiken [Ekin] Papers. "Holston Conference Minutes," II, 116. North Carolina Conference Journals, pp. 648–651, Methodist Episcopal Church Papers. *Minutes of the South Carolina Conference of the Methodist Episcopal Church for the year ending December 1844*, Charleston, 1845, pp. 18, 22, 23. *Western Christian Advocate,* October 11, 1844, p. 102; November 1, 1844, pp. 115, 116; November 15, 1844, p. 121; November 22, 1844, p. 125.

[54] George Ekin [Aiken] to George C. Naff, December 5, 1844, Aiken [Ekin] Papers. Also *Western Christian Advocate,* November 15, 1844, p. 123. *Christian Advocate and Journal,* August 8, 1844, p. 206.

[55] Norwood, *Schism in the Methodist Church,* pp. 102–125, espe-

Reports from over 70 churches in widely scattered parts of the South revealed a deep antagonism towards the North and a relieved satisfaction with division. Informed by ministers who had talked over the actions of the General Conference with the delegates, Southern Methodists were also influenced by growing resentment in their section against Northern opposition to acquiring Texas. Consequently, the Methodist laity's statements were violently anti-Northern, attributing to the majority in the General Conference such characteristics as an "unprincipled" desire for "political power," "fanaticism and ignorance," and a "reckless disregard for the rights of the slaveholding portion of the Church." A very small minority claimed that the action of the New York meeting would do grave harm to the Mission to the Slaves, and a few people anathematized everyone who voted against Bishop Andrew. Almost unanimously, however, Southern Methodists praised Andrew's conduct and eulogized him as a wonderful Christian gentleman who had been terribly abused by an unfeeling, cynical majority. The general consensus was that an abolitionized North had tyrannized over an innocent South for its connection with a civil institution which no one save "fanatics" could call a moral evil.[56]

---

cially pp. 117–120. Elliott, *The Great Secession,* columns 417ff. *History of the Organization of the Methodist Episcopal Church, South,* Nashville, 1925, pp. 155–220.

[56] *Western Christian Advocate,* August 9, 1844, p. 66; August 16, 1844, p. 70; August 23, p. 74; August 30, 1844, p. 78; September 6, 1844, p. 81; September 13, 1844, pp. 86–87; September 20, 1844, p. 89. *Christian Advocate and Journal,* June 26, 1844, p. 183; July 31, 1844; p. 203; August 7, 1844, p. 207; October 17, 1844, p. 195. *Southern Christian Advocate,* June 28, 1844, p. 11; July 5, 1844, pp. 14–15; July 12, 1844, p. 19; July 19, 1844, p. 23; July 26, 1844, pp. 25, 26, 27; August 2, 1844, pp. 29, 30, 31; August 16, 1844, p. 37. *Southern Watchtower* (Athens, Georgia), July 18, 1844, p. 1; August 8, 1844, p. 3. T. M. Hudson to Joseph Doub, December 7, 1844, William C. Doub Papers. Minutes of the Salisbury District of the North Carolina Conference,

The secessionist vanguard was led by the editors of Southern denominational newspapers who, some Southerners admitted, greatly increased the antagonism between South and North.[57] William Wightman of the *Southern Christian Advocate* was particularly vitriolic and unbending in attacking the North and repudiating compromise. He insisted that the South would always demand that the Church "GIVE UP ALL ANTI-SLAVERY ACTION WHATEVER." Such a demand Wightman believed to be ultimately just; he pointed out that the Church had flourished in a slaveholding country, intimating that if slavery were really a moral evil as the North had said it was, God would not have allowed such success.[58] The North had endangered the prosperity of the Southern Church, Wightman insisted, and he followed an editorial policy derived from the assumption that a separation was inevitable and necessary. "The North may relent," he wrote, "but no repentence can avail now. Tears of blood cannot wash away the record of the proceedings of the late conference."[59]

John McFerrin of the *Southwestern Christian Advocate*

October 7, 1844, Peter Doub Papers, Emory University. Quarterly Conference resolutions from Lenoir, Montgomery, Pleasant Grove, Chesterfield, Hind, and Cumberland circuits of the South Carolina Conference in South Carolina Conference Papers. C. D. Smith to Captain Thomas Penn, August 6, 1844, Green W. Penn Papers, Duke University. Memorials to the Baltimore Conference, Baltimore Conference Papers for 1845 and 1846.

[57] See Robert Paine to Nathan Bangs, January 31, 1846, Bangs Papers.

[58] *Southern Christian Advocate,* July 26, 1844, p. 26; also August 16, 1844, p. 38. Wightman's antagonistic and insolent attitude was quite unlike that of old Lewis Myers who had been involved in the earliest antislavery work of the South Carolina conference. He wrote to Wightman, July 22, 1844, "I tell you, my dear Brother, there is more *humility,* and *self-abasement* necessary among the *whole of us*—Yes.—a selfsinking into Christ—and a feeling, that he is *ALL* in *ALL.* Then might we rise into God in ONE body, undivided and undividing—Conquering Slavery and the World without shedding one drop of Blood." Papers of Methodist Leaders, Emory University.

[59] *Ibid.,* June 28, 1844, p. 10.

agreed with the Charleston editor and printed a series of articles to vindicate the South's position at the General Conference.[60] McFerrin pretended to be disappointed with the impossibility of compromise, but he was actually doing his best to insure separation. He cautioned Wightman against alienating the Kentucky Conference by criticizing its mildness towards the North, and observed that William Capers would probably have to retract some of his conciliatory statements. He suggested that he and Wightman discourage the Louisville convention from changing the *Discipline* lest the world not realize that Southern Methodism was the "true Methodist Epis[copal] Church." He added, "We must be firm but prudent."[61]

The goal of the ardent secessionist arguments and manipulations was achieved in May 1845 at Louisville, Kentucky, where Southerners began the process of organizing the Methodist Episcopal Church, South. Delegates from 15 conferences heard Bishop Joshua Soule's assurances of the unanimous support which Southern Methodists gave to the convention. Then, after perfunctorily sweeping aside conciliation with the North, the delegates spent over ten days voicing their approval of William A. Smith's resolution to reject the ecclesiastical jurisdiction of the General Conference because of its action on slavery. The convention named committees to provide for the publications, finances, education, and missions of the new sect. Finally, on May 17, the delegates voted 94 to 3 to dissolve the South's connection with the North and named Joshua Soule and James O. Andrew as the superintendents.[62] The Methodist Episcopal Church was no longer a national institution.

[60] *Southwestern Christian Advocate,* July 19, 1844, p. 133.

[61] J. B. McFerrin to William Wightman, September 19, 1844, Eugene R. Hendrix Papers. *Southwestern Christian Advocate,* August 9, 1844, p. 154.

[62] *History of the Organization of the Methodist Episcopal Church, South,* pp. 252, 262. The conferences: Kentucky, Missouri, Holston, Tennessee, North Carolina, Memphis, Arkansas, Virginia, Mississippi, Texas, Alabama, Georgia, South Carolina, Florida, Indian Mission.

The disjunction of American Methodism exemplified the crisis of which it was a part. That crisis, whether the result of too much democracy, sectional imperialism, or economic disparity, involved the acceptance or rejection of slavery as an American institution. The test case for many Americans in 1844 was the problem of whether or not to annex Texas to the United States. To do so would have strengthened slavery by increasing its power in the federal government; not to do so would deprive Americans of their destiny. The power and preservation of slavery was no academic moral issue for many Southerners, especially those who relied upon John C. Calhoun for guidance. In April 1844, John Tyler's Secretary of State had written to the British Foreign Office explaining that American policy demanded the preservation of slavery in Texas. Calhoun's letter was published to good advantage by Northern antislavery and anti-Southern men who for various reasons refused to have their nationalism identified with the South's peculiar institution.[63] Abolitionists had for years been descrying the basic inconsistency between slavery and professed American ideals; now others less dedicated to the Negroes' rights were beginning to see the demands of Southerners as impudent aggressions upon American democracy. American policy demand the preservation of slavery? Many Northerners thought not—nor the extension of slavery either!

The same kind of relationship between North and South was revealed in the two largest Protestant churches in the United States. The Andrew case, for example, was not only peculiar to the Methodist Episcopal Church, but also indicative of general Southern demands that slavery be accepted as a national institution. While politicians demanded political sanction to make slavery an "American" institution, Southern Methodists ministers demanded moral sanction to define slavery a "household reality in the Methodist Episco-

[63] Charles Wiltse, *John C. Calhoun, Sectionalist, 1840–1850*, New York, 1951, pp. 163–171.

pal Church in the United States." If Andrew were allowed to keep both his slaves and his office he would have been the personification of the fact that slavery was now accepted by Methodists throughout the nation regardless of their circumstances.

The situation was exactly the same among the Baptist churches. After 1840, Southern Baptists were becoming increasingly restive because of the abolitionism of many of their Northern coreligionists. Southerners complained that Northern Baptists did not accept them on the basis of "entire social equality." Therefore, in November 1844 the Alabama Baptist state convention demanded that the Board of Managers of the Baptist General Convention explicitly avow that slaveholders were as eligible to become missionaries as were nonslaveholders. The Southerners as much as dared the conservative antiabolitionists of the Board of Managers to come right out and condemn slavery—and they did. The Baptist officials were taken aback by the Southerners' aggressiveness, but explained unequivocally that they could "never be a party to any arrangement which would imply approbation of slavery." Because Northerners would not affirm Negro servitude as an amoral fact of life acceptable to all Baptists, dissidents formed the Southern Baptist Convention in 1845.[64] Slavery was simply demanding more than some Americans were willing to concede.

The results and implications of ecclesiastical schism were of course not altogether clear to contemporaries. John C. Calhoun invited a few Southern Methodist ministers to discuss the division of their church, and Henry Clay feared that the schism was "fraught with imminent danger" for the Union should it be combined with other unstabilizing

[64] Alabama Baptist State Convention to Daniel Sharp, president of the Board of Managers of the Baptist General Convention, November 25, 1844 and the reply of December 17, 1844 in *Baptist Missionary Magazine*, August, 1845, pp. 220–222; also Putnam, *Baptists and Slavery*, pp. 21ff.

events.[65] Clay's apprehension was not shared by Governor James Hammond of South Carolina, however, who hailed the secession of the "patriotic Methodists of the South" as earning for them the "lasting honor and gratitude" of their fellows.[66] The Charleston *Mercury* was more reflective, calling the action of the General Conference the "most ominous event of our times," and adding: "If the clergy whose business is peace and good will cannot tolerate each other of the same sect, what will become of the politicians whose vocation is strife and dissention?"[67]

The rhetorical question was answered much later with the Civil War that resolved the issues so intensely debated in 1844. The division of the Methodist Episcopal Church, however, neither portended that war nor "snapped" a bond of union: it merely became one of many events which contributed to increased sectional antagonism. After the General Conference of 1844 over one and one-half million Americans (and with the Baptists, perhaps three million) had a more definite, personal reason to dislike their compatriots and coreligionists in the other section of the nation. An antislavery/proslavery dichotomy between North and South could be more easily alluded to and emphasized; more people would believe it and fewer people would make distinctions. Both the North and the South now had a church to emphasize the morality of their section, the righteousness of their cause. The churches lacked the institutional power and independence of popular morality to have acted as bonds of union, but they did have enough influence and identification with their people to provide poles of discord once their own national identity had been shattered.

[65] John C. Calhoun to Whitefoord Smith, June 4, 1844, Whitefoord Smith Manuscripts. Henry Clay to W. A. Booth, April 4, 1845 in Calvin Colton, ed., *The Private Correspondence of Henry Clay*, New York, 1856, p. 525.

[66] *Western Christian Advocate*, January 4, 1845, p. 150.

[67] *Charleston Mercury*, June 14, 1844 in Granville T. Prior, "A History of the Charleston Mercury, 1822–1852," unpublished Ph.D. thesis, Harvard University, 1946, pp. 351–352.

EPILOGUE
Of Slavery and Morality

T HE story of the slavery controversies within the Methodist Episcopal Church is a story of American morality. Although these controversies often reflected economic, political, social, and psychological facts, they were always framed in moral and ideological terms. Consequently, the moral discourse of the period from 1780 to 1845 reveals something about the nature of American society during that time. More specifically, a discussion of slavery and Methodism explains the fate of antislavery thought among Southerners, the significant relationship between the early and later antislavery movements, the character of the abolitionist crusade, and its effect upon the majority of Americans.

The discussion of social responsibility, at least among common folk, was directed by the moral importunity and oratorical urgency of revivalistic preachers. But nowhere were the limits of that discussion more clearly exemplified than in the fate of the early Methodist regulations on slavery. The white Democracy would not yield to an antislavery ethic, and there was no necessity for it to do so. The Church was not established; its constituency was determined by religious experience rather than birth, and it existed by the suffrance of society. Moreover, the morality valued by preachers was not essentially at odds with the social structure of early America, rather it could very easily complement or, as in the case of the Mission to the Slaves, supplement it. The morality of many Americans was characterized by personal dutifulness within the social structure. Methodists, for example, were taught to obey the law, abstain from injurious habits, and be charitable to those less fortunate than they. Thus, when emancipationist preaching failed, the

Mission to the Slaves and the colonization cause could very easily become conscientious instruments of ecclesiastical and moral concern for the Negroes. These philanthropies were quite acceptable to a slaveholding society because they not only avoided emancipation, but also emphasized the duties inherent in personal piety: honesty, charity, sobriety, prayerfulness, hard work, and a devotion to fulfilling the demands imposed by one's station in society.

Such morality was a very weak force with which to "extirpate" slavery. Emancipationists were never very popular in the South, and long before the inhabitants of that section had heard of abolitionists they had proscribed antislavery preaching. In Virginia, South Carolina, and the Old Southwest, as well as in the tramontane areas, antislavery sentiment was being smothered or driven out by the 1820's. Political sectionalism, economic investment in slaves, fear, and years of ineffective and erratic opposition to slavery such as that of the Methodists—all these factors helped to destroy emancipationist activities. Had the early antislavery Methodists and their confreres in other denominations strictly indoctrinated their successors with their own hatred of slavery, their preaching might have helped to effect emancipationist sentiment. But the primary lesson passed on from one generation of preachers to the next was that antislavery activities were doomed to failure. Compromises which had once tortured the conscience became virtuous in themselves.

To a later generation whose morality was not informed by the compromises, antislavery preaching became not a lesson in futility, but a challenge to greater efforts. Abolitionists, or at least those in the Methodist Episcopal Church, had had nothing to do with early antislavery preaching. That preaching had been institutionally permissible, but when it failed, the Church institutionalized its concern for the Negro in the Mission to the Slaves and the American Colonization Society. The abolitionists discounted the effectiveness and

284

purity of the former and the practicability and morality of the latter. Thus, they were cut off from institutional association with the old antislavery tradition. Nevertheless, they were related to the early antislavery preachers by their values and by their demand that the Church and America readopt Christian and American ideals of freedom.

Methodist abolitionism began under the aegis of men converted by William Lloyd Garrison and the lecturers of the American Anti-Slavery Society. Appealing to the Wesleyan antislavery heritage, evangelists such as Orange Scott, La Roy Sunderland, and George Storrs converted hundreds and, through those hundreds, thousands of Americans to abolitionism. Although the Methodist Episcopal Church never became "abolitionized," it did provide an excellent institutional framework within which to direct an antislavery revival. Itinerant lecturers addressed annual conferences whose members in turn harangued their congregations and organized local Wesleyan antislavery societies. When the church leaders objected, abolitionists complained of ecclesiastical tyranny and thereby enticed even more Methodists into the antislavery movement. New England Methodism was almost completely won over and became a base for Wesleyan abolitionism. Although the West was fertile ground for Theodore Dwight Weld, Methodist abolitionists moved from East to West with almost as good results. And it is not surprising that Southern Methodists singled out New England as their special enemy.

Of the many reformers in American history, the abolitionists have often been singled out as being particularly reprehensible for their fanaticism, their extremism, and their responsibility for causing the Civil War. It is quite true that among the abolitionists there were many like George Storrs, who perfected the art of personal abuse and condemnation; reform movements, however, as self-conscious affronts to the status quo and authority, are quite likely to attract such people. It is also true that men like La Roy Sunderland and the incomparable Garrison harangued, accused, and denounced in the style of the political newspapers and the revivalists of their day. But all were part of an aggressive age characterized by the wild election of 1840 and the hysteria surrounding the issue of war with Mexico, as well as by the hyperbole and exaggeration commonly used in this era of speculation and manifest destiny. Furthermore, those who opposed the abolitionists were not exactly lambs among wolves. Antiabolitionists such as David Reece and Nathan Bangs leveled their own simplified and extreme charges from the viewpoint of their own "fanaticism." And the mobs which assailed the abolitionists could hardly be vindicated as the popular expression of reasonable argument. The manners of the abolitionists were probably little worse, if at all, than those of their antagonists.

Furthermore, the abolitionists' revivalism naturally placed them in a position of being liable to the accusation of being fanatics and moral aggressors. They were single-minded in their denunciation of slavery as a moral evil and in this they had committed a double error so far as moderates were concerned. First of all, the Methodist radical antislavery preachers had neglected to pay homage to the initial compromise between the Church and slavery. They had not learned that antislavery activity would only make slaveholders more adamant, and so they appeared to be irresponsible and indifferent to the welfare of the slaves. Secondly, in condemning slaveholders as sinners, abolitionists were in the position of telling good and pious men that they were morally responsible for an evil institution and that they should do something about it. In so doing, the abolitionists merely alienated Southerners from the moral influences of a section of the nation and Church which was not engulfed by slavery. The "senselessness" and the urgency of their message marked them as immoderate and therefore "fanatic" to men who valued moderation above all else. The abolitionists knew that their difficulties were compounded because the slaveholders were often good and moderate men, but they nevertheless maintained the revivalist hope of conversion.

That that hope was doomed is revealed in the reaction of Southern and conservative Methodists to the new antislavery revival. Northern church leaders, when first confronted by the abolitionists saw them as enthusiasts and insurrectionists and refused to try to understand their arguments and explanations. Although Orange Scott and La Roy Sunderland explained that abolitionists proposed that emancipation be begun in a sensible and orderly fashion, they also suggested that it be begun as soon as possible. Afraid of proven Southern sensitivity to antislavery preaching, and dedicated to the genteel reform of colonization as well as the Mission to the Slaves, Northern churchmen scurried to put down abolitionism. Although the abolitionists converted enough Northern Methodists to affect the policies of the responsible churchmen, they utterly failed with Southerners. Methodists, along with other Southerners, simply repudiated the abolitionists' moral authority and social relevancy: they would not listen, and the results of their refusal were disastrous.

What, therefore, does the story of the Methodists and slavery reveal of the abolitionists? Within the context of their own self-image, their values, their goals, their antecedents, and the perspective of history, they were a "righteous remnant." In the prophetic tradition of the Old Testament is a recurring theme that the Lord God would condemn the apostate Children of Israel but save a remnant which had been faithful to His law. That law as the prophets understood it, required radical obedience to "hate the evil, and love the good." The people of God were to repudiate accepted standards of piety and let "judgment run down as waters, and righteousness as a mighty stream." The words and meaning were not strange to the abolitionists within the context of American history and the tradition of the

Methodist Episcopal Church. Appealing to the Declaration of Independence, the antislavery prophets demanded that a society justifying its existence upon the principles of equality should extend those principles to all men. They applied the principles of one revolution in anticipation of effecting another. The Declaration was used as the measure by which to judge American society and society was found wanting. Although the appeal to principles of equality should not have been revolutionary to Americans who had used these principles and phrases to justify securing their own freedom from England, they were. American society simply was not egalitarian so far as black men were concerned, and to demand that it can be made such was to demand a revolution in thought and social relationships.

As the prophets demanded that the Children of Israel turn again to the Law of God, so the abolitionists demanded that the inheritors of the Declaration of Independence turn again to the principles professed in it. This analogy with the prophets of Judah and Israel is quite appropriately applied to the abolitionist revivalists because of their Biblicism and their continuation of a tradition of prophetic preaching. The Methodist abolitionists demanded their church be true not only to the spirit of the Christian religion, but also to the historic Wesleyan antislavery tradition. They were often not pleasant, but what they saw in slavery was not pleasant. And the sight of the Church and the Republic condoning what they understood as evil was not pleasant. A prophetic remnant in regard to American equality and Christian and Methodist evangelism, the abolitionists attempted to keep the faith of American freedom, a just God, and Christian compassion.

The abolitionists were no more conscientious in their devotion to morality than their antagonists. Southerners did not yield anything to antislavery evangelists in appeals to moral responsibility; they made the Mission to the Slaves into the proper work of the Church and condemned abolitionists as demonic subverters of benevolent philanthropy. Northern antiabolitionists or conservatives were also conscientiously dedicated to doing all that could be done for the slaves. They thought abolitionists hopelessly irresponsible for preaching a message that had failed miserably before. Being no less dedicated to moral suasion than abolitionists, they did differ in the emphasis they placed on the proper way to apply suasion. The abolitionists wanted Northerners and Southerners to be made aware of the evil of slavery and to begin its destruction at once. The antiabolitionists thought such haste psychologically unsound and politically impossible and urged reliance upon the gradual processes deriving from colonization, Christian preaching, and the mere passage of time. Although there is no evidence that the antiabolitionists would eventually have succeeded, they nevertheless believed that they were realists who were trying to fend off unrealistic idealists.

In their opposition to abolitionism, however, the churchmen had to admit that slavery was wrong. And in this admission they were vulnerable to abolitionist pressure. When the South tried to seduce the North into accepting slavery without qualification, Northern churchmen balked. Although they argued on grounds of expediency as well as morality, their conscientious opposition to slavery made them choose a course which Southern ministers could not accept. Slavery seemed to be demanding more of everything in the Republic—more power, more land, more representation, more moral sanction. Like many Northerners, Methodist churchmen felt they had yielded enough; they decided that slavery should remain a Southern rather than become a national institution.

When the Church divided in 1844 on the question of accepting slavery as a national, domestic institution, thoughtful men wondered if the Union could remain as it was. They were realistic in their anxiety, for the Methodists' problems were only one indication of the alienation between

289

the North and the South: the admission of Texas, the imposition of a gag rule in Congress, and the character of the national political parties also caused bitter disagreement. The Methodist slavery controversies reflected the common man's willingness to identify himself with slavery. They also revealed that many Northerners were determined to refuse moral as well as political sanction to slavery, while men of conscience gave their ethical certitude to both sides of the conflict. In the dissolution of a national identity within the churches, the moral disjunction of the United States was institutionalized. This fact did not necessarily portend civil war, but it was a warning sign, a prophecy of the hostility and bitterness which could come were sectional fears and antagonism extended beyond the moral realm into the world of force and power.

APPENDIX

BIBLIOGRAPHY

INDEX

Methodist Rules Concerning Slavery

GENERAL RULES

(The General Rules listed particular sins which Methodists should avoid: trading in smuggled goods or slaves, lying, etc. They remained the same from year to year. The Sections on Slavery were special legislation of the General Conferences and tried to deal with far more than trading in slaves.)

1789

There is one only condition previously required of those who desire admission into these societies, *a desire to flee from the wrath to come,* i.e. *a desire to be saved from their sins:* But wherever this is really fixed in the soul, it will be shewn by its fruits. It is therefore expected of all who continue therein, that they should continue to evidence their desire of salvation,

First, By doing no harm, by avoiding evil of every kind; especially that which is most generally practiced: Such as

. . . .

The buying or selling of men, women, or children, with an intention to enslave them.

1796

(The 1798 edition of the *Discipline* was annotated by Bishops Francis Asbury and Thomas Coke. The note to the General Rule on Slavery reads as follows.)

The buying and selling the souls and bodies of men (for what is the body without the soul but a dead carcase) is a complicated crime.* It was indeed, *in some measure,*

* *Are there not many proprietors to be found on this continent,*

293

overlooked in the Jews by reason of the wonderful hardness of their hearts, as was the keeping of concubines and the divorcing of wives at pleasure, but it is totally opposite to the whole spirit of the gospel. It has an immediate tendency to fill the mind with pride and tyranny, and is frequently productive of almost every act of lust and cruelty which can disgrace the human species. Even the moral philosopher will candidly confess, that if there be a God, every perfection he possesses must be opposed to a practice so contrary to every moral idea which can influence the human mind. Nehem. v. 8, 9. 'I said unto them, We, after our ability, have redeemed our brethren, the Jews, which were sold unto the heathen; *and will ye even sell your brethren? or shall they be sold unto us?* Then held they their peace, and found nothing to answer. Also I said, It is not good that ye do: ought ye not to walk in the fear of our God, because of the reproach of the heathen our enemies?' Isai. lviii. 6. 'Is not this the fast that I have chosen? to loosen the bands of wickedness, *to undo the heavy burdens,* and *to let the oppressed go free,* and that *ye break every yoke,*' Ezek. xxvii. 13 (This chapter is written on the destruction of Tyrus, and the causes of it) 'Javan, Tubal, and Meshech, they were thy merchants: they *traded the persons of men.*' Acts xvii, 24–26 '*God—hath made of one blood all nations of men* for to dwell on the face of the earth.' I Tim i. 9, 10. 'Knowing this, that the law is not made for a righteous man, but for the lawless and disobedient, for the ungodly and for sinners, for unholy and profane, for murderers of fathers, and murderers of mothers, for man-slayers,—for *man-stealers,*' &c. Rev. xiii. 10. 'He that leadeth into captivity shall go into captivity.'

---

who restrain their slaves from enjoying the privileges of the gospel, and thereby invade the rights of the souls *and* consciences *of their slaves, as well as their* bodies? *At the same time we must give the credit due to multitudes who do not thus enslave* the minds *of their servants, but allow them full liberty to attend the preaching of the gospel, wherever they think they are most profited.*

Rev. xviii. (On the fall of Babylon and the causes of it) ver. 11–13. 'No man buyeth their merchandise any more: the merchandise of gold, and silver,—and *slaves,* and *souls of men.'*

SECTIONS ON SLAVERY

(The first Section on Slavery was passed by the General Conference of 1796; the earlier rules were agreed upon by annual conferences except in the case of the Christmas Conference which organized the Methodist Episcopal Church.)

1780

Quest. 16. *Ought not this conference to require those travelling Preachers who hold slaves, to give promises, to set them free?*

Ans. Yes.

Quest. 17. *Does this conference acknowledge that slavery is contrary to the laws or God, man, and nature, and hurtful to society, contrary to the dictates of conscience and pure religion, and doing that which we would not others do to us and ours?—Do we pass our disapprobation on all our friends who keep slaves, and advise their freedom?*

Ans. Yes.

1783

Quest. 10. *What shall be done with our local Preachers who hold slaves contrary to the laws which authorize their freedom in any of the United States?*

Ans. We will try them another year. In the meantime let every Assistant deal faithfully and plainly with every one, and report to the next conference. It may then be necessary to suspend them.

1784

Quest. 12. *What shall be done with our friends that will buy and sell slaves?*

Ans. If they buy with no other design than to hold them as slaves, and have been previously warned, they shall be expelled; and permitted to sell on no consideration.

Quest. 13. *What shall we do with our local Preachers who will not emancipate their slaves in the states where the laws admit it?*

Ans. Try those in Virginia another year, and suspend the preachers in Maryland, Delaware, Pennsylvania, and New Jersey.

Quest. 22. *What shall be done with our travelling Preachers that now are, or hereafter shall be possessed of slaves, and refuse to manumit them where the law permits?*

Ans. Employ them no more.

CHRISTMAS CONFERENCE 1784

Quest. 42. What methods can we take to extirpate slavery?

Ans. We are deeply conscious of the impropriety of making new terms of communion for a religious society already established, excepting on the most pressing occasions: and such we esteem the practice of holding our fellow-creatures in slavery. We view it as contrary to the golden law of God on which hang all the law and the prophets, and the unalienable rights of mankind, as well as every principle of the revolution to hold in the deepest abasement, in a more abject slavery than is perhaps to be found in any part of the world except America, so many souls that are all capable of the image of God.

We therefore think it our most bounden duty to take immediately some effectual method to extirpate this abomination from among us: and for that purpose we add the following to the rules of our society, viz.:

1. Every member of our society who has slaves in his possession, shall, within twelve months after notice given to him by the assistant, (which notice the assistants are required immediately and without delay, to give in their

respective circuits,) legally execute and record an instrument, whereby he emancipates and sets free every slave in his possession who is between the ages of forty and forty-five immediately, or at farthest when they arrive at the age of forty-five.

And every slave who is between the ages of twenty-five and forty immediately, or at the farthest at the expiration of five years from the date of the said instrument.

And every slave who is between the ages of twenty and twenty-five immediately, or at farthest when they arrive at the age of thirty.

And every slave under the age of twenty, as soon as they arrive at the age of twenty-five at farthest.

And every infant born in slavery after the above-mentioned rules are complied with, immediately on its birth.

2. Every assistant shall keep a journal, in which he shall regularly minute down the names and ages of all the slaves belonging to all the masters in his respective circuit, and also the date of every instrument executed and recorded for the manumission of the slaves, with the name of the court, book, and folio, in which the said instruments respectively shall have been recorded: which journal shall be handed down in each circuit to the succeeding assistants.

3. In consideration that these rules form a new term of communion, every person concerned, who will not comply with them, shall have liberty quietly to withdraw himself from our society within the twelve months succeeding the notice given as aforesaid: otherwise the assistant shall exclude him in the society.

4. No person so voluntarily withdrawn, or so excluded, shall ever partake of the supper of the Lord with the Methodists, till he complies with the above restrictions.

5. No person holding slaves shall, in the future, be admitted into society or to the Lord's supper, till he previously complies with these rules concerning slavery.

N.B. These rules are to affect the members of our society

no farther than is consistent with the laws of the states in which they reside.

And respecting our brethren in Virginia that are concerned, and after due consideration of their peculiar circumstances, we allow them two years from the notice given, to consider the expedience of compliance or non-compliance with these rules.

Quest. 43. What shall be done with those who buy or sell slaves, or give them away?

Ans. They are immediately to be expelled: unless they buy them on purpose to free them.

1796

Quest. WHAT regulations shall be made for the extirpation of the crying evil of African slavery?

Ans. 1. We declare that we are more than ever convinced of the great evil of the African slavery which still exists in these United States; and do most earnestly recommend to the yearly conferences, quarterly meetings, and to those who have the oversight of districts and circuits, to be exceedingly cautious what persons they admit to official stations in our church; and in the case of future admission to official stations, to require such security of those who hold slaves, for the emancipation of them, immediately or gradually, as the laws of the state respectively, and the circumstances of the case will admit: and we do fully authorize all the yearly conferences to make whatever regulations they judge proper, in the present case, respecting the admission of persons to official stations in our church.

2. No slave-holder shall be received into society, till the preacher who has the oversight of the circuit, has spoken to him freely and faithfully on the subject of slavery.

3. Every member of the society who sells a slave, shall immediately, after full proof, be excluded the society. And if any member of our society purchase a slave, the ensuing quarterly meeting shall determine the number of years, in

which the slave so purchased would work out the price of his purchase. And the person so purchasing, shall immediately after such determination, execute a legal instrument for the manumission of such slave, at the expiration of the term determined by the quarterly meeting. And in default of his executing such instrument of manumission, or on his refusal to submit his case to the judgment of the quarterly meeting, such member shall be excluded the society. *Provided also,* That in the case of a female slave, it shall be inserted in the aforesaid instrument of manumission, that all her children who shall be born during the years of her servitude, shall be free at the following times, namely—every female child at the age of twenty-one, and every male child at the age of twenty-five.—*Nevertheless,* if the member of our society, executing the said instrument of manumission, judge it proper, he may fix the times of manumission of the children of the female slaves before mentioned, at an earlier age than that which is prescribed above.

4. The preachers and other members of our society are requested to consider the subject of negro-slavery with deep attention, till the ensuing general conference; and that they impart to the general conference, through the medium of the yearly conference, or otherwise, any important thoughts upon the subject, that the conference may have full light, in order to take further steps towards the eradicating [of] this enormous evil from that part of the church of God to which they are united.

1800

(The General Conference of 1800 retained the Section on Slavery passed in 1796, and added two paragraphs.)

Q. 13. Shall any further steps be taken for the promoting of the emancipation of the slaves?

A. 1. The annual conferences are directed to draw up addresses for the gradual emancipation of the slaves, to the legislatures of those states in which no general laws have been passed for that purpose. These addresses shall urge, in the most respectful but pointed manner, the necessity of a law for the gradual emancipation of the slaves; proper committees shall be appointed, by the annual conferences, out of the most respectable of our friends, for the conducting of the business; and the presiding elders, elders, deacons, and travelling preachers shall procure as many proper signatures as possible to the addresses, and give all the assistance in their power, in every respect to aid the committees, and to further this blessed undertaking. And this shall be continued from year to year, till the desired end be fully accomplished.

2. When any travelling preacher becomes an owner of a slave or slaves, by any means, he shall forfeit his ministerial character in the Methodist Episcopal Church, unless he execute, if it be practicable, a legal instrument of emancipation of such slave or slaves, conformably to the laws of the state in which he lives.

1804

Quest. WHAT shall be done for the extirpation of the evil of slavery?

Ans. 1. We declare, that we are as much as ever convinced of the great evil of slavery; and do most earnestly recommend to the yearly conferences, quarterly meeting conferences, and to those who have the oversight of districts, circuits, and stations, to be exceedingly cautious what persons they admit to official stations in our church; and in the case of future admission to official stations, to require such security of those who hold slaves, for the emancipation of them, immediately or gradually, as the laws of the state respectively, and the circumstances of the case will admit: and we do fully authorize all the yearly conferences to make whatever regulations they judge proper, in the present case, respecting the admission of persons to official stations in our church.

300

2. When any travelling preacher becomes an owner of a slave or slaves, by any means, he shall forfeit his ministerial character in our church, unless he execute, if it be practicable, a legal emancipation of such slaves, conformably to the laws of the state in which he lives.

3. No slave-holder shall be received into full membership in our society, till the preacher who has the oversight of the circuit, has spoken to him freely and faithfully on the subject of slavery.

4. Every member of the society who sells a slave, shall immediately, after full proof, be excluded the society. And if any member of our society purchase a slave, the ensuing quarterly meeting shall determine the number of years, in which the slave so purchased would work out the price of his purchase. And the person so purchasing, shall immediately after such determination, execute a legal instrument for the manumission of such slave, at the expiration of the term determined by the quarterly meeting. And in default of his executing such instrument of manumission, or on his refusal to submit his case to the judgment of the quarterly meeting, such member shall be excluded the society. *Provided also,* That in the case of a female slave, it shall be inserted in the aforesaid instrument of manumission, that all her children who shall be born during the years of her servitude, shall be free at the following times, namely—every female child at the age of twenty-one, and every male child at the age of twenty-five.—*Nevertheless,* if the member of our society, executing the said instrument of manumission judge it proper, he may fix the times of manumission of the children of the female slaves before mentioned, at an earlier age than that which is prescribed above. *Nevertheless,* The members of our societies in the States of North-Carolina, South-Carolina, Georgia, and Tennessee, shall be exempted from the operation of the above rules.

5. Let our preachers from time to time as occasion serves, admonish and exhort all slaves to render due respect and

obedience to the commands and interests of their respective masters.

1808

(The Section on Slavery remains the same in paragraphs 1 and 2. Paragraphs 3, 4, and 5 are deleted, and the following added.)

3. The general conference authorises each annual conference to form [its] own regulations, relative to buying and selling slaves.

1812

(The only change is the wording of paragraph 3.)

3. Whereas the laws of some of the states do not admit of emancipating of slaves, without a special act of the legislature; the general conference authorises each annual conference to form [its] own regulations, relative to buying and selling slaves.

1816

Quest. WHAT shall be done for the extirpation of the evil of slavery?

A.1. We declare that we are as much as ever convinced of the great evil of slavery; therefore no slaveholder shall be eligible to any official station in our Church hereafter, where the laws of the state in which he lives will admit of emancipation, and permit the liberated slave to enjoy freedom.

2. When any travelling preacher becomes an owner of a slave or slaves, by any means, he shall forfeit his ministerial character in our church, unless he execute, if it be practicable, a legal emancipation of such slaves, conformably to the laws of the state in which he lives.

3. Whereas the laws of some of the states do not admit of emancipating of slaves, without a special act of the legislature; the general conference authorises each annual conference to form [its] own regulations, relative to buying and selling slaves.

1820

Quest. What shall be done for the extirpation of the evil of slavery?

Ans. 1. We declare that we are as much as ever convinced of the great evil of slavery; therefore no slave holder shall be eligible to any official station in our Church hereafter, where the laws of the State in which he lives will admit of emancipation, and permit the liberated slave to enjoy freedom.

2. When any travelling preacher becomes an owner of a slave or slaves, by any means, he shall forfeit his ministerial character in our church, unless he execute, if it be practicable, a legal emancipation of such slaves, conformably to the laws of the state in which he lives.

1824–1844

(The Section on Slavery remains the same as that of 1820 with the addition of three new paragraphs.)

3. All our preachers shall prudently enforce upon our members, the necessity of teaching their slaves to read the word of God; and to allow them time to attend upon the public worship of God on our regular days of divine service.

4. Our colored preachers and official members shall have all the privileges which are usual to others in the district and quarterly conferences, where the usages of the country do not forbid it. And the presiding elder may hold for them a separate district conference, where the number of colored local preachers will justify it.

5. The annual conference may employ colored preachers to travel and preach where their services are judged necessary; provided that no one shall be so employed without having been recommended according to the form of discipline.

Manuscripts

Most of the manuscript collections used in this study provided depth rather than important facts indispensable to understanding the story. The most useful papers, or those which scholars might find interesting for other aspects of social history, are marked with an asterisk (*). The other collections were helpful in providing bits and pieces to fit the story together. They would be most interesting to scholars who wished to study the Methodists.

* American Colonization Society Papers, Library of Congress
  George Aiken [Ekin] Papers, Emory and Henry College
  Charles Wesley Andrews Papers, Duke University
  Francis Asbury Papers, Emory University
* Baltimore Conference Papers, Lovely Lane Museum and Library, Baltimore
  Nathan Bangs Papers, Drew University
  George Coles Letters, Drew University
  Silas Comfort Papers, Syracuse University
  Ezekiel Cooper Papers, Garrett Theological Seminary
  Peter Doub Papers, Emory University
  William C. Doub Papers, Duke University
* Edward Dromgoole Papers, University of North Carolina
  John Early Papers, Randolph-Macon College
  James B. Finley Papers, Ohio Wesleyan University
* Willbur Fisk Papers, Wesleyan University
* William Lloyd Garrison Papers, Boston Public Library
  Eugene R. Hendrix Papers, Duke University
  John McClintock Papers, Emory University
  William McKendree Papers, Emory University
* Maryland State Colonization Society Papers, Maryland Historical Society, Baltimore
  Methodist Church Papers, Randolph-Macon College
  Methodist Episcopal Church Papers, Duke University

New England Methodist Historical Society Papers, Boston University School of Theology

Papers of Methodist Leaders, Emory University

Green W. Penn Papers, Duke University

* Amos A. Phelps Papers, Boston Public Library

Philadelphia Conference Historical Society Papers, Old St. George's Church, Philadelphia

Matthew Simpson Papers, Library of Congress

Whitefoord Smith Manuscripts, Duke University

Joshua Soule Papers, Drew University

South Carolina Conference Papers, Wofford College

George Storrs Papers, New York Public Library

Thomas Stringfield Papers, University of North Carolina

* Weston Family Papers, Boston Public Library

* William Winans Collection, Mississippi Conference Historical Society, Millsaps College

* Elizur Wright Papers, Library of Congress

PERIODICALS

Periodicals revealed the extent and the public nature of the slavery controversies. Much of what church-going Americans read came from denominational journals which printed political and foreign as well as religious and domestic news. The abolitionist papers helped to spread antislavery sentiment, and provide a good source for understanding just what the abolitionists were saying.

Abolition Intelligencer and Missionary Magazine (Shelbyville, Kentucky)

African Repository and Colonial Journal (Washington, D.C.)

Anti-Slavery Examiner (New York)

Anti-Slavery Lecturer (Utica, New York)

Anti-Slavery Reporter (New York)

Christian Advocate and Journal (New York)

Christian Register (Boston)

Christian Sentinel (Richmond)

Colonizationist and Journal of Freedom (Boston)
Colored American (New York)
Emancipator (New York and Boston)
Friend of Man (Utica, New York)
Genius of Universal Emancipation (Baltimore, place varies, name varies)
Herald of Freedom (Concord, N.H.)
Liberator (Boston)
Maine Wesleyan Journal (Hallowell, Maine)
Maryland Gazette (Annapolis)
Maryland Journal (Baltimore)
Methodist Magazine (New York, title varies)
National Anti-Slavery Standard (New York)
New York Herald
Niles' National Register (Washington, D.C.)
Northern Christian Advocate (Auburn, New York)
Philanthropist (Cincinnati)
Pittsburgh Christian Advocate
Signal of Liberty (Ann Arbor, Michigan)
Southern Christian Advocate (Charleston)
Southwestern Christian Advocate (Nashville)
True Wesleyan (Boston)
Virginia Gazette (Alexandria)
Wesleyan Anti-Slavery Herald (Concord, N.H.)
Wesleyan Journal (Charleston)
Western Christian Advocate (Cincinnati)
Zion's Herald (Boston)
Zion's Watchman (New York)

OFFICIAL RECORDS

Although not all of the relevant official records are extant, those of the Methodist General Conferences and the colonization and antislavery societies are. They were useful in outlining what happened in the general meetings, but lack adequate reports of the debates which would answer many important questions. Furthermore, the reporters often neglected to keep full accounts. The same is often true of annual conference journals, many of which have been misplaced or lost.

MAJOR CHURCH RECORDS

Doctrines and Discipline of the Methodist Episcopal Church, Place of publication varies, 1789, 1791, 1798, 1804, 1808, 1812, 1820, 1824, 1828, 1836, 1840, 1844.

History of the Organization of the Methodist Episcopal Church, South (Journal of the Louisville Conference), Nashville, 1925.

Journal of the General Conference of the Methodist Episcopal Church, Baltimore, 1840.

Journal of the General Conference of the Methodist Episcopal Church, New York, 1844.

Journals of the General Conference of the Methodist Episcopal Church, 1796–1836, New York, 1855.

Minutes of the Annual Conferences of the Methodist Episcopal Church, 3 vols., New York, 1840–1845.

ANNUAL CONFERENCES AND OTHERS

American Anti-Slavery Society, *Annual Report of the American Anti-Slavery Society* (title varies with the designation of which annual report), New York, 1834–1839.

American Colonization Society, *Annual Report of the American Society for Colonizing the Free People of Colour of the United States* (title varies with the designation of which annual report), Washington, D.C., 1826–1845.

Journals of the Baltimore Conference, 3 vols., Lovely Lane Museum and Library, Baltimore.

"Journals of the Genesee Annual Conference of the Methodist Episcopal Church, 1810–1848" (typescript copy at Duke University), 3 vols.

Journals of the Virginia Conference, 3 vols. Randolph-Macon College.

Minutes of the General Assembly of the Presbyterian Church in the United States of America, Philadelphia, 1836.

"Minutes of the Holston Annual Conference, 1824–1844" (typescript copy at Duke University).

"Minutes of the Illinois Annual Conference of the Methodist Episcopal Church" (typescript copy at Duke University).

Minutes of the Maine Annual Conference of the Methodist Episcopal Church, 1841–1845. New England Methodist Historical Society Papers, Boston University School of Theology.

Minutes of the Methodist Conferences [English], vols. 7, 8, London, 1838, 1841.

"Minutes of the Michigan Annual Conference of the Methodist Episcopal Church" (typescript copy at Duke University).

"Minutes of the New England Conference of the Methodist Episcopal Church" (typescript copy at Duke University prepared by the New England Methodist Historical Society at Boston in 1912), 2 vols.

Minutes of the New Hampshire Annual Conference of the Methodist Episcopal Church for the year 1844–45, Claremont, N.H., 1845.

Minutes of the Providence Annual Conference of the Methodist Episcopal Church, Providence, 1845.

Minutes of the South Carolina Conference of the Methodist Episcopal Church (Annual publication), Columbia and Charleston, 1831–1845.

North Carolina Conference Journals, 1838–1849, Methodist Episcopal Church Papers, Duke University.

Sweet, William Warren, *Circuit Rider Days in Indiana: Containing the Minutes of the Indiana Conference, 1832 to 1844,* Indianapolis, 1916.

Sweet, William Warren, *The Rise of Methodism in the West, 1800–1811: The Journal of the Western Conference,* Nashville, 1920.

Contemporary Works

The pamphlets and other contemporary writings which were most helpful in this study are listed below. Those interested in a complete bibliography of antislavery works should consult Dwight L. Dumond, *A Bibliography of Antislavery in America,* Ann Arbor, 1961.

Adams, Charles, *An Address to Abolitionists of the Methodist Episcopal Church,* Boston, 1843.

Bangs, Nathan, *The Substance of a Sermon Preached on opening the Methodist Church on John Street,* New York, 1818.

Barnes, Gilbert H. and Dwight L. Dumond, eds., *The Letters of Theodore Dwight Weld, Angelina Grimké Weld and Sarah Grimké, 1822–1844,* 2 vols., New York, 1934.

Bascom, Henry Bidleman, *Methodism and Slavery,* Frankfurt, Ky., 1845.

Birkbeck, Morris, *An Appeal to the People of Illinois on the Question of a Convention,* Shawneetown, Ill., 1823.

Birney, James G., *The American Churches the Bulwarks of American Slavery,* Boston, 1843.

———, *Letter on Colonization Addressed to the Rev. Thornton J. Mills,* New York, 1834.

Bourne, George, *Man-Stealing and Slavery Denounced by the Presbyterian and Methodist Churches,* Boston, 1834.

———, *Picture of Slavery in the United States of America,* Middletown, Conn., 1834.

Child, Lydia Maria, *An Appeal in Favor of that Class of Americans Called Africans,* Boston, 1833.

Clark, Elmer T., ed., *The Journal and Letters of Francis Asbury,* 3 vols., Nashville, 1958.

Colton, Calvin, ed., *The Private Correspondence of Henry Clay,* Boston, 1856.

Controversy between Caius Gracchus and Opimius in reference to the American Society for colonizing the Free

People of Colour of the United States, Georgetown, D.C., 1827.

Debate on Modern Abolitionism in the General Conference of the Methodist Episcopal Church held in Cincinnati, May, 1836, Cincinnati, 1836.

Dumond, Dwight L., ed., *Letters of James Gillespie Birney, 1831–1857,* 2 vols., New York, 1938.

Dunwody, Samuel, *A Sermon upon the Subject of Slavery,* Columbia, S.C., 1837.

Exposition of the Causes and Character of the Difficulties in the Church in Charleston in the year 1833, Charleston, 1833.

Exposition of the Object and Plans of the American Union for the Improvement of the Colored Race, Boston, 1835.

Foster, Stephen S., *The Brotherhood of Thieves,* Boston, 1844.

Furman, Richard, *Rev. Dr. Richard Furman's Exposition of the views of the Baptists Relative to the Coloured Population of the United States, in a Communication to the Governor of South Carolina,* Charleston, 1823.

Garrettson, Freeborn, *A Dialogue Between Do-Justice and Professing Christian,* Wilmington [n.d., 1820?].

Garrison, William Lloyd, *Thoughts on African Colonization,* Boston, 1832.

Glennie, Alexander, *Sermons Preached on Plantations to Congregations of Negroes,* Charleston, 1844.

Hoff, John F., *A Manual of Religious Instruction Specially intended for the Oral Teaching of Colored Persons,* Philadelphia, 1852.

Holland, Edwin C., *A Refutation of the Calumnies Circulated Against the Southern and Western States, Respecting the Institution and existence of Slavery Among Them,* Charleston, 1822.

Jay, William, *An Inquiry into the Character and Tendency of the American Colonization and American Anti-Slavery Societies,* New York, 1835.

Jefferson, Thomas, *Notes on the State of Virginia* (Edited by William Peden), Chapel Hill, 1955.

Jenkins, James, *Experience, Labours, and Sufferings of Rev. James Jenkins of the South Carolina Conference,* Charleston, 1842.

Jones, Charles Colcock, *Catechism of Scripture Doctrine and practice, for families and Sabbath School Designed also for the Oral Instruction of Colored Persons,* Savannah, 1844.

———, *The Religious Instruction of the Negroes in the United States,* Savannah, 1842.

Lane, Lunsford, *Narrative of Lunsford Lane,* Boston, 1842.

Lee, Jesse, *A Short History of the Methodists,* Baltimore, 1810.

Longstreet, Augustus Baldwin, *Letters on the Epistle of Paul to Philemon,* Charleston, 1845.

Meade, William, *Sermons, Dialogues, and Narratives for Servants to be Read to them in Families; abridged, altered and adapted to their condition,* Richmond, 1836.

Ninth Annual Report of the Association for the Religious Instruction of the Negroes in Liberty County, Georgia, Savannah, 1844.

O'Kelly, James, *Essay on Negro-Slavery,* Philadelphia, 1789.

Parker, Franklin N., ed., *A Diary-Letter Written from the Methodist General Conference of 1844 by the Rev. William Justice Parks* (Emory University Publications, Sources and Reprints, Series II), Atlanta, 1944.

Peck, George, *Slavery and the Episcopacy,* New York, 1845.

Phelps, Amos A., *Lectures on Slavery and Its Remedy,* Boston, 1834.

Pinckney, Charles Cotesworth, *An Address delivered in Charleston before the Agricultural Society of South Carolina at its anniversary meeting,* Charleston, 1829.

Practical Considerations founded on the Scriptures relative to the Slave Population of South-Carolina, Charleston, 1823.

Proceedings of the Meeting in Charleston, S.C. May 13–15, 1845 on the Religious Instruction of the Negroes together with the Report of the Committee and the Address to the Public, Charleston, 1845.

Report of the Committee of the South Carolina Conference of the Methodist Episcopal Church, on the subject of the Schism in Charleston with the accompanying Documents, Charleston, 1835.

Reese, David M., *A Brief Review of the First Annual Report of the American Anti-Slavery Society,* New York, 1834.

———, *Letters to the Hon. William Jay, being a Reply to his 'Inquiry into the American Colonization and American Anti-Slavery Societies,'* New York, 1835.

Rice, David, *Slavery Inconsistent with Justice and Good Policy,* Philadelphia, 1792.

Scott, Orange, *Address to the General Conference of the Methodist Episcopal Church by the Rev. O. Scott, A Member of that Body,* New York, 1836.

———, *An Appeal to the Methodist Episcopal Church,* Boston, 1838.

———, *The Grounds of Secession from the M.E. Church,* New York, 1848.

———, *The Methodist E. Church and Slavery,* Boston, 1844.

Storrs, George, *Mob, under pretence of law, or, the Arrest and Trial of Rev. George Storrs at Northfield, N.H.,* Concord, N.H., 1835.

Sunderland, La Roy, *Anti-Slavery Manual Containing a Collection of Facts and Arguments on American Slavery,* New York, 1837.

Thrift, Minton, *Memoirs of the Rev. Jesse Lee with Extracts from his Journals,* New York, 1823.

de Tocqueville, Alexis, *Democracy in America* (Translated by Henry Reeves), 2 vols., New York, 1945.

Washburn, E. B., ed., *The Edwards Papers* (Chicago Historical Society Collection, vol. 3), Chicago, 1884.

Wesley, John, *Christian Perfection* (Edited by Thomas Kepler), New York, 1954.

————, *The Journal of the Rev. John Wesley, A.M.* (Edited by Nehemiah Curnock), 8 vols., London, 1909–1916.

————, *Thoughts Upon Slavery,* London, 1774.

West, Robert Athow, *Report of Debates in the General Conference of the Methodist Episcopal Church, Held in the City of New York, 1844,* New York, 1844.

METHODIST HISTORY AND BIOGRAPHY

As with most denominational history, studies of the Methodist Church, its conferences, and its ministers are frequently uncritical hagiographies. This is especially true of those written in the nineteenth century. Wade Crawford Barclay, and William Warren Sweet are twentieth century exceptions to the rule. The former's history of Methodist missions is truly monumental and Sweet's contributions to American historiography are well known. Despite the short-comings of many of the following works, they were especially useful in filling in the great gaps left by inadequate or missing official records. The authors did historians a great service by printing long sections of original source material without comment. And the biographers usually provided interesting sketches of American life during the early nineteenth century. These works, despite their weaknesses, are well worth perusal by social historians. A more complete bibliography can be found in Emory Stevens Bucke, ed., *The History of American Methodism,* 3 vols., New York, 1964.

Allen, Stephen and W. H. Pilsbury, *History of Methodism in Maine 1793–1886,* Augusta, 1887.

Arnold, W. E., *A History of Methodism in Kentucky,* 2 vols., Louisville, 1936.

BIBLIOGRAPHY

Bangs, Nathan, *A History of the Methodist Episcopal Church*, 4 vols., New York, 1838–42.

————, *The Life of the Rev. Freeborn Garrettson*, New York, 1830.

Barclay, Wade C., *Missionary Motivation and Expansion* (*Early American Methodism, 1769–1844*, vol. 1), New York, 1949.

————, *To Reform the Nation* (*Early American Methodism, 1769–1844*, vol. 2), New York, 1950.

Bennett, William, *Memorials of Methodism in Virginia*, Richmond, 1871.

Betts, Albert D., *History of South Carolina Methodism*, Columbia, 1952.

Bucke, Emory Stevens, ed., *The History of American Methodism*, 3 vols., New York, 1964.

Buckley, James M., *Constitutional and Parliamentary History of the Methodist Episcopal Church*, New York, 1912.

Cartwright, Peter, *Autobiography of Peter Cartwright*, Cincinnati, 1856.

Chreitzberg, A. M., *Early Methodism in the Carolinas*, Nashville, 1897.

Clark, D. W., *Life and Times of Rev. Elijah Hedding, D.D.*, New York, 1855.

Clark, Robert D., *The Life of Matthew Simpson*, New York, 1956.

Conable, F. W., *History of the Genesee Conference of the Methodist Episcopal Church*, New York, 1876.

Drew, Samuel, *The Life of the Rev. Thomas Coke, LL.D.*, New York, 1818.

Drinkhouse, Edward J., *History of Methodist Reform*, 2 vols., Baltimore, 1899.

Elliott, Charles, *History of the Great Secession from the Methodist Episcopal Church in the year 1845*, Cincinnati, 1855.

Emory, Robert, *History of the Discipline of the Methodist Episcopal Church*, New York, 1844.

————, *The life of the Rev. John Emory, D.D.,* New York, 1841.

Fitzgerald, O. P., *John B. McFerrin: A Biography,* Nashville, 1893.

Fradenburgh, J. N., *History of the Erie Conference,* 2 vols., Oil City, Pa., 1907.

Grissom, W. L., *History of Methodism in North Carolina,* Nashville, 1905.

Hall, B. M., *The Life of Rev. John Clarke,* New York, 1856.

Harrison, W. P., *The Gospel Among the Slaves,* Nashville, 1893.

[Haven, Gilbert], *Memorials of Gilbert Haven, Bishop of the Methodist Episcopal Church,* Boston, 1880.

Henkle, Moses M., *The Life of Henry Bidleman Bascom,* Louisville, 1854.

Holdich, Joseph, *The Life of Willbur Fisk, D.D.,* New York, 1842.

Holliday, F. C., *Indiana Methodism,* Cincinnati, 1873.

————, *Life and Times of Rev. Allen Wiley, A.M.,* Cincinnati, 1853.

Jewell, Horace, *History of Methodism in Arkansas,* Little Rock, 1892.

Jones, John G., *Complete History of Methodism as connected with the Mississippi Conference of the Methodist Episcopal Church, South,* 2 vols., Nashville, 1908.

Leaton, James, *History of Methodism in Illinois from 1793 to 1832,* Cincinnati, 1883.

Lee, Leroy, *The Life and Times of the Rev. Jesse Lee,* Charleston, 1848.

McFerrin, John B., *History of Methodism in Tennessee,* 3 vols., Nashville, 1875.

Matlack, Lucius C., *The Anti-Slavery Struggle and Triumph in the Methodist Episcopal Church,* New York, 1881.

————, *The History of American Slavery and Methodism from 1780 to 1849,* New York, 1849.

————, *The Life of the Rev. Orange Scott*, New York, 1848.

Mudge, James, *History of the New England Conference of the Methodist Episcopal Church, 1796–1910*, Boston, 1910.

Norwood, John Nelson, *The Schism in the Methodist Episcopal Church: 1844*, Alfred, N.Y., 1923.

[Olin, Stephen], *The Life and Letters of Stephen Olin, D.D., LL.D.*, 2 vols., New York, 1854.

Paine, Robert, *Life and Times of William M'Kendree*, 2 vols., Nashville, 1870.

Peters, John L., *Christian Perfection and American Methodism*, New York, 1956.

Price, Richard Nye, *Holston Methodism from its Origin to the Present Time*, 3 vols., Nashville, 1903–1914.

Redford, A. H., *The History of Methodism in Kentucky*, 3 vols., Nashville, 1870.

Roche, John A., *The Life of John Price Durbin, D.D., LL.D.*, New York, 1890.

Smith, George G., *The History of Georgia Methodism from 1786 to 1866*, Atlanta, 1913.

————, *The Life and Letters of James Osgood Andrew, Bishop of the Methodist Episcopal Church, South*, Nashville, 1882.

Stevens, Abel, *Life and Times of Nathan Bangs*, New York, 1863.

Strickland, W. P., *The Life of Jacob Gruber*, New York, 1860.

Swaney, Charles, *Episcopal Methodism and Slavery*, Boston, 1926.

Sweet, William Warren, *Methodism in American History*, New York, 1932.

————, *The Methodists* (*Religion on the American Frontier*, vol. 4), Chicago, 1946.

————, *Virginia Methodism: A History,* Richmond, 1955.

Tigert, John J., *A Constitutional History of American Episcopal Methodism,* Nashville, 1916.

West, Anson, *A History of Methodism in Alabama,* Nashville, 1893.

Wightman, William M., *Life of William Capers, D.D.,* Nashville, 1858.

GENERAL HISTORY AND JOURNAL ARTICLES

Adams, Alice Dana, *The Neglected Period of Anti-Slavery in America (1808–1831),* Boston, 1908.

Adams, Charles Francis, ed., *Memoirs of John Quincy Adams,* 12 vols., Philadelphia, 1874–1877.

Aptheker, Herbert, *A Documentary History of the Negro People in the United States,* New York, 1951.

————, *American Negro Slave Revolts,* New York, 1943.

Barnes, Gilbert H., *The Anti-Slavery Impulse 1830–1844,* New York, 1933.

Barnhart, John D., "Sources of Southern Migration into the Old Northwest," *Mississippi Valley Historical Review,* XXII (June, 1935), 49–62.

Birney, William, *James G. Birney and His Times,* New York, 1890.

Bond, Beverly W., Jr., *The Civilization of the Old Northwest,* New York, 1934.

Boyd, William K., ed., "A Journal and Travel of James Meacham—Part I, May 19–August 31, 1789," *Historical Papers* (Trinity College Historical Society), IX (1912), 66–95.

————, ed., "A Journal and Travel of James Meacham Part II, 1789–1797," *Historical Papers* (Trinity College Historical Society), X (1914), 87–102.

Carroll, Joseph Cephas, *Slave Insurrections in the United States, 1800–1865,* Boston, 1938.

Carroll, Kenneth L., "Religious Influences on Manumission of Slaves in Caroline, Dorchester, and Talbot Counties," *Maryland Historical Magazine,* LVI (June, 1961), 176–197.

Catterall, Helen Tunnicliff, *Judicial Cases Concerning American Slavery and the Negro,* 5 vols., Washington, D.C., 1926–1937.

Chapman, John Jay, *William Lloyd Garrison,* Boston, 1913.

Coleman, J. Winston, *Slavery Times in Kentucky,* Chapel Hill, 1940.

Craven, Avery, *The Coming of the Civil War,* New York, 1942.

Cross, Whitney R., *The Burned-Over District,* Ithaca, 1950.

Davis, David Brion, "The Emergence of Immediatism in British and American Antislavery Thought," *Mississippi Valley Historical Review,* XLIX (September, 1962), 209–230.

Donald, David, *Lincoln Reconsidered,* New York, 1956.

Doyle, Bertram W., *The Etiquette of Race Relations in the South,* Chicago, 1937.

Drake, Thomas, *Quakers and Slavery in America,* New Haven, 1950.

Du Bois, W. E. B., *The Negro Church,* Atlanta, 1903.

Dumond, Dwight L., *Antislavery: The Crusade for Freedom in America,* Ann Arbor, 1961.

Earnest, Joseph B., *The Religious Development of the Negro in Virginia,* Charlottesville, 1914.

Eaton, Clement, *Freedom of Thought in the Old South,* Durham, 1940.

Elkins, Stanley M., *Slavery: A Problem in American Institutional and Intellectual Life,* Chicago, 1959.

Fairbank, Calvin, *Rev. Calvin Fairbank during Slavery Times,* Chicago, 1890.

Fickling, Susan Markey, *Slave-Conversion in South Carolina 1830–1860* (Bulletin of the University of South Carolina, September, 1924), Columbia, 1924.

319

Filler, Louis, *The Crusade Against Slavery 1830–1860,* New York, 1960.

Fortenbaugh, Robert, "American Lutheran Synods and Slavery 1830–1860," *Journal of Religion,* XIII (January, 1933), 72–92.

Fox, Early Lee, *The American Colonization Society 1817–1840* (Johns Hopkins University Studies in Historical and Political Science, Series XXXVII, Number 3), Baltimore, 1919.

Fox, Henry Clay, *Memoirs of Wayne County and the City of Richmond Indiana,* 2 vols., Madison, 1912.

Franklin, John Hope, *From Slavery to Freedom,* New York, 1947.

Garrison, Wendell Phillips, and Francis Jackson Garrison, *William Lloyd Garrison, 1805–1879,* 4 vols., Boston, 1894.

Gewehr, Wesley, M., *The Great Awakening in Virginia 1740–1790,* Durham, 1930.

Gray, Lewis Cecil, *History of Agriculture in the Southern United States to 1860,* 2 vols., Washington, D.C., 1938.

Henry, H. M., *The Police Control of the Slave in South Carolina,* Emory, Va., 1914.

Hurd, John C., *Law of Freedom and Bondage,* 2 vols., Boston, 1863.

Jackson, Luther P., "Religious Instruction of Negroes 1830–1860, with Special Reference to South Carolina," *Journal of Negro History,* XV (January, 1930), 72–114.

Jenkins, William Sumner, *Proslavery Thought in the Old South,* Chapel Hill, 1935.

Jernegan, Marcus W. "Slavery and Conversion in the American Colonies," *American Historical Review,* XXI (April, 1916), 504–527.

Litwack, Leon F., *North of Slavery: The Negro in the Free States 1790–1860,* Chicago, 1961.

Lloyd, Arthur Young, *The Slavery Controversy 1831–1860,* Chapel Hill, 1939.

Locke, Mary S., *Anti-Slavery in America from the Introduction of African Slaves to the Prohibition of the Slave Trade 1619–1808,* Boston, 1901.

McGill, A. T., *American Slavery, as viewed and acted on by the Presbyterian Church in the United States of America,* Philadelphia, 1865.

McLoughlin, William G., *Modern Revivalism,* New York, 1959.

Martin, Asa Earl, *The Anti-Slavery Movement in Kentucky prior to 1850,* Louisville, 1918.

Mays, Benjamin E., *The Negro's Idea of God as Reflected in His Literature,* Boston, 1938.

Mode, Peter G., *The Frontier Spirit in American Christianity,* New York, 1923.

Moore, Glover, *The Missouri Controversy 1819–1821,* Lexington, 1953.

Morrow, Ralph E., "The Proslavery Argument Revisited," *Mississippi Valley Historical Review,* XLVIII (June, 1961), 79–94.

Mott, Frank Luther, *A History of American Magazines 1741–1850,* 4 vols., New York, 1930.

———, *American Journalism,* New York, 1941.

Nye, Russel B., *Fettered Freedom: Civil Liberties and the Slavery Controversy 1830–1860,* East Lansing, 1949.

O'Neall, John Belton, *The Negro Law of South Carolina,* Columbia, 1848.

Paul, James C. N., *Rift in the Democracy,* Philadelphia, 1951.

Pease, Theodore Calvin, *The Frontier State 1818–1848* (*Centennial History of Illinois,* vol. 2), Springfield, 1918.

Phillips, Ulrich Bonnell, *American Negro Slavery,* New York, 1940.

Pillsbury, Parker, *The Acts of the Antislavery Apostles,* Concord, N.H., 1883.

Poole, William Frederick, *Anti-Slavery Opinions Before the Year 1800,* Cincinnati, 1873.

Porter, James, "General Conference of 1844," *Methodist Quarterly Review,* LIII (April, 1871), 234–250.

Posey, Walter B., *The Baptist Church in the Lower Mississippi Valley 1776–1845,* Lexington, 1957.

————, *The Presbyterian Church in the Old Southwest 1778–1838,* Richmond, 1952.

————, "The Slavery Question in the Presbyterian Church in the Old Southwest," *Journal of Southern History,* XV (August, 1949), 311–324.

Putnam, Mary B., *The Baptists and Slavery 1840–1845,* Ann Arbor, 1913.

Quarles, Benjamin, *The Negro in the American Revolution,* Chapel Hill, 1961.

Rice, Madeleine Hooker, *American Catholic Opinion in the Slavery Controversy,* New York, 1944.

Robbins, Roy M., "Crusade in the Wilderness, 1750–1830," *Indiana Magazine of History,* XLVI (June, 1950), 121–132.

Scarborough, Ruth, *The Opposition to Slavery in Georgia Prior to 1860,* Nashville, 1933.

Sellers, Charles G., Jr., ed., *The Southerner as American,* Chapel Hill, 1960.

Sellers, James Benson, *Slavery in Alabama,* Tuscaloosa, 1950.

Smith, Timothy L., *Revivalism and Social Reform,* New York, 1957.

Staiger, C. Bruce, "Abolitionism and the Presbyterian Schism of 1837–1838," *Mississippi Valley Historical Review,* XXXVI (December, 1949), 391–414.

Stampp, Kenneth M., *The Peculiar Institution,* New York, 1956.

Staudenraus, Philip J., *The African Colonization Movement 1816–1865,* New York, 1961.

Stroud, George M., *A Sketch of the Laws Relating to Slavery in the Several States of the United States of America,* Philadelphia, 1856.

Sweet, William Warren, *The Baptists 1783–1830* (*Religion on the American Frontier,* vol. 1), New York, 1931.

———, *Religion in the Development of American Culture 1765–1840,* New York, 1952.

Sydnor, Charles, *Slavery in Mississippi,* New York, 1933.

———, *The Development of Southern Sectionalism 1819–1848* (*A History of the South,* vol. 5), Baton Rouge, 1948.

Taylor, Orville, *Negro Slavery in Arkansas,* Durham, 1958.

Thomas, Benjamin P., *Theodore Weld, Crusader for Freedom,* New Brunswick, 1950.

Thomas, John L., *The Liberator: William Lloyd Garrison, a Biography,* Boston, 1963.

Troeltsch, Ernest, *The Social Teaching of the Christian Churches* (translated by Olive Wyon), 2 vols., New York, 1931.

Wade, Richard C., "The Vesey Plot: A Reconsideration," *Journal of Southern History,* xxx (May, 1964), 143–161.

Weeks, Stephen B., *Southern Quakers and Slavery* (John Hopkins University Studies in Historical and Political Science, extra vol. 15), Baltimore, 1896.

Weisberger, Bernard A., *They Gathered at the River,* Boston, 1958.

Willey, Austin, *The History of the Antislavery Cause in State and Nation,* Portland, 1886.

Wolf, Hazel Catherine, *On Freedom's Altar,* Madison, 1952.

Woodson, Carter G., *The Education of the Negro Prior to 1861,* New York, 1915.

———, *The History of the Negro Church,* Washington, D.C., 1921.

Theses and Other Unpublished Materials

Burrows, Edward F., "The Literary Education of Negroes in Ante-Bellum Virginia, North Carolina, South Carolina, and Georgia with Special Reference to Regulatory and Prohibitive Laws," unpublished M.A. thesis, Duke University, 1940.

Colbert, William, "A Journal of the Travels of William Colbert, Methodist Preacher through parts of Maryland, Pennsylvania, New York, Delaware and Virginia in 1790 to 1828," typescript copy at World Methodist Building, Lake Junaluska, N.C.

Dillon, Merton L., "The Antislavery Movement in Illinois, 1809–1844," unpublished Ph.D. thesis, University of Michigan, 1951.

Grant, Minnie Spencer, "The American Colonization Society in North Carolina," unpublished M.A. thesis, Duke University, 1930.

Haskins, Thomas, "Journal, November 17, 1782–September 28, 1783," typescript copy at World Methodist Building, Lake Junaluska, N.C.

Holmes, Marjorie Moran, "The Life and Diary of the Reverend John Jeremiah Jacob (1757–1839)," unpublished M.A. thesis, Duke University, 1941.

Howard, Victor B., "The Anti-Slavery Movement in the Presbyterian Church, 1835–1861," unpublished Ph.D. thesis, Ohio State University, 1961.

Myers, John Lytle, "The Agency System of the Anti-Slavery Movement, 1832–1837 and its antecedents in other Benevolent and Reform Societies," unpublished Ph.D. thesis, University of Michigan, 1960.

Prior, Granville T., "A History of the *Charleston Mercury* 1822–1852," unpublished Ph.D. thesis, Harvard University, 1946.

Smith, Warren Thomas, "Thomas Coke and Early American Methodism," unpublished Ph.D. thesis, Boston University, 1953.

Senior, Robert C., "New England Congregationalists and the Anti-Slavery Movement 1830–1860," unpublished Ph.D. thesis, Yale University, 1954.

Williams, Thomas Leonard, "The Methodist Mission to the Slaves," unpublished Ph.D. thesis, Yale University, 1943.

INDEX

abolitionism, as revival, 166–67
abolitionists, on missions to slaves, 85; rise of, 113ff, 117ff, 133; attack *Christian Advocate and Journal,* 127; dilemma of, 146; oppose bishops, 151ff; nature of controversy with opponents, 160–62; in ecclesiastical trials, 161; influence of, 165ff; evaluated, 174–76; South on, 188; as conscience of church, 209; on Few resolution, 214; repudiate moderate antislavery sentiment, 216; in West, 219–20; in General Conference of 1844, 262–64; on General Conference of 1844, 269–71. *See also* Methodist abolitionists

Africa, mission to, 98ff

agents, Methodist ministers as, for colonization, 94; for antislavery societies, 166–67

Allen, Richard, 64

amalgamation of races, charged against abolitionists, 102–03, 105

American Colonization Society, founding of, 89; financial aid for, 93–94

American Revolution, spurs antislavery activity, 6

American Union for the Improvement of the Colored Race, 106, 108

American Wesleyan Anti-Slavery Missionary Society, 218

American Wesleyan Anti-Slavery Society, 216–19

Andrew, James Osgood, supports missions to slaves, 68–70, 73; mentioned, 82, 108; elected bishop, 116–17; becomes slaveholder, 245, 248, 256–57;

Andrew, James Osgood (*continued*), asked to resign, 258; debate on status of, 258–64

annual conferences, character of, vii–viii; regulate slave trade, 32; support colonization, 93; oppose abolitionists, 133f, 161–62

antiabolitionists, entrenched in church, 124f; refuse to defend slavery, 137; shocked by Southerners, 178ff, 184f; Chapter VII

antislavery Methodists, first efforts of, 5, 7–9, 14; pamphlets, 14–17; last bastion in South, 46ff; in Kentucky and Tennessee, 53–54; Chapters I, II. *See also* abolitionists

"Appeal on . . . Slavery," 127f

Asbury, Francis, 3, 5, 7–9, 10–11; writes against slavery, 14; optimistic about results of antislavery preaching, 17; mentioned, 19, 21; compromises, 23, 26, 47

Baltimore Conference, 27, 33–37, 251f; accused of supporting slave trade, 182–83; as example of moderation, 244

Bangs, Nathan, 58–60, 91, 98, 102–03, 109, 125, 126, 131, 136, 158, 161, 178, 186–87, 195, 198, 202, 203, 215, 272

Baptists, 31, 42, 47, 63, 83, 206; face problem comparable to that of Methodists in Andrew case, 281

Bascom, Henry Bidleman, colonizationist, 95, 105; apologist for South, 266ff

Beckley, Guy, 220

Birney, James G., 131, 169, 171, 223, 246

DATE DUE

APR 9 '68			
DEC 3 '68			
NOV 12 '69			
DEC 2 '69			
DEC 10 '69			
NOV 17 '70			
NOV 18 70			
DEC 5 '70			
MAR 22 '71			
NOV 10 '71			
NOV 24 '71			
DEC 8 71			
APR 2 '75			
NO 23 '77			
DE 14 '77			
FE 4 '82			
GAYLORD			PRINTED IN U.S.A.